Born to Translate

Born to Translate

The Life and Works of
Barclay Moon Newman, Jr.

Jean Butler Newman

Acclaim Press
MORLEY, MISSOURI

Acclaim Press
— Your Next Great Book —

P.O. Box 238
Morley, MO 63767
(573) 472-9800
www.acclaimpress.com

Editorial Consultant: Paul Bass
Book Design: Rodney Atchley
Cover Design: M. Frene Melton

ISBN: 978-1-948901-11-6 | 1-948901-11-0
Library of Congress Control Number: 2018910080

First Printing: 2018
Printed in the United States of America
10 9 8 7 6 5 4 3 2 1

Contents

Dedication

Tina and Dana
Christy and Chris
Malea
Andrea

I wish to thank Paul and Jan Bass
who spent many meticulous hours
editing and organizing this volume
thus making it all worth while…
You are all the greatest!

Introduction

It was during the May 1984 United Bible Societies Triennial Workshop in Stuttgart, Germany that Eugene Nida approached Barclay and asked him if he would be willing to serve as the drafter for a Literary Liturgical translation of the Bible for the American Bible Society. Barclay agreed and soon began prayerfully to prepare some sample texts of materials for the Gospels, which he (Nida) agreed to review. Barclay never forgot the statement Gene made that day, "Translators are not made. They are born." Barclay reasoned that this could possibly be true, but not always. Thus the title for this book. To help educate the initiated reader, Jose Ruiz of the Paper Wood Publishers in Birmingham, New York, wrote the following about Barclay M. Newman:

> Dr. Barclay M. Newman was chair and Chief Translator of the *Contemporary English Version (CEV)* of the Bible, first published in 1995 by the American Bible Society (ABS), then in 2006 by G. P. Putnam's Sons (Penguin Books) as *Seek Find: The Bible for All People.*
>
> He was a member of the Old Testament Committee for the *Good News Bible (Today's English Version)* published in 1976 by the ABS, and he chaired the revision that was published by the ABS in 1982 as the *Good News Translation.*
>
> In 1974, Newman was invited to establish a Department of Translation at the University of Malaysia, where he also lectured in both English and Malay for two years. At the request of the Malaysian Ministry of Education, he translated from Malay into English a novel, several books of poetry, and a collection of short stories, all of which reflected Islamic perspectives and culture.
>
> He has written extensively on issues of translation, both religious and secular, including *A Concise Greek-English Dictionary of the New*

Testament, and translator's handbooks on Judges, Matthew, John, Acts, Romans, and Jeremiah, as well as almost one hundred articles on various subjects. Most recently he prepared an On-Page Greek English Dictionary of the New Testament that was published in 2007 by the German Bible Society (GBS) in conjunction with the latest edition of the United Bible Societies' Greek New Testament. He has recently completed a thorough revision and expansion of his *Concise Greek-English Dictionary*, and it is scheduled to be published this year (2009).

Dr. Newman's hobby is writing serious satire, semi-poetry, and other sensible and nonsensible stuff. In 2006 the National Liberty Museum (Philadelphia) in conjunction with the Satell Foundation and the Interfaith Institute named him Interfaith Person of the Year.

Barclay's story is one of the true love of God and fellow mankind. May it inspire and motivate us all to a closer walk and work for God.

Author's Notes

Note to the Reader:

Certain parts of this manuscript (especially in the discussions of Translation Principles of the ***Contemporary English Version*** *and other American Bible Society Scripture publications) represent a composite of quotations made by Barclay M. Newman, Jr. in various publications.*

Born to Translate

The Life and Works of
Barclay Moon Newman, Jr.

Chapter I

Birth, Parents, and Ancestors

While most of America was celebrating George Washington's 199th birthday, Lillie Mae Whitman Newman and Barclay Moon Newman, Sr. had a very private celebration of their own. Their first and only child, a son, Barclay Moon Newman, Jr., was born in the early morning hours of February 22, 1931. The event took place in Princeton, West Virginia, Mercer County. A few years earlier in 1928, the proud father had graduated from Princeton University in Princeton, New Jersey at the age of 22.

At the time of his son's birth, Barclay, Sr. was teaching high school in Princeton, West Virginia. This would be their home for the next six weeks, until the family of three moved on to Brooklyn, New York, where they remained for the next three years.

Barclay, Sr. and his siblings, the children of Katherine M. Newman Clement of Lynchburg, Virginia, and Walter G. Newman, were educated at home under the guidance of private tutors. They were introduced to music and several European languages. Barclay, Sr. enrolled at Princeton University. Scientific discovery was the "rage of the age" so it seemed, and Barclay, Sr. became a serious student of science. Biology was his field of choice.

Barclay, Jr., on his father's side of the family, inherited an interesting ancestry. Both his first and last names attest to his English and Scottish background. Barclay, Sr.'s ancestors had settled in Virginia when they first came to the United States. In recent years it has been confirmed that Barclay, Jr. is the first cousin, four times removed to Lottie Moon, a pioneer woman missionary to China. Lottie was born December 12, 1840 in Viewmont, Albermarle County, Virginia, near Charlottesville.

Lottie – at four feet three inches – was an outstanding student, and would have pursued her calling to become a missionary to the Far East, immediately after receiving her master of arts degree in 1861, except that the Southern Baptist Convention did not allow women to serve in that capacity. By 1873 the Convention had relaxed its restrictions, and she soon left her teaching position for China. During the famine of 1911, she unselfishly gave her food and money to help the Chinese, and when she died December 24, 1912 en route to the States, she weighed only fifty pounds.

Barclay's mother, Lillie Mae, was born and raised in Greenwood, Mississippi. Barclay, Sr. had moved from New York sometime in 1928 to Greenwood, where he rented the front bedroom from Lillie Mae's sister, Mrs. Ovieda Wells, who considered him a soft-spoken and thoughtful gentleman. At this time, Barclay, Sr. was employed by the Public Health Service.

While Barclay, Sr. was in Greenwood, Mississippi, he won Lillie Mae's heart and hand and subsequently promised her a life of ease.

It was on April 6, 1929 at a quiet, private service that Barclay, Sr. and Lillie Mae Whitman were married in the home of Ovieda Wells, Lillie Mae's older sister.

Early in 1931 Barclay, Sr. began his second teaching opportunity at the Brooklyn Academy in Brooklyn, New York City. He was driven by two passions – writing and eventually drinking. He was obsessed with writing, and the drinking kept him going. For long hours – many nights way into the wee hours of the morning and on into the following day – the typewriter's clicking could be heard all over their small New York apartment. Lillie Mae found it hard to sleep and almost impossible to keep a baby quiet while daddy became more and more prolific with his writing.

By the time Barclay, Sr. was in his early thirties, he had produced a significant number of biology textbooks, which were used in schools across the United States for years to come.

Barclay, Sr. had taken on a heavy load of writing responsibilities. Not only was he producing textbooks, but he was also frequently contributing articles to *Scientific America, Literary Digest, Science for Today.*

Having a baby to care for filled Lillie Mae's days, but the nights were another story. She loved her son dearly and was always a good mother. But living in the big city of New York became more and more oppressive. The new mother felt tied down and neglected. She was far from home, relatives, and everything that had been familiar to her all her life. She became dreadfully homesick.

In 1934, by the end of Barclay, Jr.'s third year, Lillie Mae began to make plans to take him and move back to Mississippi, where they could be near her family once again.

When Lillie Mae returned to Mississippi, Barclay, Sr. wrote to her and declared his love for her and their little son. He promised to quit drinking, but insisted that his writing must continue in earnest and would still consume all his time, "It was," as he stated in a letter, "the only activity he did not blunder."

In less than a year after Lillie Mae had taken Barclay, Jr. to Mississippi, Barclay, Sr. wrote on January 1, 1935, saying he had resigned from his teaching position at the Brooklyn Academy.

Partly at the urging of her older sister, Lillie Mae was persuaded not to rejoin her husband, and over a period of time a divorce ensued, although she never stopped deeply loving her husband.

The letters to Barclay, Jr. from his father were infrequent and always filled with promises to correspond more often, to send him gifts and books, and help his mother financially, but the gifts and money rarely came.

In the fall of 1935, Lillie Mae wrote the publisher of Barclay, Sr.'s biology textbooks and asked if some of his royalties could be diverted directly to help with finances for his son. The President of COLLEGE ENTRANCE BOOK COMPANY of Fifth Avenue in New York responded promptly with a very kind but firm letter:

> Mr. Newman has not received any royalties from this company and will not receive any royalties, because Mr. Newman had entered into agreement to have all his work purchased on an outright basis. The monies were given to him as per agreements, and Mr. Newman has no interest any longer in the sale of his books.... I wish to place myself on record that it was against my advices and better judgment for him to decide to sell his manuscripts. I tried to convince him that he ought to work on a royalty basis, but his claim was that money was very urgent and he would rather have the cash in hand than the income from royalties in the future. signed: Theodore Cohen.

The most painful broken promise to Barclay, Jr. was when his father offered to send his mother money for train fare for the two of them from Greenwood, Mississippi to New York City, so father and son could have a visit. After waiting hopefully for a long time, the money did not arrive. On at least three occasions he did send Barclay, Jr. a book. One was a thick child's pictorial dictionary, another became his favorite book, entitled "Desert Friends," and the third book was published by Whitman Publishing Company, "Wonders of the World" – an illustrated guide book.

As those early years came and went, Barclay realized that he had indeed received one very special gift from his father, for which he has always been grateful – the heritage of a brilliant mind, the ability to write, and a good, if not fierce, work ethic.

Barclay, Jr. wrote of his early days in Greenwood:

> When I first moved to Greenwood from New York – more specifically, from Brooklyn – my roguish northern accent apparently amazed all of the southern elite, and they continuously encouraged me to talk, until it was discovered that a little encouragement went a long way, in fact much too far, and they soon made a concerted effort to discourage my "constant chatter." Habits learned in childhood are difficult to change, though I ultimately was conquered by a sluggish southern accent that I spoke with the speed of a Brooklyn bookie, rendering my speech unintelligible to all but the most astute ears.

After leaving New York and living in Greenwood, Mississippi for only a short interval, Barclay's mother moved for a brief time to Greenville, Mississippi to take care of her ailing sister, Ruby Westbrook, and her two young children, Ruby Frances and Jimmy. (Following the example of Jimmy's father, Barclay called him "Buddy.") Barclay remembers those days as good days because he always had someone close by to play with. But on a sadder note, he had his first experience with death when his Aunt Ruby died.

All that he can remember about that first death process and funeral was that Buddy, his little cousin who was very near his age, went out in the yard someplace (Barclay couldn't recall the place) with a shovel and tried to dig his mother up. After Ruby passed away, Lillie Mae took Barclay, Jr. and moved back to Greenwood, Mississippi.

Barclay recently wrote of his preschool years:

> Life for me has frequently been a dialogue between excitement and embarrassment, because more often than not my innate overexuberance for life has been a contributing factor to many embarrassing moments.
>
> As a preschooler (a term unknown in my time) I was invited to the home of Emily Johnson for her birthday party. This was my first invitation of this sort, and I wanted to make a lasting impression, which I ultimately did – at least upon myself. Her mother instructed all us miscreants to line up for a game of Pin the Tail on the Donkey. I had never played this game before, and for as much as I knew about the game, I may as well have been the donkey itself.
>
> When it came my time to bestow the honors upon this clumsy looking four-legged creature on the kitchen wall, a blindfold was

> placed over my eyes, but not with great effectiveness, because I was still able to see everything perfectly well (a fact I revealed to no one)...
>
> This humiliating loss of face (known only to me, of course) inspired me to even greater heights in the next game – that of Hide and Seek, which definitely required more cunning than the previous game of pure chance. I was determined to defeat all participants in this match of wits, and I decided exactly where to hide so no one could ever find me, "One, two, three, four, five, six, seven, eight, nine, ten. Coming, ready or not!" echoed the announcement. But to me it was barely audible, because I was safely tucked away in the rear of the giant pantry in this huge country home. No one – not even my dog Spot – could have found me.
>
> And no one ever did find me – or had even missed me. I waited and waited, then waited some more, all the while listening to happy voices of children laughing and running around. Finally, after concluding I had taught them a lesson about hiding that they would never forget, I emerged from this dark cavern and found everyone sitting around eating ice cream and cake. Greatly embarrassed and red-faced, I slunk up to Mrs. Johnson and asked if I could have some dessert, which by now had been mostly devoured by those less talented at hiding than me. After asking my name, she said, "Oh" and hurriedly presented me with a thin slice of cake topped by a teaspoon of vanilla ice cream.

Barclay's mother, not being trained in any particular field, worked hard at various jobs to support herself and her young son. She sometimes clerked in large department stores and later worked in a "variety" store that stayed open until past midnight on Saturday, in order to accommodate the black workers, who were hauled in from the cotton plantations for their one day of freedom. But soon after World War II erupted, Lillie Mae moved to Memphis, Tennessee to accept employment in an aircraft factory, where she worked at riveting Billy Mitchell B-25 Bombers.

She soon became a skillful worker and as a result earned merit awards, thus enabling her to better support her son and herself. Barclay, Jr. joined her in Memphis a few months later.

Barclay once wrote of his father:

> From the few photographs of him, I know he smoked a pipe. Although I have occupied myself with a lifelong tirade against smoking and smokers (except for the one occasion I foolishly sucked

> fiery fumes from a flaming segment of a possum grape vine), as a boy I occasionally imitated him by pretending my black plastic whistle was a pipe…

Because Barclay's mother and all her family had always lived in the south, there was a certain mystique about Barclay, Jr.'s father, whose family was raised and educated in the "north." Years later he recalled hearing his mother and her sisters talking in hushed tones about his dad's shameful negligence and his broken promises to his only son. After Barclay, Jr. was married to Jean, she remembers him telling her that for years as a child he had dreamed about and longed to be allowed to see his father just once more in person.

After his third birthday, Barclay, Jr. never saw his father alive again. But some 35 years later, while at a United Bible Societies Translation Workshop in Spain, he received a phone call from New York, informing him of his father's death. So he immediately returned to the States and attended his funeral in White Plains, New York.

Chapter II

Early Childhood Through High School

Although in his early years Barclay frequently wished that he had a dad like the other kids, his young life was surrounded by loving aunts, uncles, cousins, and friends. His days were filled with lively activity, happiness, and more fun than can possibly be imagined. That was his nature. Funny things almost always happen to fun-loving people! Naturally a good student, he quickly grasped all the teachers had to offer, and, in the meantime, gave them fits with his antics. He always brought home excellent report cards – except for Deportment.

Barclay affectionately wrote about one of his teachers, Ms. Eggleston:

> As it happened, there were two maiden sisters teaching at North Greenwood Grammar School – Ms. Eggleston # 1 and Ms. Eggleston # 2 – one who never understood me, and one who didn't want the opportunity to do so. All of my "academic" grades were good, but I always managed to receive the lowest possible marks on "Deportment," which was consistently accompanied by the comment, "Lacks self-control." Actually, I controlled myself very well, practically always doing exactly what I wanted – the problem was their lack of control over me.
>
> Ms. (Sarah) Eggleston # 1 taught grades two and three, while Ms. (Frances) Eggleston # 2 taught grade four … So when it came time for me to be promoted to grade four, Ms. Egg # 1 – in order to benefit her sister Ms. Egg # 2 – recommended to my mother that I skip that grade and proceed directly to the fifth grade, something my mother refused to let me do…

Years later, Barclay figured the teacher didn't know what to do with him, so she thought if she could have him promoted to the next higher grade, he would, at least, be out of her and her sister's hands and hair. When Barclay's mother had been approached about this development, she considered the long term effects on her son, and decided she wanted more than anything else to keep him a child and at home as long as she possibly could. No grades were to be skipped.

Barclay's early religious training had its beginning in the Cradle Roll Department of the First Baptist Church in Greenwood, Mississippi, his new hometown. At Sunday school, Barclay's behavior was always closely monitored by his mother's older sister, Aunt Beda.

Barclay, at the request of Jean, wrote of his early years:

> For most of my somewhat extensive lifetime, school has been an integral part of my existence. Therefore, I feel duty bound to expound on certain of my exploits – both inside and outside the classroom – at the same time exercising as much restraint as humanly possible, so as neither to embellish nor to diminish the truth – at least, the truth as it either would have been or could have been, had the events actually transpired as described herein…

Barclay recounted several of his more embarrassing moments in his early grades and on into junior high and high school:

> On my very first day in the very first grade, I headed home the very first minute school was out, rejecting any advice from the teachers and the older students on what route to follow. Somehow I ended up at the Planters Cotton Seed Oil Mill at the extreme end of Claiborne Street, which was quite a distance from my intended destination. Fortunately, however, I remembered 1270 -- my Aunt Beda's phone number – and she soon came to my rescue in her car.
>
> … It was the second grade, and Ms. Sarah Eggleston had us lined up around the classroom, singing patriotic songs. She leaned over to me and inquired, "Why aren't you singing?"
>
> "I am singing!" came my cautious response.
>
> "No, you're not," she informed me, and I never tried singing again, except once in the shower…

Barclay recalled the occasion, when the teacher announced that tomorrow would be "Pet Day." All the children were encouraged to bring their pets to school – dogs, of course were required to be on leashes. Barclay did not have a dog at the time or even a goldfish, so he improvised:

> Pets have become such an essential part of life both in and out of the classroom that "Pet Day" is often celebrated in primary schools with far more enthusiasm than Independence Day. Such was my experience in North Greenwood Grammar School. Instead of one or two pets, I had captured and collected a shoebox full of my favorite

living things – those little brown lizards, whose tails automatically disengaged from the torso, if touched by the human hand.

From vast experience, I had developed a scientific technique for capturing these squirmy creatures with their entire anatomy still in tack by grabbing that portion of their body between the two sets of legs. Sometimes, however, a lizard would get so excited that its tail would automatically pop off and start dancing around on its own, even if untouched by the hand of a homo erectus.

Before the official opening of Pet Day in the second grade, we went through the routine of saying the pledge of allegiance to the flag of the United States of America. That day we never completed the pledge of allegiance, and Pet Day was postponed. Worst of all, before my own personal pets could be recaptured by all male – and a few female – volunteers, brown body parts like wiggling worms had found refuge on the top of almost every desk in class. And – worst of all – in an abortive attempt to avoid contact between her legs and the lizards, Ms. Eggleston started performing an Irish jig and accidentally squashed a few of the slower and less fortunate of God's little creatures. The next year as Pet Day was approaching, a message appeared in massive bold font on the school bulletin board: **NO lizards are allowed on Pet Day.**

Desirous to be cooperative and to help maintain a semblance of order, I was glad to leave my remnant of lizards at home. So when the long-awaited day finally arrived, I took my shoebox – with its mixture of green and garden snakes.

These misfortunate events, however, didn't keep Barclay from his antics in the third grade:

One of my most stressful moments at school took place in the third grade, when C.V. Bruce handed me a note to pass along to Shirley Atkinson, who was two seats beyond me. Just as I reached over to hand her the note, the long arm of Ms. Eggleston reached out and intercepted the folded piece of paper that had written on it a rather vulgar proposition. I immediately informed her that the note had originated with C.V., a fact he fervently denied. I was devastated. How could I possible prove my innocence – this one time when I actually *was* innocent? But Ms. Eggleston had it all figured out, and I was saved – the writing was obviously produced by someone who wrote with the left hand, and C.V. Bruce was the only left-handed person in our class.

Barclay has almost complete recall of his first date, which took place in the fourth grade. Even today, to the great astonishment of many of Barclay's friends and relatives, he remembers the names of almost every boy and girl in each grade, as well as the names of their teachers:

> My first date with a girl was in the fourth grade. On Monday morning, I asked Sethelle if she could accompany me to the Saturday afternoon movie, and on Tuesday morning she reported her mother had agreed that we could meet at the theatre, then after the movie I could walk her down Riverside Drive to their home. I arrived at the theatre long before time and stood there waiting. After what seemed forever, Mrs. Belle drove up in a cream-colored Cadillac, and Sethelle stepped out. The two of us waved goodbye to her mother and proceeded to enter the theatre (I'd already bought the tickets.). I don't remember anything we said before the feature started, and I don't remember anything that transpired either during or following the movie, except that Earl Wyatt (a suave sixth grader) was standing there as we came out. He greeted us both with a smile, and I said, "Earl, would you mind walking Sethelle home?" This must have been the right thing to say, because I can still picture them in my mind, walking in the direction of her house, holding hands. That was my last date with Sethelle.

There is no such thing as a free lunch, but Barclay could attest to paying for his "free" lunch in the "free" lunch line:

> In the fourth grade, after transferring from North Greenwood Grammar School to Jefferson Davis Grammar School, I also experienced some "disorientation" – but of a different sort. There were two cafeterias in the building where students from junior high and senior high joined the grammar school group for lunch. I always ate in what was known as the "little cafeteria," because the line there was shorter and moved considerably quicker. All you had to do was to hand the lady your money, grab a bowl of soup, a piece of bread, and apple or an orange, and a half-pint of milk, then head straight for the playground after gobbling down this gourmet grub. One day someone from the principal's office came to our classroom to take a survey, and she asked, "If you eat in the little cafeteria, would you please hold up your hand?"
>
> "I do!" burst forth my response with great gusto, while at the same time I was stretching my hand up as high as humanly pos-

sible. Not until the fifth grade did I learn that "little cafeteria" was a euphemism for "free lunch line."

One summer day when Barclay was eight or nine, he found a box turtle with a high-domed shell. He wondered why it had ventured so far away from the river. So he picked it up, put it in a shoebox, and headed for the land. Carefully he released it just at the shallow edge of the river with its head pointed toward the water.

When the turtle slowly turned around and crawled back in his direction, he repeated this process, but again the turtle turned around and headed for dry land. Barclay took his bare toes and nudged the turtle away from the graveled embankment and towards the water.

Again the turtle began to turn and Barclay decided he must help this poor dumb creature get to where he belonged. He picked up the defenseless turtle and threw him as hard as he could right out into deep water where Barclay thought he belonged. Later, to his dismay, he learned that not all turtles live in the water.

Barclay wrote about an incident that took place when he was between the ages of nine and ten. He gave a good description of the part of Mississippi he lived in and the waterways that surrounded Greenwood:

> **GREENWOOD: WORLD'S LARGEST INLAND LONG STAPLE COTTON MARKET, Welcomes You.** When I was a boy, this sign appeared over the bridge that separated Greenwood proper from North Greenwood, and you saw it as you prepared to cross the Yazoo River, going from north to south.
>
> Greenwood is, in fact, defined by this river. Born of the confluence of the Tallahatchie and Yalobusha Rivers just north of the town, the Yazoo leisurely worms its way south and southwest for somewhat less than two hundred miles, almost as a microcosm of the Mighty Mississippi River, which becomes the benefactor of its muddy resources at Vicksburg.
>
> The Yazoo was – and remains – a proud river, and in many ways it was my personal mentor when I was young. From this river I learned both courage and fear, but most of all respect for this silent, subtle, and secretive stream that seemed determined to decide its own course, regardless of any attempts on my part to become its master in any small degree.
>
> ... Marvin Tillman (that was his real name, and the one I preferred, though most others called him Jake) lived next door and was something of a role model for me, though I had never heard of that

term at the time. He was older and even let me play neighborhood football with the boys his age, because I could catch the ball and wasn't scared of getting pounded into the ground, which generally happened once I made the catch. On the other side, when I played monopoly with him and his younger sister Sue (a year older than me), he'd borrow heavily from me when he was in need, but vehemently refused to loan, even when I was desperate.

... Although my mother lacked a formal education and the financial advantages of such, she always managed to convince Santa Claus to deliver precisely what I begged for. One year it was a type of wall tent, not quite high enough for me to stand up in, but large enough for a cot.

By now you may wonder what all this has to do with the Yazoo River. I'll explain. After I had gotten good use from the tent for a few seasons (it stayed in the back yard year round), Marvin decided he'd like to build a one-and-a-half-person kayak – he would be the one, and I would be the half. Marvin had easy access to the small amount of lumber that was required for framing the envisioned vessel, but this skeleton would also require a skin, and the most likely candidate was my tent!

Convinced by Marvin of how glamorous it would be to become part owner of a kayak, I lowered the tent, which he then took into the small building behind his house that served for a storage shed and other, less noble purposes, such as dissecting a boy's tent in order to transform it into the skin of a kayak. He did this when I wasn't around... By some strange coincidence, the next Sunday both Marvin and I suffered from the same malady – a headache and a stomachache, though with no fever. My mother's traditional remedy for stomachaches – especially those accompanied by fever – was a volatile solution of castor oil and orange juice. However, since she detected no fever and no obvious reason for me to want to stay at home and miss Sunday school (I attended regularly, as did Marvin, who "grew up" to become a deacon at First Baptist Church in Greenwood, Mississippi), I was allowed to stay at home when she and Aunt Beda left in the car on their way to church. Uncle Paul, my Aunt Beda's husband, left not much later in his pickup truck for the local "pool hall," where he spent most Sunday mornings with his buddies. And their son, Paul Alexander Wells, Jr. (nine years my senior) was away at "prep" school, the ancient equivalent of modern "boot camps" for undisciplined students who otherwise would have flunked every course in school. Marvin had also managed to win the good graces of his parents, and when all adults of the two households were safely out of sight, we each scampered for the shed where the kayak was hidden. It was almost eight feet long and two feet wide in the middle, then it tapered to about six inches at either end. The "cockpit" was large enough to accommodate the two of us, if we scrunched up tightly enough, with me in the front and Marvin sitting with his long, lanky legs stretched out alongside me. When we were both in the vessel, we each had a paddle, though Marvin acted as the helmsman and determined the course we would follow. It was a beautiful summer day, and we had to carry the kayak only about two blocks before reaching the levee, then approximately a hundred yards down to our designated "port of departure." As soon as we attempted to go aboard ship, we discovered that kayaks have a stubborn streak as well as a sadistic sense of humor. No matter which of us attempted to enter the cockpit first, our creation spontaneously started rolling over and over like a barrel on a greasy hillside. Finally, Marvin stood on one side and held this rebellious monster firm, while I crawled in...

The water nearest the bank flowed at a less rapid pace than did the water of the main channel, so we didn't venture far out. Time! Time quickly became our nemesis. How were we going to reverse our course and get back to our point of origin in time enough to reach home before the church crowd returned? It was obvious to the entire crew that any attempt to head back upstream by circling around would cause the skinny boat to capsize as soon as the current struck it broadside.

Finally, we decided that Marvin would grab a low branch of a tree and hold on with both hands, after which I would momentarily abandon ship and hold securely to the same branch, while he turned around and faced the opposite direction. Once he was settled, I was to crawl into position, and we would begin our journey back upstream. This was the plan ... not the reality.

Marvin did manage to take hold of a tree branch, and I was able to bail out of the boat; he turned around as planned, and I crawled up on the kayak as planned. But the branch suddenly slipped from his grasp, the kayak went into reverse gear, and I was left sprawling across its upper ribs. Fortunately, the current was propitious and swept us into a shallow inlet, where we managed to arrange ourselves in our original positions and began slowly – ever so slowly – paddling upstream, hugging the shore as though it was our mother's bosom.

Favorable also was the "soft water" we encountered in our climb upstream, and we docked at our homeport in sufficient time to hurriedly put our clothes back on. (We had not wanted to leave any traces of our adventure, so we had completely disrobed before setting sail, fearing we might otherwise have ruined our clothes.) Then we ran as fast as we could with the kayak and returned it to its hidden dock, after which we immediately separated and headed to our respective homes. When my mother returned from church, she was glad to see that I had made such a miraculously swift recovery, and all went well until Monday afternoon, when she asked me to turn in my dirty underwear and socks, so she could wash them. She didn't own a washing machine – not many people did in those days – and she would usually hand wash undergarments and socks twice a week. I turned in all I had, but still came up lacking one pair of undershorts.

In my rush to get back home on Sunday, I had hastily thrown on my outer shirt and trousers and had failed to notice that I had not picked up my undershorts when I had grabbed my undershirt. Now I was in serious trouble. But I told mother I had been swimming in the Yazoo and had forgotten to pick up my shorts when I walked home in my swimming trunks. This was not the *exact* truth, but it was the best I could produce on the spot, and it was damaging enough, since she had forbidden me to swim in the river.

Mother immediately marched me out to the weeping willow tree in our back yard, broke off a few of its torturous tentacles, then proceeded to walk behind me at close quarters down to the riverbank, all the while rhythmically reminding my legs of my premeditated sin. I was ordered to pick up my shorts and carry them to the house, as she gave a repeat performance of her previous activities en route to the river. This punishment was more humiliating than painful, and it was a full week before I dared slip off to the river again. My only compensation was remembering that Jesus had been forced to carry a cross, while his captors beat him with a whip and boisterous crowds followed behind, jeering at him.

More than a year later – after Marvin had tired of the kayak – he gave it to me, and I hid it among some of the greenery of the wooded area between the levee and the river. Once I felt very adventuresome, so I took the boat out on my own. By this time, it was not in good shape – the canvas skin was more like a sieve – but I was obligated to answer the call of the river. So I placed my newly acquired possession in the water, jumped in, and was off for adventures in paradise. But the inevitable happened – the boat began taking in water and soon turned upside down. I was forced to abandon ship, though I held on to the craft until I managed to get it within five or six feet of the riverbank.

Then I let go, thinking the water was shallow enough for me to walk the rest of the way to safety. I was wrong – almost fatally wrong – the water was far deeper than I had anticipated, and I plunged downward until my head was completely immersed. Although I was a good swimmer, the suddenness of the near catastrophe had caused me to panic momentarily, and I thought I would drown. Somehow I struggled to dry land, and vowed never again to swim in the river – not unless absolutely certain of a divine summons, which came much sooner than I had expected at the moment I uttered this inexorable vow of abstinence.

Barclay entered the fifth grade with renewed expectations and in his own words much later wrote:

As much as I loved the classroom, I occasionally had the opportunity to spend time outside, and I recall one occasion when this resulted in something of a disaster. This particular occurrence happened in the fifth grade, when there was some misunderstanding in the classroom about who should do most of the talking, Mrs. Boswell or me. Although there was strong support for my position, she controlled the majority vote, and one morning she ordered me out of the room for the rest of the day.

Not wanting to waste my "release" time, I decided to explore the school grounds in the course of which I finally became thirsty and went to the artesian well that flowed through drinking fountains in one large stone structure at the center of the schoolyard. This quartet of water fountains also happened to be directly beside the shortcut pedestrians used on their way downtown.

As soon as my thirst was quenched, I looked up and saw a familiar sight – my mother – she was heading in my direction with a quizzical expression on her face. "Hi, Mom, it's sure good to see you" I blurted out, with as much enthusiasm as I could possibly muster under the circumstances.

"What are you doing here?"

"Drinking some water. I was thirsty."

"I can see you were drinking water – but why are you outside the building? Nobody else is out here."

"There aren't any artesian wells inside, Mom."

"Artesian wells or not, go back to your classroom this very minute, before I take you there myself!"

"Mom, I'm on my way – I've had all the water I want." Then I immediately ran inside the building, flew up the stairs to the second floor, and stood like a sentinel on guard duty outside the classroom door.

A few minutes later, Mrs. Boswell came out into the hallway and asked if I thought I could be quiet, if she would let me come back into the room. "Yes Mam," I answered. "But could I please get some water first and go to the restroom? I got awful thirsty, just standing in this same spot for so long."

It seems that all Barclay's teachers had to think of ways to keep him out of trouble. He recalls just such a time in the sixth grade:

Mrs. Lewis, my sixth grade math teacher, employed a similar method of punishment for disruptive scholars. I was enjoying a conversation with Sethelle Belle, who sat across the aisle from me and was as beautiful as her name, when Mrs. Lewis interrupted without warning and suggested I seat myself in the desk placed in the hallway for such perpetrators. While there, it would be my responsibility to solve a list of math problems provided especially for such an occasion. I learned quickly there was no easy way out of this dilemma – as soon as I solved one list of problems and proudly presented the correct answers to her, she merely handed me another list and sent me right back. Apparently, except for math, I was a very slow learner.

Also significant in Barclay's memory was one of the few letters he received from his father:

World War II was in full swing, and my dad wrote to inform me that he was involved in a "secret" project for developing germ warfare. Apparently the "Evil Axis" isn't the only – and perhaps not even the first – group of guys to have dirtied their hands with such infectious experimentations. Of course, he didn't supply any details, nor did I know enough to ask any. He was my father, and I was proud of him – now I really had something to brag about. He signed the letter: "Lieutenant Commander Barclay M. Newman of the U. S. Navy."

Many years later, Barclay, Jr. would read an article his aunt had cut out and saved from *The Commercial Appeal* (Memphis, Tennessee, Sunday Morning, July 15, 1944). The caption was "Disease in Warfare Basis of Japan's Secret Weapon, Chemistry Professor (Barclay Newman, Sr.) Says" – the subtitle read, "Nipponese Dropped Infected Rice and Wheat On Six Chinese Towns Which Caused Spread of Deadly Bubonic Plague."

The article was attributed to Howard W. Blakeslee of New York, and in it he said, "Japan's secret weapon, as described in a new book of that title by Barclay Newman, Sr. is bacterial, fungus, virus, and cancer warfare."

In April 1967, the article "Malaria and Pneumonia Killed off Men Like Flies," published by Rodolfo G. Tupas in Manila's *The Sunday Times Magazine,* confirmed what Newman had written:

> According to my official records, the No, 1 killer in the (Japanese prison) Camp was malaria. As of June 1, 1942 at the peak of the Disease Graph, there were 5,278 prisoners downed with it ... On that day (June 1) there were 12,515 sick prisoners: 5,278 with malaria ...Early each morning, the usual greeting (in the camp) would be not "How are you?" but "How many died?" It was a common experience for one to awaken on the morrow beside a still companion.

It seemed that the Japanese were releasing malaria-carrying mosquitoes in the prison camp. Allied troops were dying by the hundreds from malaria, while the Japanese personnel were not dying, because they were all regularly given quinine to combat the disease.

From a very early age it seems that Barclay, Jr. always had a fascination for guns. First, he imagined his wooden rubber gun in the shape of a long barreled pistol, with a clothespin fastened to the handle, to be a deadly weapon. He also had a water pistol and a slingshot, but none of these would suffice for what his heart truly desired. From this primitive start, he advanced to an authentic Red Ryder B-B gun, and later to a "lethal" bow and arrow. He remembers shooting sparrows with his B-B gun. After all, these little creatures were a real nuisance... He took great pride in his ability to hit them squarely in the head at a respectable distance.

Barclay recalled his "worst – and by far most painful experience" with his B-B gun:

> It took place in a clandestine clump of chinaberry trees along the Yazoo riverbank, where a mother dove was sitting on a nest of eggs. I shot her several times through the bottom of the nest, but she

tenaciously sat there, protective of her eggs until she died among the shattered eggshells. Sometimes what "boys will be" is subhuman – unfortunately, men are too often merely boys at their worst.

Once I was allowed to go hunting with (my older friend) Marvin, who let me tag along, toting a single shot bolt action twenty-two rifle, while he pompously paraded beside me with his double-barreled shotgun of whatever gauge. We were out for big game this time – something more impressive than the nameless English sparrows of my previous repertoire.

We came upon a bluff that reached only a few feet above the ground below where two pigeons were feeding side-by-side. "When I say shoot, take the one on the right, and I'll take the one on the left," whispered Marvin. Seconds later, "Shoot!" came the command, but only the sound of the shotgun resounded across the open field, and only one blood-spattered bird lay writhing below us in its tortuous death throes.

"Why didn't you shoot the pigeon like I told you to?" questioned the curious inquisitor.

"I just couldn't" was all I said, but I was thinking how closely the grayish pigeon assigned me had resembled a certain mother dove.

In the summer of 1945 Barclay joined his mother in Memphis, Tennessee, where she was now working in a defense factory. Barclay was enrolled in Bellevue Junior High School. He recalls a date he had in the eighth grade:

By the time I was an eighth grader at Bellevue Junior High in Memphis, I'd learned more about the fine art of dating in a movie theatre. I had something of a crush on Delores Weaver, who – on this occasion – was sitting beside her boyfriend in the Saturday matinee. I didn't know what to do, until my friend Harold Summers (known as Peewee) advised, "There're two sides to everything." So I sauntered down the aisle and casually flopped into the seat on the other side of Delores. Although Peewee had been philosophically correct, I soon discovered an unexpected "side" to this sad state of affairs, when Delores and her date silently swapped seats.

... Our English teacher, Ms. Yarborough, had her own unique way of dealing with classroom troublemakers, especially if the disturbance happened to be generated by a cross-gender dialogue. I was very innocently enjoying such a conversation with Joanne Carter (a brilliant student of the English language), when Ms.

"Yard Bird" (as she was affectionately called – though only in her absence) suddenly approached and said, "If you feel you really *must* talk to that little gal, take her home with you!"

Although that sounded like a pretty good idea to me, neither Ms.Yard Bird nor Joanne seemed at all pleased when I shot back, "Can I take her home now, or do I have to wait till school's out?"

Throughout Barclay's early school years, he showed a wide interest in his studies with his academic marks revealing excellence in some areas more than others. He remembers well and with great pleasure his fourth grade teacher. According to him, Miss Marshall understood him, and in her class he made straight "A's". At the end of the school year, she wrote a note to him and his mother, "… enjoyed having you in my room and you have done excellent work. (signed): Love, Miss Marshall." That first ever kind of commendation from one of Barclay's primary school teachers gave his mother hope for her son's success in life.

In the sixth grade Barclay had excelled in Language Usage, and a few years later Science and Math were his favorite subjects. Deportment almost always showed a need for improvement. It was not until high school that he received an outstanding mark in that area; it was his first "Excellent."

After moving to Memphis, Barclay wrote about a time when he was able to go back to Greenwood to visit with his aunt and uncle for the first time after moving away:

> Thanksgiving was approaching and I had returned to Greenwood … Upon threat of abandonment and abuse by my mother, I dared not even think about hunting with a shotgun, but a rifle was still an option, so I borrowed my uncle's rifle and left for a wooded area just outside the city limits, where I thought a few friendly squirrels would surely be cooperative enough to volunteer for participation in a pot of stew. I was wrong – although squirrels were plentiful, they were equally bashful and cautiously tucked their heads back into the safety of their nests each time they perceived I was peering in their direction.
>
> "Anything is better than nothing," I said to myself, when a (turkey) buzzard alighted toward the top of a dead tree not far from where I was standing. After lining up this foul smelling fowl in my trusty rifle sights, I slowly squeezed the trigger, and my target tumbled ungracefully to the ground. I strolled over, picked it up, and was examining it (I'd never seen a buzzard that close up before), when an old beat-up, nondescript vehicle pulled over and stopped.

"What you'uns got thar?" inquired the not-too-bright looking driver.

"A turkey! Thought I'd get one for Thanksgiving."

"Bird's got a funny color."

"It's mating season – Wild turkeys blush a lot in mating season."

"Neck's kind of crooked like."

"Got bent when it fell from the tree."

"Wanna sell it?"

"'Don't know. My uncle will beat me, if I don't come home with a turkey. We didn't have one last year, and he's mighty hungry for turkey meat right now."

"Ah, come on, I'll give you two bits – then you'uns can keep the money and tell yer uncle twern't none 'bout."

"Wouldn't take less than four bits."

"How about three bits?"

"I really hate to do this, but if you'uns sure you'uns want the turkey, and if you'uns promise not to tell my uncle, he's yer'n for three bits."

At this, the country gentleman handed me the seventy-five cents and drove off with his prize turkey buzzard, sprawled across the rumble seat of his antiquated automobile.

Occasionally my conscience feels a bit uncomfortable – especially at Thanksgiving time. In such moments of weakness I silently pray, "Lord, forgive my sins of the past, but most of all, please protect me from the anger of merciless men."

Sometime in 1945 Barclay's mother Mae married a man who was a barber at the Baptist Hospital in Memphis. He was Rayburn Holman Frey. Barclay has told Jean many times that this man was a very gentle, sweet, and very patient person. There was an adjustment that the three of them had to make, and Barclay testifies that his stepfather always had a loving and kind spirit as situations were worked through.

Like his great-grandfather, Ulysses L. Whitman, on his mother's side of the family, Barclay loved playing the drums. His great-grandfather was a drummer in Company "C," 46th Regiment Infantry Co. during his tour of service in the Civil War. Young Barclay played the drums in the Treadwell High School Band (Memphis, Tennessee) for three years. In his last year at Treadwell, his school's paper, *The Eagle*, featured him as, "'Red' Newman is the boy with the drums. He plays them well and best of all he enjoys playing. Drums are his hobby.

At one Tennessee State competition a judge said to Barclay, "You play a golden drum." As a result of his many long hours of practice, he became proficient enough in playing the snare drums and timpani to be offered a band scholarship in 1950 by Dr. Hugh Gunderson of Western Kentucky State College in Bowling Green, Kentucky.

From 1947 to 1949, Barclay showed a penchant for the military. He joined ROTC, and at the end of the three years, he was ranked "Cadet Captain, Barclay Newman." In this last year of school he also was included on the "I-DARE-YOU" Honor Roll sponsored by the Danforth Foundation. With this honor he was given the book *I Dare You!* by William H. Danforth, who challenged young people to "Think Tall, Stand Tall, Smile Tall, and Live Tall." All during Barclay's life, he has taken seriously the challenges this small book offered.

Barclay was an energetic, well-rounded teenager. Along with his interest in music, he played football and basketball at Treadwell High from 1947 to 1949, earning his letters in football in his senior year. He was not a heavily built youngster, rather tall and skinny, but he could run like the "dickens," which made him a valued member of the team. His mother believed that football was too dangerous, and Barclay did not seriously pursue the sport after entering college.

In May 1949, just before high school graduation, Barclay exhibited another side to his fun-loving personality. His high school friend, Nellie Ann Kilpatrick, was chosen by the Treadwell High faculty to be the Co-operative Club Cinderella. She would be their representative in the Cotton Carnival and would reign at several functions. The school's paper *The Eagle* announced, "Immediately upon being chosen, she pronounced Barclay Newman also of Treadwell, her 'Prince Charming'." Barclay would escort Nellie Ann during the festivities.

On April 13, 1949 the Memphis, Tennessee *Commercial Appeal* declared Barclay to be "Nellie Ann's Prince, who would accompany his Cinderella to the various functions she attends during Carnival Week and ride with her on a float at the Children's Ball at Crump Stadium." Pictures of the two young people were spectacular – all white formal wear from head to toe.

Chapter III

Calling and Higher Education

After graduating from Treadwell High School in 1949, Barclay's plans were to enroll in Memphis State for his four-year college education. He never got there. In his senior year Barclay had felt that God was calling him into some capacity of Christian Ministry. Barclay had made known his plans to enter Memphis State as a freshman in the fall of 1949, but one late summer morning, Rev. William E. Lyles, pastor of the National Avenue Baptist Church of Memphis, Tennessee, came to Barclay's home and said, "Get in the car. I'm taking you to Jackson, Tennessee, where there is a school for young men and women entering Christian ministry."

Rev. ("Brother," to Barclay) Lyles never had a formal education; he struggled with his studies of the Bible and wanted to see Barclay succeed to his highest potential. This would be possible in a Christian oriented college. Barclay liked what he saw at Union University and allowed "Brother" Lyles to help him enroll on the spot.

When Barclay, Sr. heard indirectly that his son had decided to answer the call to Christian ministry and planned to pursue his PhD degree in Religion, he had occasion to visit his former major professor at Princeton University. When he told him of his son's intentions, the elderly gentleman, for some reason, dropped dead on the spot.

In the fall of 1949, it was at Union University in Jackson, Tennessee that Barclay began his first year with great expectations. As promised in the school's annual, "Union University is dedicated to the purpose of preparing young people for maximum Christian service." It was a sacrifice for his mother and his stepfather, Rayburn Frey, to send him to a private denominational school, and for this reason among others, Barclay took the annual's statement seriously.

In his freshman year, Barclay joined the Union Ministerial Society, led by Dr. R. C. Briggs, who taught New Testament and New Testament Greek from 1946 to 1956, and became Dean of the college midway of Barclay's tenure there. In its weekly meetings, this organization provided an atmosphere of genuine fellowship and support for ministerial students, where there were almost always discussions of common problems for the beginning student-minister.

As a freshman Barclay also became an active member of the "Life Service Band," an organized group, which encouraged members to participate in prayer, study, fellowship, and the conducting of mission services.

In his second year, Barclay became obsessed with the study of New Testament Greek. At this time, the most outstanding college professor of Greek in that part of the country was Dr. R. C. Briggs, and he led Barclay into a new world of study, of learning, and of searching for truth that could be found only in the Greek New Testament. This kind of endeavor has continued to be a life-long pursuit for Barclay.

Barclay preached his first sermon on October 3, 1949 at a Baptist Church in Holly Springs, Mississippi. His mother and stepfather, Rayburn Frey, were able to make the trip to Mississippi with him, and their prayerful and loving support, immensely encouraged Barclay.

Barclay's early years were so filled with wholesome fun one might think he had already had a lifetime of fun. And even though he was rapidly becoming a serious academic student in college, he still had time for an occasional joke on his fellow students. He tells about one incident and vows even today that he had nothing to do with it -- except for a healthy and hearty laugh. It seemed that one of his fellow students had returned to their notorious pre-Civil War dormitory, Adams Hall, on Union's campus and saw that a mattress had been thrown over the winding banister from the third floor down to the first. Boys all over the dorm came running to see what all the excitement was about. When they saw what was taking place, they joined in the fun. And so, while hanging over the banisters, they poured water from the two upper floors onto the mattress down below. Some even joined in pouring cold colas on the mattress.

When Eddie Prather returned to the dorm, he joined with gusto the fun and took the record for pouring the most liquid on the already soaked mattress. When the fun had subsided, Eddie climbed the stairs two steps at a time to reach his room on the third floor. There he found everything in his room was in place just as he had left it, except for one item – his mattress was missing from the bed frame.

It was sometime in January during Barclay's freshman year, when he met his future wife and mother-in-law. Barclay and Jean Butler were in the same speech class. Neither of the two had especially noticed one another in particular, until one day the professor, Dr. Lloyd, asked each class member to give an impromptu speech. When Barclay's turn came, he did a take off on the poem, "Little Boy Blue." The class roared with laughter, and Jean recalls that this would be the young man she would like to invite to her church's "Sadie Hawkins" Valentine party and banquet coming up in February.

The girls were encouraged to invite the boys for the party. In the meantime, Jean's best friend, June Bennett, informed her that she should not invite Barclay Newman, because he had a girlfriend back in Memphis, the attractive Cotton Festival Princess. With this input, Jean decided definitely not to invite Barclay and began to think of someone else to accompany her to the social. Still she reasoned that this Barclay would be a lot of fun at any party, and surely nothing serious would come of a Valentine party date at her church.

And for some reason, he remained her first choice. Even today, if you ask Jean, she honestly cannot tell you why she changed her mind and did indeed invite Barclay to the Party. If the truth were revealed, her friend June Bennett likely shared this information with her boyfriend and word got back to Barclay. As in small towns so in small colleges, most news travels fast. What harm could a Valentine party and dinner invitation be? After all, he had to eat, and the food was guaranteed to be good. Barclay accepted Jean's invitation with a pleasant grin.

So on the designated evening, Barclay made his way to Jean's home across town and found that she, her two sisters, Ann and Lucy Nell Butler with their boyfriends, her brother Carlton (the driver) with his girlfriend, and Jean's mother, who had been asked to help out with the party, would be going to the festive occasion – nine people all in one mid-sized car.

Fortunately in those days, the number of passengers in a car didn't attract the attention of the police. Four of the group hurriedly scrambled into the front seat and Barclay, being a gentleman, helped the remaining four get into the back seat before taking his turn at getting in. There was just no space left to sit, as the four occupants tried in vain to make room for him. Not to be outdone, and with his sense of humor, and the anticipation of a delicious meal, he ended up half of himself sitting on the edge of the seat and the other half of himself almost on the lap of Jean's mother.

When school was out in May, Barclay went back to his home in Memphis, and found himself working most of his vacation time in Afro-American Vacation Bible schools, sponsored by the Shelby County Baptist Association. He actually enjoyed this experience with the exception of the high temperatures reached in the basement of these small black churches. There were not nearly enough fans to cool the multitude of excited children, and worst of all the children's favorite mid-morning treat was a big, sweet sucker with wooden sticks stuck in an even bigger dill pickle. To this day, Barclay abhors dill pickles, especially the smell.

Barclay's sophomore year at Union University went about the same as his first year – concentrated study seasoned with just enough antics between himself and his roommates to keep life interesting. Barclay and Jean spent many happy hours together doing their homework (Jean's mother's oak dining room table still today bears the faint impressions of assignments being prepared), and going to campus and church activities. During his second year Barclay had added responsibilities. He was elected Religion Editor on the BSU (Baptist Student Union) Council at Union University.

At the end of his second year Barclay spent the summer working in the mountains of East Tennessee, where he conducted Vacation Bible Schools and Bible study courses, working with children in the mornings and with adults at nights. Barclay shared his experience of his first encounter as a "summer missionary":

> … of the six different places where I stayed for a week during the summer, only one home conjures up negative memories about the "vittles," as they were called. Mrs. Tindall served as my first hostess for the six-week stay as a missionary in these mountains. She and three of her six children met me on Saturday afternoon at the designated "drop off" point in the county seat town where the other "ad hoc missionaries" were picked up as well by the families that would be their hosts for the coming week … most of them smelled pretty good, considering their bodies were reeking of a certain type of overpowering toilet water that I quickly learned was the alternative for a bi-weekly bath.
>
> The drive to their home was pleasant, considering the condition of the car and the rugged ridge-ridden gravel roads. Pleasant, because the two sisters and their brother felt obligated to entertain me with their expertise at inflating the massive wads of purple and pink bubble gum that was consistently blown in my direction and beyond their control and often landed in my lap – sometimes simultaneously from two sides, and once from three directions.
>
> This was Saturday evening and apparently the one evening of the month dedicated to the bathing event that required less water than the baptism of a single infant in a Catholic Church. Mrs. Tindall stood beside a table whereupon she had placed a large wash pan filled with water, and the children lined up without any sense of false modesty, facing their mother. Then one by one they approached her, beginning with the youngest, and she washed first the face, then the hands, then the feet – and finally other, more sensitive parts, beneath the loose fitting clothing – after which she

rinsed out the rag and invited the next in line to step up and "be made clean," beginning again with the face!

The Sunday spread (at noon) had everything imaginable – fried chicken and fried chicken and fried chicken, together with a wide variety of farm vegetables and homemade rolls. The pastor – who sat across from me – was asked to "say grace" which he did in record time and, even before I was able to lift my head and open my eyes, he had covered his plate with several choice pieces of chicken and had filled his mouth with mashed potatoes and gravy. I could see this meal was going to be quite a challenge.

Flies preyed on every meal.

Monday – Tuesday – Wednesday: This fare was repeated, in fact the same food exactly (without refrigeration) in precisely the same serving bowls as Sunday noon, and by Wednesday night I was sick! The house had been built along side a hill, with the outhouse on the upgrade directly from the window in my room, allowing me the full benefit of the aroma produced by the decaying feces, which intensified my illness. I assume they had intentionally placed the "guestroom" in this location, knowing that sooner or later their guests would be driven by diarrhea to seek refuge there, as I constantly did that night.

About Thursday noon, it was decided I should go to the doctor in the county seat, a proposal I whole-heartedly accepted, and so I headed off to the main road, where I had to hitchhike, because the family car was already in town. As soon as the doctor looked at me – even before the examination – he asked, "Did you come into town with the carnival last Saturday night?"

"No," I replied, "but if they are leaving today, I'll be glad to go with them!" According to the doctor, I had a touch of ptomaine poison for which he prescribed medication that happened to be available for free in his office. When I returned to the source of my discontent, I told my hostess that I had overeaten the rich, country food to which I was unaccustomed, and that the doctor had instructed me to fast and imbibe only "Kool-Aid" until my departure … on Saturday.

By the end of the six weeks of being a "missionary" in the mountains, Barclay never again complained about being an only child. Neither did he ever object to the food served at his mother's table.

Many good things happened to Barclay during the year of 1952. Almost every week presented a new challenge, but he received the good news with gratitude and excitement.

On May 27th, near the end of Barclay's junior year at Union, he was declared the winner of the M. E. Dodd Expository Writing Contest. On May 30, Dr. Roland Q. Leavell of the New Orleans Baptist Theological Seminary wrote a letter to Dr. M. E. Dodd, "On May the 27th it was my pleasure to hear the 'M. E. Dodd Expository Writing Contest' at Union University. Three young men named Booker, Jones, and Newman delivered three very excellent expository sermons in the contest. The award was given to Barclay Newman of Memphis, (Tennessee) who preached on Isaiah 6.1-8. His sermon would have done credit to any mature preacher."

Soon Barclay received a check with which he purchased *The Expositor's Greek New Testament* (a five volume set) to add to his library. Dr. M. E. Dodd wrote a brief but sincere note to Barclay in June after receiving a copy of Barclay's sermon, "I have read the address with great interest. I congratulate you on it. It is good."

During this same month, Barclay was elected President of both the Union University and the State Baptist Student Union (BSU). He would serve in both capacities during his senior year.

Sometime in late May of the same year, Barclay had been invited to preach at the Fruitland Baptist Church, a small church near Humboldt, Tennessee in view of a possible call as the new pastor. They had preaching services on the first and third Sundays of the month.

On June 2nd, Barclay received a letter from E. A. Thomas of the China Grove Baptist Church at Rutherford, Tennessee, inviting him to present both morning and evening sermons on June 8th in view of a calling as pastor to their Church. A Committee of members from the China Grove Church had attended a service at Fruitland to hear Barclay preach, without his knowing they would be coming. China Grove Baptist Church was also a small, well established, rural church of more than a 100 years old at this time, and on June 16th Mr. Thomas again wrote to Barclay, "This is to advise that China Grove Church went into conference yesterday and elected you as their new pastor for the balance of this church year at a salary of $1080.00 per annum … Second and fourth Sundays (each month) are the regular preaching days with two services, and you are to begin next Sunday which is June 22nd."

Then on July 7th, Barclay received a letter from Douglas Nix, the Church Clerk of the Fruitland Baptist Church, "The Fruitland Baptist Church held a special Conference July 6th, and extended you a call to be our pastor."

Between August 17th and 23rd Barclay, together with the dedicated church members at Fruitland, conducted his first revival. After Barclay had completed his third year at Union, he was ordained by the National Avenue Baptist Church of Memphis. Rev. Chester R. Parker, the pastor at that time, preached the ordination sermon. Then both he and Rev. William E. Lyles, Barclay's former pastor, together with others, signed the certificate of ordination.

Years later on September 13, 1981 Barclay was invited back to National Avenue Baptist Church to deliver the morning worship sermon for the Church's "Note-burning on Debt Retirement" and Homecoming Celebration. William E. Lyles was there for the special occasion, and after that wonderful visit with him, Barclay never got to see him again.

It was a very warm summer evening on August 2, 1952 that Barclay and Jean became engaged. Barclay had practically no money at that time. But his mother had given him a blue diamond that Barclay, Sr. had given to her many years before, and he proudly presented the ring to Jean with the diamond, which had been mounted in gold for her. The incident took place in Jean's front yard, where they were sitting in a couple of metal lawn chairs her Dad had freshly painted. Those same two chairs, only in a different color, may be found at their home today, tucked away under a small arbor in the back yard.

In Barclay's senior year at Union, he was elected the Student Council's Religious Activities Representative; he was President of both the "Life Service Band," and the Ministerial Society, and on November 1st, along with eight other students (including Jean), he was elected to Who's Who in American Universities and Colleges. The students were selected by members of the Union University faculty according to the standard set up by the national organization, which includes scholarship, leadership and participation in extra curricular and academic activities; citizenship and services to the school, and the promise of future usefulness to business and society.

At the same time, Barclay also served as the Senior Class Chaplain. What a year it was! Barclay had also accepted the call to pastor two half-time churches in West Tennessee, where he would preach twice a month at one and twice a month at the other.

It was during the summer months preceding Barclay's senior year at Union, that he was made aware he needed a car to get him to his two preaching assignments four Sundays out of the month. As a rule, he went from his boarding house near the campus back home to Memphis on Friday afternoon or else early Saturday morning. Then he would leave early on Sunday morning, (earlier than necessary, but in case of car trouble, he would have some time leverage) to drive either to Rutherford or to Fruitland, depending on which Sunday of the month it was.

A "friend" of the family recommended a really ancient 1937 colorless Dodge coupe, which could be had for just a few hundred dollars. It's hard to say how much trouble that car came to be, stranding Barclay more than once on his way to preach. But he never missed a Sunday; he managed to get there and on time one way or the other. When it seemed impossible to keep the old Dodge, he traded it in for a '48 Chevrolet coupe. This car was an exceptionally good car – again the color almost colorless. There was only one big problem. The back seat was considered a "full" seat, though very limited in leg space – much like the manufacturer had somehow failed to make the frame long enough. The actual legroom was half the space you would expect in a normal car.

Barclay and Jean had spent their brief and exciting four years at Union University, attending meetings on and off the campus, going to church together whenever possible, working diligently on their class assignments, and attending many campus and church socials. Barclay and Jean today look back on that time as being one of the grandest highlights in their entire lives. They graduated together on May 26, 1953. At the conclusion of these wonderful days filled with much activity, on a Saturday afternoon four days after graduation, Barclay and Jean were married on May 30, 1953 at the West Jackson Baptist Church in Jackson, Tennessee, Jean's hometown. The minister chosen to perform the ceremony was Barclay's Greek and New Testament professor at Union University, Dr. R.C. Briggs.

The young couple recalls the day Dr. Briggs sat down with them in the Dean's Office at the college. He gave them excellent advice, most of which they don't remember verbatim today, but one statement he made still stands out significantly from all the rest as he said with a twinkle in his eye, "You think you're in love today. But just wait a few years from now, and you'll see that your love for one another will grow and become much stronger and deeper as the years go by."

On the day before the wedding, the newlyweds were pre-warned that some of Barclay's good college "buddies" had planned to really "dress" up their car during the reception. And Barclay feared the worst. After all, these were the same young men that Barclay had played pranks on for the last four years, and of course, they on him. So a day or two before the ceremony was to take place, Barclay arranged with Jean's brother Carlton Butler to whisk them away in his car. Barclay had gotten up very early on the morning of the Big Day and driven his car to the little town of Humboldt, Tennessee, about twenty miles from Jackson and parked it in a safe place. This plan worked out quite well, and the couple did not have to leave the church in a vehicle that had been painted with bright letters and decorated with flowing streamers and with old shoes dragging behind.

Now Barclay and Jean, sporting a clean car, headed for a honeymoon in East Tennessee. It had become quite dark, and what they both remember most about that drive was a sight, which took their breaths away. The old highway to Nashville, Tennessee from Jackson was more winding at that time than it is today. Just as they were coming out of a rather sharp curve in the road with low hills on either side of the highway, they simultaneously tensed as they saw a harvest moon so low and so large that they immediately thought they were about to run into a humongous brightly lit Shell sign within inches of the road.

Another thing they remember vividly was going to the big First Baptist Church in Nashville, Tennessee the next day to hear Dr. W. F. Powell preach. After a few days in East Tennessee, it was a mutual decision that they would return one day early in order to buy a good, sturdy card table, so Barclay would have a temporary desk for the summer months before moving to Louisville, Kentucky, where they would enroll in the Baptist Theological Seminary. Trenton, Tennessee was to be their very first home together from early June through the middle of August.

The newlyweds had rented two upstairs rooms with a shared bath in an old, but elegant house, which today is on the register in Tennessee for historical homes. It was built in 1868 by a Mr. Marshall.

In Trenton Barclay obtained work in the Brown Shoe Company, and Jean always found activities to keep busy while Barclay worked away from their upstairs apartment. She remembers one such activity. With the dozens of beautiful wedding gifts – most of which were now packed and stored away in Jean's parents' attic -- there was not a single bedspread among them. So she began the task of making a double yellow bedspread by hand to have ready when they reached the Seminary. There was no sewing machine in their newly rented quarters, but this just served as a challenge for Jean.

Barclay and Jean were happy to be living near their Church "fields" at Fruitland and Rutherford, and Barclay knew there would be times when Jean would need to drive their car. In fact, their first Vacation Bible School was approaching, and Barclay's job with the Brown Shoe Company involved five full days a week. Jean had taken a course in Drivers' Education in High School but did not feel that she either wanted to or could drive a car.

But Barclay insisted that she learn. Very patiently he went through all the steps with her over and over again. Every day in the late afternoon, he would take her out for a practice drive. But Jean thought she would never be able to start the car without jerking it and complained to Barclay that she did not even want to learn to drive.

Barclay had grown up eating his mother's good food, and he and Jean received an abundance of gourmet dishes on the weekends at the two half-time churches where Barclay was pastor. Mrs. Leslie Scruggs, Mrs. Lester Hicks, Mrs. Bernice Wilson, Mrs. Douglas Nix, Mrs. C. O. Hardison, and Mrs. Carl Coleman, among others, must surely have outdone any fare found in the pages of *Southern Living*. Once, Jean said about Mrs. Lois Scruggs, "If she prepared it, I would even eat chitlins."

To Barclay's delight, Jean decided she would have to become a good cook. With recipes from the ladies at both churches and a few gracefully shared hints, she first began that summer in their tiny upstairs kitchen with no stove. Barclay's mother had given them a one-unit electric hot plate and another electric hotplate with a rounded hood-like cover that could convert the hotplate to a small oven. So when one of the church members presented them with a large pail of blackberries, Jean decided to make a blackberry cobbler. The dough was no problem. It was put together like an old timer and arranged in a nice new casserole dish and placed in the hooded hotplate.

Jean checked it often, and after a considerable amount of time, when the outside turned golden brown and the sugar on top bubbled, she decided it was done. It was beautiful! The deep purple juice had oozed out around the pastry. Barclay smiled with proud approval, and at the end of the meal each had a large serving. Looks are deceiving! The cobbler was nice on the outside, but the berries inside were as raw as they had been while hanging from the blackberry bushes, and the thick dough was only cooked on the outside.

Towards the middle of August, Barclay and Jean once again packed their meager belongings – mostly clothes, Barclay's books, and a few cooking and eating utensils and began their trip to Louisville, Kentucky where they would enroll at the Baptist Theological Seminary. On arrival at the big campus, Barclay and Jean were assigned student housing on their very first day. Their new address would be Barnard Hall.

This building was a huge mansion – at one time someone's beautiful private home situated on a large immaculately manicured lawn. The house had tall white columns in front and a drive circling around to the back of the house, where you entered a marble floored vestibule with a winding staircase to your left. On inspecting the house, they discovered it had at least eight bedrooms with an enormous formal living room and separate formal dining room.

As it turned out, the Newmans were the first couple to arrive and therefore had their choice of which bedroom they would occupy for their first year. They chose the Master bedroom, which went the full width of the house with a walk-in closet and had a hidden safe deposit box at the side of a huge fireplace. In order to disengage the door to the safe deposit box, you pressed a button hidden under the molding of the fireplace.

There were two full-sized stoves in this kitchen – much to Jean's delight. Now would be the right time to make those delicious yeast rolls that the church ladies served every Sunday. She had been given their no-fail recipe and one day went to work. She did every thing according to directions, but the dough simply refused to rise. The ample mass was placed in a big mixing bowl, covered over by a nice thin cloth, and placed in a warm spot next to the oven. After several hours when the dough wouldn't rise, Jean became disgusted and threw the whole batch in the kitchen trash receptacle, then served Barclay a slice of store-bought sandwich bread and vegetables for dinner.

The next morning when the two of them went downstairs for breakfast, the yeast dough had risen until it popped open the lid and draped over the side of the trashcan, almost reaching the floor. Jean was tempted to rescue it, but thought better of that. But from then on, the Newmans had good homemade yeast rolls during the week – that is, until someone commented on Barclay's putting on extra pounds.

Barclay was given the job of custodian for this massive, formally, private home called Barnard Hall. Barclay and Jean came to feel very much at home in these beautiful surroundings. But Jean will testify today that for the next nine months, she saw more of Barclay's back while sitting at his desk in their large combination bedroom-sitting room than anything else.

When classes resumed their second year, Barnard Hall had been selected by the Seminary to house the Music Department, and now the Newmans were reassigned to a very old, on campus, unfurnished couples' dormitory, Judson Hall. They knew before they left school for the summer months where they would be living, so they returned to the campus in the fall, prepared with furniture – mostly "home made".

Barclay continued to pastor his two small churches in Tennessee after he had enrolled as a seminary student, and more often than not he would have a fellow-student pastor hitching a ride with him from the Seminary to designated drop-off places in fairly close proximity to where Barclay had to travel four Sundays out of the month.

By this time Barclay and Jean were into the late winter months of their second year at the Seminary. Jean often went with Barclay to the churches in Tennessee, and as usual had gone on this particularly cold winter weekend. When Sunday night came, the plan for the three of them was as usual to begin driving back, approximately 320 miles, to the Seminary after the Sunday night worship services at the Fruitland Baptist Church, hoping to arrive at the seminary campus in the wee hours of Monday morning. At its best, it was an all night drive. When Jean went along, which she often did, she always felt "dead in the head" on Mondays at the lawyer's office, where she worked in downtown Louisville. Sunday was always an extremely tiring day.

As soon as Barclay and Jean finished lunch each Sunday in one of the church member's home, they would immediately begin visiting as many members of the church as possible in the length of time they would have before eating an evening meal and arriving back at the church for the evening services. Fortunately, there were no Monday classes, a plan designed to let the all night traveling preacher boys catch up with their rest by early Tuesday morning when classes resumed.

On this weekend, as they headed north in the direction of the Seminary, Barclay's car broke down in a small town soon after they got out of Tennessee. It looked serious to Barclay and Wayne Jones, and neither of them knew a lot about the mechanics of an automobile. So they decided to get Jean to the nearest train station, since she was scheduled to be at work in Louisville at the Greenbaum, Barnett, and Carroll Law Office by 8:00 on Monday morning. After riding all night by car and then train, Jean went straight to her receptionist job from the train station in downtown Louisville, Kentucky.

Tired and disheveled, she powdered her face, brushed her teeth, and fluffed up her now wrinkled Sunday clothes. All day she couldn't stop thinking of Barclay and Wayne and wondering what the outcome had been with the car. She returned from work to the small apartment at half past five Monday evening to find that Barclay and Wayne had never gotten back to the campus at all. She kept telling herself that after the car had been repaired, the two men had likely run into bad weather on those narrow winding highways between Tennessee and Kentucky. But even with very bad weather, something had to be wrong. And that turned out to be a pretty good guess!

Jean recalls as she puttered around in the apartment, worried sick, a knock came at the back door. By this time, she was in tears. The visitor turned out to be their next-door neighbor in the apartment complex – Judson Hall on the Seminary campus. It was Emanuel Dahunsi. He immediately knew something was wrong even before Jean could pour out her worry in one quick breath. Emanuel was the most godly man she had ever known, and when he prayed, everyone present felt God's Spirit so close that they could reach out and touch him. Emanuel offered without hesitation to pray with her that Barclay and Wayne would return safely.

Not two hours had gone by before the two men returned with the most horrific tales Jean had ever heard. It was the '51 Chevrolet. It broke down on them time and time again. Finally, they were forced to spend the night in a small town, resting uneasily on hard benches at the jail, which also housed the police station. Neither of the two had more than a very few dollars cash with them – only the small checks from their respective churches. The policemen told them about a man who could fix the car, and they even hauled the car to the mechanic, only to find him drunk and unable to do an adequate job. However, he was lucid enough to tell them to go to the bank when it opened the next morning and cash their checks they each had received from their churches on Sunday evening. Why not just use their cell phone? Good idea, but cell phones had never been heard of in those days. Moreover, there was no phone in the Newman's apartment in Judson Hall – only a pay phone in the basement of that building.

Barclay later related what happened. The radiator began to leak water rapidly, and the two weary preachers stopped often to fill it up so they could drive on. Once they had to break the ice in a large water barrel to get to the water. This filling up the radiator was repeated over and over, every few miles. Of course, there was no working heater now in the car. Finally, the timing belt went out, and they found themselves close to the police station and city jail in a small town, where the police came somewhat to their rescue.

When the two finally dragged in that night, they were fairly frozen to the bone and ravenously hungry, not to mention their state of exhaustion.

The next day Barclay and Jean partly drove and partly pushed the car to a dealer there in Louisville not far from the Seminary and told the salesman that they never wanted to look at another second-hand car for as long as they lived. "We want a new car – the least expensive one on your lot." It turned out to be a new, darker than royal blue Ford. "We'll take it." Their bargaining power was very limited at this stage, and they never knew if they had gotten a good deal or not.

From the beginning, Jean disliked the color, but the car always got them to where they were going. Once she took the car along with her sister, Lucy Nell (Butler) Sawyer, who was now married to James Sawyer, to Jackson, Tennessee for a Friday/Saturday visit with their parents. Barclay would follow the next day with one of the other student preachers. The minute Jean and Lucy arrived at their parents' home, Jean announced to Lucy that she wanted to wash the car as a surprise for Barclay. On Sunday morning, the two drove to one of their churches in the cleanest, shiniest cars on the road – a slightly faded, less than royal blue, but clean, because Jean had scrubbed the car with her mother's laundry detergent, Tide.

In April of 1955 during Barclay's second year at the Seminary, he was elected Executive Secretary of the Student Executive Committee of Southern Seminary with major responsibility for guiding the Seminary's total program of student activities during the academic year of 1956.

When the third year rolled around at the Seminary, Barclay and Jean were assigned to still other living quarters. They were soon to become proud parents, and married couples with one child were being housed at Fuller Hall, a beautiful and convenient new complex on the campus.

During the summer of this year, Barclay and Jean remained on the campus rather than move to Trenton, Tennessee, the small town near his church at Fruitland. In the meantime, Jean was working at the American Printing House for the Blind in Louisville, though at the end of her seventh month of pregnancy, she had left the office of the Printing House.

Jean was allowed to bring home enough work for one month, and on the day the work was completed and turned in, she realized suddenly that evening after dinner that she and Barclay needed to hurry to the Baptist Hospital in Louisville, where Tina Jean was born shortly after they arrived. Tina was a tiny, red-haired, doll-like baby weighing only 5 pounds and 6 ounces. When the parents took her home in five days, she weighed only 4 pounds and 15 ounces. The doctor assured them, "She's little, but loud, and fortunately healthy. Keep her room slightly darkened for about a month until her eyes have had time to develop fully."

The Newmans made three more moves while at the Seminary – one to a private upstairs apartment over a neighborhood grocery store and almost adjacent to the campus when Tina was about 10 months old, and later to Seminary Village, an off-campus complex for married students with children. The third move involved was to a large rural church with a parsonage next door. The church was about 90 miles north of the Seminary and not far from the Ohio State line. Here Barclay was pastor of the Ten Mile Baptist Church in northern Kentucky.

Barclay has always been a "die hard" prankster. But from the beginning Jean felt that she somehow escaped the pranks that he loved to play on her two sisters and once on Jean's first cousin. However, Jean can't forget a prank he played on her at the home of one of the church members at the Ten Mile Baptist Church.

Barclay had just recently been called as pastor of this church, but his family had not yet moved into the parsonage. So they were invited to eat lunch after the morning worship services with Mr. and Mrs. Elmore Collins. Shortly after the three Newmans arrived at Mr. Collins' home, he offered to show them a little bit of the farm – the chickens, the ducks, the cows, the vegetable garden and so on, while Mrs. Collins finished making preparations for a beautiful and abundant lunch. As Barclay and Jean strolled in the back yard of the old farmhouse, a dog crawled out from under the house wagging his tail. Mr. Collins told them something about this one-eyed dog and recounted how faithful he had always been.

Jean had all her life been a bit afraid of dogs, and so she kept her distance. She thought to herself that was the worst excuse for an animal she had ever seen. The nondescript hound was just awful looking. Its right eye, which was devoid of any sight, was glazed over and appeared to have a well-worn marble in the socket; he was mangy, skinny, and just generally the most pathetic animal she had ever encountered.

After a minute or two, Jean excused herself and left the two men and went gladly back to the kitchen in hopes of lending Mrs. Collins a hand with lunch. In her absence, Barclay and Elmore, although very new friends, contrived a plan that Barclay would announce soon after they all sat down to eat.

When most of the dishes had been passed around the large table, Barclay said to Jean in particular, but in the presence of all the guests around the table, "Jean, Mr. Collins wants to give us his favorite dog 'Cry Baby' as soon as we get settled in the parsonage. He will be good protection for you and Tina when I am away."

The story Barclay was telling was so sincere, Jean believed him, but didn't know what to say. She was dumbfounded. There was no way she was going to accept this pitiful pet as her own. Jean didn't say much for fear she would offend her host and hostess. But she knew in her heart what she might do if that dog came to live with them. Almost at the end of the meal, Barclay admitted it was a joke, and he and Elmore had a big laugh.

At the Ten Mile Baptist Church parsonage Jean was a full time mother and pastor's wife, and in September of 1959, she and Barclay became proud parents of their second child – another little girl. But Dana was not so little! She weighed almost 8 pounds at birth and could take her four-ounce bottle in a flash. Soon she was taking 8 ounces of her formula, eating baby food, and sleeping all night.

On one Sunday evening, before Dana was born, Jean did not attend the evening service at the church. It was either late winter or in the early spring of 1959, and the doctor had ordered her to rest in bed for a few weeks. There seemed to be some problem as to whether she could carry the baby to full term.

Frankly, going to bed almost anytime was difficult for Jean. She was born with a large dose of energy and enthusiasm for life, and she never wanted to miss out on anything. But she and Barclay had planned for months for this child, and she was determined not to jeopardize their chances of bringing another healthy baby into their family. Jean was convinced that she should follow the doctor's orders.

Home was next door to the church, and word got around quickly that Jean had been confined to bed for awhile, and many of the church members offered to help out by entertaining Tina, who was a very active young miss.

Just a short time before the Sunday evening services were scheduled to begin, one of the ladies came by the house to check on Jean and offer to take Tina into her care at the church services. It was planned that while Barclay was in the pulpit Tina would sit with her. During one of the hymns, Tina quietly and quickly slipped out from the pew, unnoticed for a minute or two by the lady in charge. The parsonage sat just yards away from the church, and she ran home, letting herself in by the front door. Their yard bordered the church parking lot, and fortunately you could walk across the side yard and go into the church without ever going into the parking lot. Jean immediately sent her back over to the church with instructions to be very quiet when she went in the big door.

Tina did as she was told, but made one quick stop from the front door to the door of the church. She picked up a kitten that lived with its mother in the church basement. Clutching the kitten with all her might, she reentered the church. Pride got the best of her. She was so happy that she had caught the unsuspecting creature that she ran straight up to the pulpit before anyone could stop her announcing, "Daddy, daddy, look, I caught the kitty all by myself." Barclay was shocked that she had apparently gotten away from the lady looking after her and stepped aside to get her corralled once again. When he made an effort to coach her back to the lady who was by now terribly embarrassed and coming forward, every light in the church suddenly and without warning went out. The church was totally black. There were no streetlights to shine on this rural church.

At this, Barclay quickly decided that this was a good time to cut his sermon short and close with a long prayer.

Barclay finished his thesis in the summer of 1959 and graduated on January 12, 1960 from the Baptist Theological Seminary in Louisville, Kentucky.

Barclay has always felt indebted to his professors at Southern Seminary. During his tenure there, he felt privileged to have Dr. W. W. Owens (better known as "Redtop" to his peers), who, with his unique sense of humor, brought the Old Testament to life. Barclay always enjoyed his studies with Dr. T. C. Smith, who was equally as passionate about the

New Testament and who later became a close and treasured friend of the Newmans. Barclay and Jean were fortunate enough to have T. C. and his wife Ellen to come to Springfield, Missouri for a number of years after he retired. Ellen's mother, Mrs. Flossie Stewart, lived there and attended First Baptist Church, when Dr. T. T. Crabtree was their pastor.

Barclay has gained valuable insights from T. C. Smith's writings over the years. Dr. Bill Morton and Dr. Henry Turlington rank high on Barclay's list for great professors during his time at the Seminary. Dr. Turlington was a missionary to China prior to lecturing at Southern Seminary. While Barclay was doing his residence work at the Seminary, Henry chose him to serve as his Teaching Fellow in the Department of New Testament Interpretation and Greek.

Those were wonderful days of delving deeply into the Scriptures and putting to use the Greek language that Barclay had learned and grown to appreciate under the guidance of Dr. R. C. Briggs at Union University.

Chapter IV

First Academic Teaching Opportunity

In the very early winter months of 1960, Barclay learned that Dr. Morris Ashcraft had recommended him to teach in the Religion Department at William Jewell College in Liberty, Missouri. Dr. David Moore, head of the Religion Department, wrote Barclay a letter of invitation to come to the campus for a visit and an interview.

As Barclay anticipated the trip in the cold winter months, he realized he would need to take an overcoat with him. But since he did not have a lightweight winter coat, he would have to wear the heavy winter coat his Uncle Searcy Cummins had given him. This coat was designed and made for artic wear – it was beyond heavy and fit Barclay's slender frame like an oversized black wool rug.

It looked fairly certain that Barclay would be asked to come to William Jewell College after he enjoyed the visit with David and felt he could make a contribution to this Baptist College. And now it looked like the Newmans would soon be moving again – this time from Kentucky to far away Missouri. This was what Barclay had prepared himself for during all those years of study, and the challenge was really exciting.

After a short wait, Barclay received another letter from David Moore, offering Barclay the position as Assistant Professor of Religion at William Jewell College, which he readily accepted.

There was just one sad aspect of this new move. Barclay and Jean would be saying "good-bye" to some of the most wonderful people in the world. While at Ten Mile Baptist Church in Kentucky, the Newmans had become very close friends to Glenna and Bud McMichael and their two little girls, Lesa and Lori, who were very close to Tina and Dana's ages. The Newmans spent many happy hours in their comfortable and delightfully furnished home.

The Moreheads – Jim and Rae, fellow Seminary students, were serving a nearby church in downtown Glencoe, Kentucky. They also had two little girls, and the Newmans often had good meals and good fellowship with them. At Ten Mile the Newmans would have to say their "good-byes" to their neighbors and church members.

Kay and Lou Ann Collins, members of Ten Mile, were beautiful people and remained good friends, even after an almost catastrophic incident in their home, when they invited the Newman family for lunch one Sunday after the worship service. Their daughter Tina was not yet three and always took a long nap after the noon meal. Barclay had been the pastor at Ten Mile for just a short time, and he and Jean were looking forward to another great meal at this church member's farm home.

As soon as the meal was over, Jean asked Lou Ann if it was all right to put Tina down for a nap. Jean always looked forward to those afternoon naps because it gave her a break from watching a very active little girl for that hour or so. Then too, that day she could slip in the kitchen undistracted and help clear the dishes and chat with her new friend. Lou Ann showed Jean where to put Tina down for her nap. On the big bed, Jean put a warm blanket over Tina, since that room was not well heated. Then she closed the door and rejoined the adults. She helped Lou Ann do the dishes, and afterward the four of them sat down in the living room.

Time went by quickly, and after an hour Jean tiptoed to the door of the room where Tina was napping and listened to hear her stirring – not a sound. Jean did this several times, and when two hours had gone by, Jean became concerned and opened the door to check on Tina. What Jean saw shocked, embarrassed, and astounded her. She called Lou Ann quickly, while apologizing profusely and offering to clean up the whole dresser.

Tina had awakened and spotted a large round jar of deodorant on the low dresser with a huge attached round mirror. She had managed to open the jar, climb up on the dresser stool, and meticulously paint every inch of the dresser and mirror with the white deodorant. Jean was a little relieved when Lou Ann started laughing. She was a big lady, and she laughed till she shook. Jean wasn't laughing. She could see Barclay having to buy Lou Ann and her husband Kay a new dresser. By now both men had joined the two ladies staring at the artwork, and only one of them was laughing, and it wasn't Barclay. As it turned out, the deodorant came off with a lot of scrubbing and polishing and without damaging the finish on the dresser. To say the least, Barclay and Jean were relieved.

When the Newmans were still living in the parsonage at Glencoe, Kentucky next door to the Ten Mile Church, Jean's sister and her husband came for a visit. James (known as Buz) Sawyer and Lucy lived in another church community in Kentucky as well, but a good many miles away. Barclay wanted to show Buz a good time. So on the second night of their visit, Barclay suggested the two of them go frog gigging in a nearby pond. Of course, they waited until dark before they set out with flashlight and gig in hand.

Barclay doesn't remember if he and Buz came home that night with a lot of frogs or not, but he clearly remembers frantically freeing himself from thorns and brush and definitely leaving the pond in a hurry. Buz had unintentionally let the flashlight beam tilt upwards just enough for Barclay to see that he had come eye-to-eye with a huge water moccasin hanging over a partly submerged barbed wire fence. This snake may have been real dead but there surely must be a brother or two lurking around, and Barclay wasn't willing to wait around to find out.

On another occasion when Barclay and Jean were visiting Buz and Lucy in their more eastern Kentucky church community, Buz offered to take Barclay fishing. As the pastor of the church, Buz had a standing invitation to fish at any time in one of his church members' pond. There was even an old boat conveniently tied up at the water's edge, and the two young men stepped in with their gear.

They rowed around from spot to spot casting their lines in every direction but didn't get a single nibble between the two of them. They both were about to give up and call it a bad day, when they noticed that someone had a trot line running across a section of the pond. And, of course, they were curious to see just what had been hooked sometime earlier and before they arrived in the late afternoon. Gingerly they rowed over to the line, picked it up slowly, and there was a three-pound catfish securely hooked or so they thought. Just as they were about to put the line and fish back in the water, the catfish gave one last effort to free himself. And whop! The fish flopped right in the boat at their feet. They dropped the line back in the water and looked at each other. Neither of them figured they could or even wanted to reattach this poor, beautiful fish to that big rusty old hook.

The two of them made their way back to the house. Lucy and Jean met them at the back door both at once asking if they had had any luck catching anything. Buz and Barclay each sported a sheepish grin on their faces, and when asked if they had caught anything, the simultaneous answer was, "sorta," and the two gave no further details until much, much later. The men proceeded to dress the hapless fish while Lucy heated the oil. Everyone agreed it was one tasty, mysterious fish.

When Barclay and Jean were forced to seriously contemplate their move, they realized they would need at least a thousand dollars for moving expenses and setting up house once they arrived in Liberty, Missouri. Barclay went straight to Mr. Frank Woods, a church member and a respected friend, and asked him if he could borrow the money from him. Barclay presented his request as a strictly business deal, offering to sign a note stating that he would make regular payments to Frank through the Bank in Glencoe, Kentucky. Frank, without the slightest hesitation, agreed to the loan.

Some years later, Barclay and Jean learned that Frank Woods would not loan money to anyone – not even his own brother. For some reason, Frank trusted Barclay, but the Newmans were not sure if he ever really expected to get that money back.

James Morehead and Jim Grubbs helped Barclay and Jean make the move. The two Jims drove the truck with all the Newman's earthly possessions, and Barclay drove their car behind the truck. Jean was kept busy trying to keep a wiggly almost four-year-old and a less than a year-old sick baby occupied and comfortable.

Soon after arriving in Liberty, Missouri, Jean took Dana to Dr. Richard Bowles, the doctor who had been recommended to her by the Edsons. Over the next six years, Dick became more than a physician to the Newman family. He and Polly proved to be their dear Christian friends. Barclay and Jean both recall the delicious fish fries they had at the Bowles' home and the good times their girls had with their four sons.

When the Newmans moved to Liberty, Barclay was asked to preach on numerous occasions. On September 25, 1960 Barclay preached at the Linneus Baptist Church in Linneus, Missouri, where he met Joe Turner, the Sunday School Superintendent, a man for whom Barclay came to have great respect. From August 27th until September 9th of that same year, Barclay held a revival at the Linneus Baptist Church.

Barclay preached the morning and evening sermons on October 16, 1960 at the Second Baptist Church in Liberty, where he and Jean had become members shortly after moving to Liberty.

Barclay had been on the staff at William Jewell College only briefly, when Dr. Heber Peacock, a faculty member of Midwestern Theological Seminary in North Kansas City, was asked by Dr. Eugene A. Nida, Translations Officer of the American Bible Society in New York, to recommend someone who could prepare a concise Greek-English Dictionary of the New Testament. This volume was designed to be used primarily by Bible translators working under the auspices of the United Bible Societies. Heber gave him Barclay's name and phone number. Soon afterward, Gene contacted Barclay by phone and described to him both what he felt these translators needed and what could also be a useful study tool for other serious students of New Testament Greek.

Together Gene and Barclay began to think about the directions in which such a dictionary should go, in order to be most helpful for translators. In the Preface to the Dictionary, Barclay summarized its most essential and unique features:

> It is distinctive, for rather than listing various meanings of words on the basis of traditional etymological methods which follow logico-historical principles, the meanings are arranged according to their usage in the New Testament, so that the more central and frequent meanings are given first and the secondary or peripheral meanings follow. Moreover, the meanings are given in present-day English, rather than in accord with traditional ecclesiastical terminology.

As soon as Barclay considered how to proceed with this project, he realized that the material would need to be typed, and Barclay explained to Gene that he had never taken typing in school and couldn't type. No problem. Gene's quick response to Barclay was, "Learn how!" Barclay obtained a college typing book and taught himself to type with fair speed and much accuracy. The little portable typewriter certainly did not have the capability to type in Greek, so all Greek words were meticulously drawn in by hand.

The dictionary should be designed to have no more than 200 pages total, since the title included the word "Concise." When the dictionary was completed, Barclay had submitted a manuscript of 203 pages.

Barclay, of course, was teaching at William Jewell College at this time, but he agreed to take on this important project, provided the College would give him permission to do so and at the same time continue to lecture. Fortunately, it was William Jewell's policy that its professors were encouraged to produce written works in their specific fields.

Barclay began the tedious process in about 1963 and continued working through all of 1964 and beyond. He decided on the format best suited for him, and his method proved helpful. He cut sheets of typing paper to an approximate size of 5" X 4" and used a separate page for each Greek entry. If memory serves him correctly, he filed them in alphabetical order in a couple of narrow shoeboxes.

When Barclay went to New York to sign a contract for this project, the administrative personnel offered him $3.00 an hour for his time and expertise. Barclay's salary at William Jewell College was meager, but he felt the amount of $3.00 an hour would put pressure on him to finish quickly. So he suggested the American Bible Society pay him $2.75 an hour for his work. When Barclay received his first small check after turning in his hours, the amount paid to him was yet smaller – all of $2.50 per hour. That was the time in Jean and Barclay's marriage when Jean decided it would be best if she were to take over the managing of the family's bills and finances in general. As it turned out, Barclay has always been perfectly happy that he doesn't have to worry about such mundane things.

Although Barclay had completed and submitted his work while living and working as a Translations Consultant in the Philippines in the late sixties, the Dictionary was not published until 1971. The United Bible Societies printed and has for years distributed around the world the widely used dictionary.

At one time or another, every father dreams of being a hero to his children on at least one occasion. Barclay was no exception, and he truly was named "hero" of the year by his oldest daughter Tina, when she was in the second grade at the Mann Hill Elementary School in Liberty, Missouri. Mrs. Elva McClard was her teacher.

The last part of October was nearing. One evening at the dinner table, the elder of the Newmans' two daughters, Tina, now in her second year at school, announced to her Dad that she would need an owl to take to her schoolteacher within the next few days. Halloween was approaching – the time of year when witches and black cats, pumpkins and owls become favorite objects of adoration and excitement to seven year olds.

For days the children in her class had been bringing a variety of large and small pumpkins and ears upon ears of Indian corn. All the boys and girls had drawn and cut out black paper cats, witches, and paper owls. But at least one child had volunteered to bring a real live owl to school for the children to observe first hand.

"My Dad will go out and catch one for me," she had announced to her teacher and all the students in her second grade class.

The day Tina came home from school and informed her mother of her plans, Jean remembers that she laughed – not a ridiculing laugh but an amused one. In the beginning, Jean was certain that she must not really be serious, but on second glance she could tell that Tina was more determined than usual when asking for a favor of her Dad. She did, indeed, intend to have an owl, and she would soon present it to her teacher and twenty-nine classmates.

Her insistence made Jean attempt to become more convincing as she explained to her that there are some things in life we just can't have, no matter how badly we want them. The kids would understand if she had to break her promise. Jean told her she could *not* have a real owl now or probably ever. Jean was keenly aware of the fact that Tina's Dad had neither the wherewithal, nor the time, nor the patience to capture a live owl.

Besides, Jean told herself, "This is pure nonsense, even for a second grader to come up with." To shoot an owl – maybe, but to bring one back alive and unharmed – well – that would be out of the question! Jean tried more than once to convince Tina that her request was a bit ridiculous, hoping perhaps she would see clearly how impossible a task this would be for her Dad. Both her Dad and I hoped she would eventually realize the absurdity of her request, laugh about it, and then forget about it.

Yet every day when Tina came home from school, before the afternoon was over, she brought up the subject very nonchalantly and inquired as to when she would be getting the owl to take to school. Jean tried everything. She promised Tina another trip to the supermarket, where she could select some nice ears of Indian corn for her class. She had already taken a bright orange pumpkin to share with her classmates.

But no. Tina never forgot nor changed her mind. The more Jean tried to dissuade her about taking a live owl to school, the more resolved she became. She didn't fuss or whine or even pout. She only set her composure and determined in silence to have the owl.

Finally, Jean tried to make a mental picture for Tina as to what it would involve for her Dad to go out into the cold night and climb up in all the trees, in a not so nearby woods, hunting for a lonely owl. He might climb a thousand trees and still never see a single owl; and if he did, how could he be quiet enough to capture it? Neither of them knew a thing about catching or trapping owls.

With all Jean's reasoning, she wasn't getting anywhere. There were two things she was deeply concerned about. Jean wanted Tina to see how ridiculous her request was, and also she felt it was her bound duty to protect her dad from loosing face with his worshipful daughter. Neither of them enjoyed seeing Tina's growing disappointment. Eventually Jean kept quiet and said nothing.

The days slipped away without much mention of the owl. Tina's days were full and happy ones. Both her dad and mom hoped that at last she had forgotten about the whole owl incident. After a time they thought that surely she had, and they were, to say the least, somewhat relieved.

Yet again more time had slipped away, when Dad and Mom learned otherwise. One afternoon Tina calmly informed her parents that she had reminded Mrs. McClard and all her classmates that she would still bring the owl she had promised, even though Halloween had long since come and gone. She would bring an owl just as soon as her Daddy found a way to capture one. "He is still trying," she had told them.

Now the classroom was decorated with paper Santa Clauses, Christmas trees, tinsel, and decorative balls of many designs and colors. It was less than a week before Christmas Day, when the Newman family of four was anticipating a trip to a southern state to enjoy the Christmas holidays with the girls' grandmother and other relatives. On this particular occasion, Jean had been busy all day making preparations for their approaching trip. Clothes for four people had to be gotten ready and packed.

Many Christmas packages had to be wrapped and checked and rechecked to make sure nothing was left behind.

Jean was tired and trying desperately to think of a way to get out of preparing the evening meal. Barclay sensed her plight and suggested that the family go out to their favorite drive-in hamburger place in North Kansas City. This was always a treat for the girls. They would eat in the car. But Barclay stated that he first needed to make a quick trip back to his office on the college campus. When Barclay had left his office building earlier in the day, his mail had not come, and he also needed to pick up some papers to take on their trip to Tennessee. He promised to return very shortly, and Jean would have the girls well bundled up for the cold night out. The three of them would be ready and waiting when he returned. He assured Jean he could be back in less than fifteen or twenty minutes.

In less time than that, the girls were ready and waiting. Twenty-five minutes passed, then thirty. Just about that time Barclay's car slowly turned into the driveway, and he came rushing in the house, completely out of breath and looking literally like he had swallowed a canary. He looked straight at Tina, and without a word motioned her to follow him to the car. Little sister Dana and Mom had to come along too. The excitement was contagious. Barclay shone his flashlight on an object in the back seat of the car. There sat, wide-eyed and frightened, an owl. It looked more like a toy bat then an owl. But it was not a wind up toy with eyes darting back and forth as it made an effort to focus on their amazed faces. Barclay had brought Tina her owl as big as life itself. Tina requested no explanation. It mattered little how he had trapped the small owl. He had done what she knew he would do.

Unlike Tina, Jean literally couldn't wait to know how and where he had gotten the owl. Barclay and Jean first herded their giggling, jumping girls back into the house. Then Barclay hurriedly put on his heavy work gloves and went back to the car to get the scared and very active bird. Jean scrambled for a box big enough to put it in until they could return that evening and borrow a cage of some description to house the shivering, long wished-for creature. Their whole house was vibrating with excitement. One might say it was rocking with all the jumping the two girls were getting away with. None of them could believe what they had just witnessed. On their way to eat hamburgers, the loud exchange of the two girls in the back seat of the car made it difficult for Jean to hear Barclay's account of how the feat had been accomplished.

Barclay had left the college campus, and his car had been moving at a moderate speed along a tree lined residential street in their small

Midwestern town of Liberty, Missouri, when a dull thud was heard on the windshield, and in the dark something large fell to the side of the car. Almost without thought Barclay stopped the car, thinking a branch had fallen from a tree. He stepped out onto the curb, and what he saw both thrilled and amazed him. Here was Tina's owl. The owl's perch had fallen out from under him, and owl and limb came tumbling down with a thunk on the car's hood.

His first thought whirred, "A dead owl is better than no owl at all." He picked it up carefully and placed the limp creature on the back seat of the car and drove toward home. In a matter of seconds, that still and helpless little animal was no longer lifeless. He had perched himself on the back of the seat and there stared at the driver as only an unhappy owl can stare. Barclay drove home in fear that the frightened captive might try to peck and scratch his way to freedom, but Tina's Dad was determined to arrive home with his heaven sent prize, whether dead or alive. And he did.

Jean called Mrs. McClard on the phone, and she was almost as excited as the Newmans were as she gave the account of how Tina had promised for so long to bring a live owl to school. Tina had her owl just in time for Christmas – only a few days before the boys and girls would be dismissed from school for the Christmas Holidays. She was the class "hero"! But Jean knew her dad was a hero too. Mother and daughter escorted the lively animal to school the next day, and the excitement among the boys and girls was ecstatic as they took turns getting a close look at the owl. The owl was not named, and when Barclay told Tina that he would need to be set free, she agreed wholeheartedly, and the family of four watched that same evening as the little creature flew from a perch in a small tree in their front yard out into the dark night.

Chapter V

Off to Africa, Leaving William Jewell College

In the early months of 1964, Barclay was now Associate Professor of Religion and Greek and Chairman of the Department of Ancient Languages at William Jewell College in Liberty, Missouri when Gene Nida of the American Bible Society called and asked if he could visit in Barclay's home for a couple of days. Of course, he was welcome! The Newman family of four enjoyed his visit immensely, and for the entire duration of his short stay, their small daughters were perfect angels, which was certainly not always the case. It was fun to see Gene playing with them, and especially enjoying their new Etch-a-Sketches which they had received at Christmas.

Gene's primary reason for coming was to sit down and talk with Barclay and to inquire if he would be willing to serve as a Translations Consultant for Bible translators in Southeast Asia. Gene explained that the American Bible Society was under the umbrella of the United Bible Societies. In 1816 a group of 60 delegates from regional Bible Societies, who were bound together by a common Christian concern to distribute the Scripture to people in need, formed the American Bible Society.

Barclay had just signed a contract in March to teach the following year at William Jewell College. So his answer was a quick, "Yes" to Gene, if he would be willing to postpone his offer for one year.

Barclay later wrote:

> I had never even heard of a "translations consultant" – but I was soon about to learn. It was the daunting task of selecting, training, and guiding prospective translators in their sacred task. My purpose was to make them aware of linguistic techniques that would enable them to produce translations that were both faithful to the biblical languages and creative in their own languages.

Gene felt that it would be beneficial for Barclay to attend a "United Bible Society Translators Institute" (an intensive workshop) to get an idea about the work and responsibilities of a Translations Consultant. So the following year (1965), Barclay was initiated when he spent the month of August at the Translations Institute in Limuru, Kenya about 20 miles from Nairobi. Such workshops were the brainchild of Gene Nida, and the purpose was to bring together a number of translators from a certain geographical region for an intensive study of biblical and translation issues.

Neither Barclay nor Jean had ever been to Africa, but the assumption was that Africa was a very hot country. The newsletter, informing him about the climate in Limuru, what kind of clothes would be needed, and other valuable information, arrived one week after he had already departed.

As Jean began to pack for Barclay, he insisted that he would need only short- sleeved summer shirts and cotton pants for the month of August in Kenya. So she packed his suitcase with these items, but for some reason unknown to her, she insisted that he take along at least one long-sleeved winter underwear. When Barclay reached the site where they would be meeting, he learned to his dismay that the high altitude (8,000 feet) of Limuru made it very cold. For four weeks, day and night, he wore that long-sleeved top under his shirts and even then practically froze.

The mornings were dedicated to lectures, the afternoons to either checking existing drafts or drafting of new material, and the evenings to reading and "homework." About midway in the month, Gene announced that he was taking the staff to Nairobi for a special linguistic study, which – to Barclay's great surprise and joy – was the movie, "My Fair Lady" with its critique of English accents.

The invitation to attend the Institute in Limuru included payment of all expenses by the American Bible Society. The agenda included lectures on linguistics, anthropology, problems of translation and communication, as well as on Biblical interpretation by men of international repute in these respective fields.

While there, Barclay was asked to have the morning devotionals for one week and also to serve as a translations consultant to some of the individual translators attending the conference. He especially enjoyed working with a young man from the Philippines, Seraphin Chavy.

On August 3rd Barclay stated, "I am more and more amazed at the complexities involved in translation. This is certainly a task that needs to be done."

Again Barclay wrote to his family on August 5th:

> It is a genuine thrill to meet these African Christians – their faith means so much to them, and it has cost some of them quite heavily. John Mpaayei, the head of the Bible House here, was from the Masai tribe. In his tribe the main food is the blood and milk of cattle.

On August 10th Barclay again wrote:

> ...I am now working with five groups of translators all of whom are working on different parts of the New Testament (and one on an Old Testament book). I am more and more excited about the possibilities of this type work.

Barclay told of two experiences he had with the two young African nationals. He wrote on the 21st and the 24th:

> When I first came here I met two teen-age boys who live nearby. We have gone swimming together and have hiked together. Last night, one of them brought me a sack containing three boiled eggs, four cookies and a potato baked in coals. This was a real gift from him, because their family lives on a very simple diet.
>
> This afternoon I went to the home of Charles Allen, whom I mentioned ... Counting him there are ten children in the family. I stayed for supper ... His mother could speak no English, so he (Charles) translated ... she asked what I was doing here. When I told her, she said that she thanked the Lord for people who translate the Bible because she had been a "great sinner, but now she was a Christian and was repenting of her sins."

From the time Barclay could walk, he took to water like a duck, and he later told the account of his swimming in the lake near Limuru with the teenage boy who took him there:

> I ... had ill-advisedly gone swimming in a nearby lake infested with dangerous parasites. I didn't know of the infestation at the time. So when I returned to Missouri and came down with a fever of 102, I was placed in the Isolation Ward of the North Kansas City Memorial Hospital. They soon discounted any exotic disease as my malady, and for a while thought I might have leukemia, because my red corpuscle count was extremely low. Finally, I was diagnosed as having contacted mononucleosis of the liver, which left me still feeling somewhat debilitated at the time we moved to the Philippines.

During Gene Nida's first visit with Barclay and Jean in their home, he had shared information about the history and purpose of the American Bible Society. When the Bible Society was formed in 1816 in New York City, the charter adopted was simply and plainly stated to eliminate any possibility of misunderstanding. The purpose of the American Bible Society was threefold: To translate, publish, and distribute the Scriptures, without doctrinal note or comment and without monetary profit. These goals remain the same today. But in recent years, an emphasis has also been placed upon new translations in contemporary English with bright colors, attractive formats, and the use of mass media (radio, television, newspapers, magazines, and internet).

Years later Barclay wrote of his experiences as a translator and Translations Consultant in Southeast Asia:

> Where does it begin – this pilgrimage of becoming a translator of the divinely inspired Word of God? For me, it began with a faith commitment to the Lord Jesus Christ, then it continued with a call to become a minister of the Gospel when I was a high school senior. This journey continued through college and seminary, after which I was offered in 1960 a position teaching Bible and Greek in a Christian College.

In the early sixties, when Barclay had just begun teaching at William Jewell College, he felt a real need to write an easy to read and understand textbook on the New Testament. So he set out to write *The Meaning of the New Testament* both as a textbook for students taking their first course of study in the New Testament and for pastors, Sunday school teachers, and other persons interested in exploring the message of the New Testament.

It was announced on February 12, 1966 in the Kansas City Times that Barclay's new textbook, *The Meaning of the New Testament*, written in a non-technical style, would be published in August by the Broadman Press in Nashville, Tennessee.

One cold evening in the early winter of 1966, the question was put to Barclay's wife Jean almost casually, "Would you sell your house to a Negro?" She answered somewhat carelessly.

"Why, of course, I would," and gave it little thought. If she had thought about it seriously, it might have gone something like this. "I don't need to worry. We would never be asked to sell our house to a black family in our small town, this little place we call home." The fact of the matter was their house was for sale at that very moment. But no black family they knew could afford to buy or even want to buy their modest house.

Selling a house is almost always a bit frightening and always a challenge, but fortunately a gentleman from nearby Kansas City was considering this property with prospects of buying since "Negroes," he said, "were moving into his present neighborhood, and he wanted to move out." With the sale of his own residence, he would sign the necessary transfer papers, give the Newmans their equity, and the transaction would be complete. But this hadn't happened yet.

It was the pastor's wife of their church who had asked Jean the question. A group of ladies was gathering. They each removed their coats, hung them in the students' cloakroom, and went up stairs at the College Union building on William Jewell's campus to enjoy a festive evening – a social affair for the "Faculty Wives." For the moment, the matter was entirely forgotten.

About this same time, the Newman's Church, Second Baptist in Liberty, Missouri had concluded a campaign on "Fair Housing" and Barclay and Jean, along with many others, had given their one dollar and signed their names to be printed and circulated saying, in truth, they would support Fair Housing in their community. It was so simple to tuck a dollar bill in an envelope, scribble their names, and drop the envelope into an offering plate at church. It was equally effortless for all those others who did the same thing. How many of them really meant what they were doing, no one may ever know. To what degree the Newmans meant it, came as a haunting question, which Barclay and Jean were faced with many times in the following weeks.

Signing their names on paper reminded them of other risks all of us take in life. Most people believe that bad things, which result from a careless act or stupid deed or from life in general, will not affect them. Most of their thoughts would run, "Others around us lose their jobs, family members die with cancer, others burn to death in a fire, people are killed in car accidents, and so on, but these things will never happen to us."

It was not until a few weeks later that Jean's almost flippant statement about selling their house to a black family came back to her. The telephone rang, and she picked up the receiver. The voice was that of a near middle-aged black man. His voice was clear and distinct, business-like. He wished to speak with Mr. Newman. Barclay did not misunderstand him. He wanted to buy their house.

Had someone told Mr. Gutheridge the Newman's house was for sale? Had Jean told his wife? Jean knew her, because their little boy attended the preschool where she taught at a Methodist Church in Liberty. Barclay placed his hand over the mouthpiece of the phone, and Barclay and Jean quickly and quietly discussed a time and date when the caller could come to see their house. In just a minute or two the time was set for his visit on the following day at three o'clock in the afternoon.

If someone overheard the conversation on their two-party line, they could not know for certain, but on the next afternoon around the exact time set for the meeting, two neighborhood children who rarely played in the Newman's yard were conspicuously perched in the branches of the tree in their front yard, playing with their two daughters, Tina and Dana.

Out of simple courtesy, the Newmans insisted that both Mr. and Mrs. Gutheridge take a look at the rooms and also the full basement, where their two children often played in the cold winter months. The four of them discussed the amount of the monthly payments, as well as the equity the Newmans had accumulated in the house over the past six years. In addition, there was the usual down payment and the additional investments they had made in the premises.

Jean remembers one outstanding question she asked of Mr. Gutheridge, "How do you feel you and your family will be affected by moving into this all-white neighborhood? Will the children withdraw, if they were mistreated by the children already living in the neighborhood? How much would they be hurt?" This question went unanswered as though they were not concerned.

The Gutheridges had three attractive children. Jean knew, because the middle one, a four-year-old boy, was a student in the preschool where she taught. Jean had been in their home, and she recalled vividly that the house was spotlessly clean. All the children dressed appropriately and behaved properly, as well brought up children do. They were, in fact, a beautiful family! Bill Gutheridge was a large man. His suit fit well and the fabric had the appearance of silk. He was a United States Marshall working out of Kansas City. His wife was tall, slender, and lovely. She worked in a very nice department store in Kansas City. She could well have been a model.

But there was that one thing different about all of them. They were black, and everyone else in the Newmans' neighborhood was white. To Barclay's and Jean's inquiries about how the children might fare, Bill answered as though it were a simple matter. "The children will probably stay close in the house," was his quick reply. Barclay was glad the basement was big and bright and provided a perfect place for children to run and play. For their own two girls, they had hung indoor swings in the basement, and these had afforded them and their friends many hours of fun during the winter months and when the summer afternoons grew too warm to play outside.

As the four talked, the Newmans hardly noticed their black skin. Here was a quiet, likable family looking for a new home – one located where the streets were paved and clean and where the yards grew lots of deep, green grass. Last of all, the matter of finances was mentioned. Did they have the money? They barely had a few hundred dollars – eight to be exact. Only $3,000 was needed.

The rest … well … that didn't seem to discourage any of them on that afternoon. Mr. Gutheridge promised he would try to get the balance. The Newmans never really expected to receive the full three thousand, but they were hoping to get back out of the house most of what they had put into it. Yet somehow it didn't seem to be the biggest of all the problems to be faced. In those days and down through the years, practically no one loses on a house sale – not anyone with any intelligence and meager business sense. The Fair Housing form the Newmans had signed had not included the clause "… if they have the down payment."

Barclay remembers how during those first two or three years, what seemed like large house payments, had put a tremendous strain on their small budget, but they had managed, and the last three or fours years had not been quite such a struggle.

When the black couple left, the Newmans followed them to their car, and it was not until then that they clearly began to see their neighbors through the eyes of those two little girls. Jean knew they couldn't wait until they could get back home with their report to their parents. By some means the news had gotten out. The Newmans were selling their house to a black family. That night or the next, the calls began, and the firecrackers started bursting soon after dark on their front and side lawn, where the bedrooms were located. It never occurred to the Newmans to call the police. They thought this behavior would last only for a short time and then blow over.

The first telephone call caught Jean quite off guard. It came from a man who lived a good block and a half away. "I understand you're selling your house to Bill Gutheridge," was his first utterance.

"Yes," was Jean's reply, although the Newmans certainly were not sure at this time, and no binding agreement of any kind had been made. The man laughed sarcastically and began to say he just wished he had been the first to sell to a "Negro." Not until later, did it dawn on her what the man meant. He was, of course, accusing the Newmans of "making a killing," a term she had never even heard. Then the caller went on to say that he and several of the neighbors were meeting that night in one of the neighborhood homes, and he felt sure the group would agree to buy the house, if we would consider selling it to them. They would, of course, try to offer a fair price or even better than that. Fortunately, Jean never knew who the caller was, and for that she was grateful.

Over the following weeks, many calls came, but the most annoying ones were the endless ones, which came from very early in the morning through to the wee hours of the night. The ringing would start, and one of the Newmans would answer. But most always there was the same nothingness – not so much as the sound of breathing. This lasted for days and days. Barclay and Jean weren't sure if this was the work of a couple of teen-age boys, or if they had help from the adults.

What the callers never knew was to the Newman's advantage. During an earlier illness of one family member, Barclay had asked the phone company to reduce the volume of the ring on the phone. This was probably illegal, but it was a godsend at the time. The sound was adjusted, so that it could be turned down very low, all but silent. You actually had to be standing within inches of the phone to hear it at all. With certainty, they could not have endured those horrendous weeks, had they not been able to be free of the ceaseless all-night ringing of the telephone.

Barclay and Jean didn't turn to anyone for advice or comfort. As a couple, they really weren't certain they even had friends anymore. They both recall that they did not want to say much about the situation, not because they were too embarrassed for what was happening to them, but because they were so disappointed in and embarrassed for their neighborhood – the place where they had lived and enjoyed such fine fellowship with neighbors for the last six years.

It didn't occur to the Newmans to involve members of their church and their pastor. This was something they felt they had to handle as best as they could on their own. It was the Newman's problem – no one else's. However, in the end, the members of Second Baptist Church proved to be gracious and helpful.

It wasn't long until their two daughters were ordered out of the yard of two neighbors by mothers with the warning for them never to come back. The children in one family threw sticks and clots of dirt at them. Not once did a single one of them face Barclay or Jean in person, but always by telephone. The Newmans couldn't keep their phone turned off all the time. They never knew if an extended family member from out of state might need to reach them.

One day a nearby neighbor called and asked to speak to Jean. She took the phone, and this caller, unlike the other ladies, was brave enough to give her name. She stated, "I just want you to know you have done the dirtiest thing you could possibly have done to your neighbors."

Another call. A man's voice was on the line this time, "Mrs. Newman, I've heard you're going to sell your house to a nigger. Well, I just wanted to know." He hung up before Jean could answer. His voice was heavily accented with a tone of warning and full of hate.

Still another call came. This time it was twelve o'clock midnight. For some reason Jean had failed to turn the ring to "off." She had just fallen asleep. Sleep was not always coming easily those nights. This lady pled with her not to sell to a Negro family, "It will lower the value of our house," she protested. Then she supported her plea with the fact that her husband was sick, and their family might be forced to sell their own house. Now they probably wouldn't be able to sell it, or if they were able, they definitely would lose heavily on it.

Another day a call came, and it went like this, "Mrs. Newman, are you a Christian?" This lady, who probably didn't go to church, had likely seen the Newman household leave for church every Sunday morning and on many Wednesday nights.

"Yes," was Jean's reply, and then she waited.

"Do you believe that God wants us to rob others?"

"No, I don't think so. Who is this?" Jean asked.

"It doesn't matter who I am. You are the biggest robber I know. You have robbed every family in this neighborhood of several thousand dollars." There was more – not as nice as that declaration.

Others who didn't call by phone stopped speaking from across the way. The firecrackers came more frequently and a measure louder, the perpetrators coming closer. One night, sleep just refused to come, and as Jean lay tossing about on the bed, she felt she must be disturbing Barclay. So she slipped out of bed and went down the hall to the living room couch. It was late. About the time sleep was slowly but surely coming, a very large firecracker burst within inches of the front door and very close to her head on that end of the opened out couch. Jean jumped hard.

One caller accused the Newmans, "You're moving out of the country, and you don't care what happens to this town and its residents. Besides," she added, "if you should ever return here, you'll probably live in an area where no black family can afford to live."

One afternoon at the barbershop, Barclay overheard a conversation intended for his hearing. The barber and a couple of customers were making disparaging remarks about "people who sell their homes (implying a great profit was to be had) to 'Negroes'…" Little did they know! Before all of this was over, the Newmans had left their home with only eight hundred dollars – nowhere near the $3,000.

It was true that the Newman family was moving to the Philippines. They were giving up their house, their town, their relatives, their friends, and yes, even their country. They kept asking themselves, "Isn't this enough to endure without being asked to sell our house to a black family and be cursed by our neighbors for doing so?" For a while, deep in her heart, Jean recalls that she blamed God for the whole affair. She felt he was dealing her whole family an unfair blow – asking so very much of them all at once. No, she didn't really blame God for any of these bad things. It was just so hard to understand. No matter how she viewed the situation, she could not get away from the fact that they had no other choice now, but to sell to this lovely family – lose or not. It ultimately became simple. They would do this simply because they called themselves Christians.

Barclay and Jean had indeed signed the Fair Housing statement, and then after all, weren't they going into a foreign country to represent the Bible Societies? Weren't they going to do a job that would help spread God's Word to a lost world? They considered at least one other angle. Does the Gutheridge family have the money to purchase this house? Barclay and Jean both knew they did not. Would Mr. Gutheridge be able to borrow the money? They were certain they would lose on their property. The Newmans, the sellers, would pay the penalty for selling. Bill had said if the penalty was too great, he would try to make up for at least some of their loss. He was never able to keep his promise.

The Newmans felt they were doing the right thing, regardless of the loss they might have to absorb. They really didn't think they had a choice in the matter now – either because this was God's will or their own responsibility to do what they had said they would do at the time they had signed their names to the Fair Housing statement. Their friends at church gave them support by simply remaining their friends when they finally learned about what was happening. Only a few frowned on what this Newman family had committed themselves to doing.

Several months later, Barclay and Jean did count the cost when papers were finalized and their loss was made plain in black and white through a small check from the realtor. Their first reaction was once again to pity themselves. Jean had prided herself for being so frugal those last six years, and now they would have practically nothing to show for their beloved home, their only property, which they had grown to appreciate so much.

During Barclay's stay at William Jewell College, David Moore's wife Loretta, Norma and Bob Ferguson, Gwen and Bill Turnage, Margaret and Bruce Thompson, Virginia and Bill Link (their pastor at the Second Baptist Church in Liberty), Polly and Dick Bowles, and many others at Second Baptist Church became valued, life-long friends to the Newman family. Robert Alley, who shared an office with Barclay at the college became a close and trusted friend. Oscar Brooks came to the College sometime after Barclay began his tenure there. He and Sally with their two sons enjoyed good times together with the four Newmans. Their two sons were close to the ages of Tina and Dana.

The Newmans had by now moved on first to Norman, Oklahoma, where Barclay attended the Summer Institute of Linguistics. The four Newmans were fortunate enough to have a two-bedroom apartment off campus during their six-week stay. The children of other Institute participants that Tina and Dana played with complained openly that living on the University campus with so many other families was noisy and extremely hot. It was July and August, and it was so hot it was difficult for them to sleep at night.

After six weeks of intensive study for Barclay at the University, the family of four moved on to Manchester, Connecticut, where Barclay enrolled in the Linguistics School at Hartford Theological Seminary. There the winter months were just as cold as Norman, Oklahoma had been hot. But before the snow fell, Barclay took his family on a number of short trips to nearby parks and to the beach where on one occasion in November Tina and Dana waded right out into the Atlantic Ocean with their Sunday dresses on. They did think to remove their good shoes and socks before venturing into the not so shallow water. And none of them could ever forget the beauty of the brilliant yellow and golden fall colors of the sugar maple trees earlier in the fall.

The four months in Manchester went by quickly, and the Newmans were making their final preparations to sail overseas. Barclay wondered why they had not heard from the Gutheridges – not a single word. Jean asked Barclay to call long distance and see if they felt they could keep their promise to them about dividing the loss on their house in Liberty, as he had volunteered in the beginning.

When the now "Gutheridge" home was reached by phone, Mrs. Gutheridge answered. She gave Barclay the news that Bill, her husband, had been taken to the hospital in Kansas City some time ago. The prognosis was not good. Barclay graciously wished him a speedy recovery and heard nothing more. Now there would be no additional check owed on the house to come in the mail. Bill died from cancer within several months.

Two years later, the Newmans received a Christmas card from a friend in Liberty, saying that the man who had bought their house had died from a long illness, cancer. The note continued, "They are such a fine family, and I believe everyone now realizes that. I believe you would be gratified to know that your courageous action had a favorable outcome in our town."

This day was the big day! The Newman family's long planned move to the Philippines had come another step closer as they were arranging to fly to San Francisco, where they would board the big ship, the President Cleveland, and at last sail to the Philippine Islands in Asia. This was the day they had for a long time been preparing. It was December 29, 1966.

The four of them had gotten up early to find the deep Christmas Eve snow still piled high with the addition of a cold rain and soft falling sleet. It was a genuinely miserable New England winter day. The tiny, one-bedroom house in Manchester, Connecticut, which had been home for the four of them for just over four months, was now scrubbed clean and ready for other occupants, that is, just as soon as the Newman family moved out with all their trunks and suitcases.

They counted the trunks, suitcases, and bags for the last time and hoped they would prove to be sufficient. Christmas had just come and gone. Holiday presents in small packages had been selected for Tina, now eleven, and Dana, just seven, but still there were treasures the young girls clung to. They had had to give up so many of their things when the family moved out of their home in Liberty, Missouri. Now Barclay, Jean, and their two girls dressed in their warmest clothes, made one last effort at stuffing in that last pair of half worn "hush puppies," the still warm foam rubber pillows they had just abandoned, and other odds and ends. And of course, there was really no room left for any of them anyway.

Eventually all was secured in the last trunk, and the keys turned. Before Jean could brush her teeth and close the overnight bag for what seemed an endless number of times during the preceding day and this last hour, their friends arrived with their big station wagon to cart the Newmans, baggage and all, to the airport in Hartford, Connecticut. On the way, they had planned to stop at an "all you can eat" waffle house, where all eight of them could enjoy a hot breakfast.

When Ken Easton, their new friend of four months and now driver first came through the front door, he looked like he had been duck hunting all night in a cold rain. He was covered with frozen sleet. He stared wide-eyed, but politely at all the trunks and suitcases as if to say – "How could you? How can we possibly get all that in and on top of my station wagon?" There was barely enough room for him to get in the front door, when his wife Brenda and their two children joined him.

Barclay and Jean had given away, thrown away, sold, and packed and repacked for months – still there they sat – five metal footlockers, four large suitcases, and four small cases. Jean had packed clothes for every conceivable climate. It would be cool in San Francisco, warm in Hawaii, cold in Japan, temperate in Hong Kong, and very hot when they arrived at their final destination – Manila, Philippines. Three seasons of clothes had to travel. Finally, Jean at last realized why their good friend and colleague, Gene Nida, had suggested they fly and have it over quickly. But no, she thought the family should experience the move to Asia gradually – go by ship, stopping off in Hawaii, Japan, Taiwan, and Hong Kong, before arriving in the port city of Manila in the Philippines. Jean was convinced the family would be better off to acclimate gradually to living overseas. Now she wondered at the wisdom of her decision.

Barclay and Jean already knew there were four in Ken's family to go along with the four of them. To make matters even worse, and because there were so many suitcases and footlockers, most of them had to go on top of the wagon, and it was raining and sleeting hard. Both men had failed to secure a tarpaulin to protect the luggage in case of rain or snow, but since the Newmans had been in the process of moving for a total of eight months in the States and at the same time preparing for an overseas move, they simply didn't remember to keep a tarpaulin for that one last trip to the airport, which would take them to the city of their ship's port of embarkation – San Francisco, California.

Jean had for weeks wondered how they would ever get all that they now possessed into those footlockers and cases. They had lived for the last eight months out of these cases and had along the way accumulated more stuff. Household furnishings had been packed in Liberty, Missouri and stored months earlier and were now supposedly waiting at some dock in San Francisco to be hoisted into the bowels of their ship way below their cabins as they all headed for Manila. (Three weeks later upon arrival in Manila, Barclay learned that their household furnishings were never loaded on to the ship.)

When all these earthly goods had been loaded this snowy morning in or on top of Ken's station wagon, and the freshly waxed floors were streaked with melted snow and big and little rubber shoe prints, the eight passengers, already damp and cold, squeezed in among baggage and drove in the direction of the airport in Hartford. From there they would fly to New York to continue on to the west coast.

As planned the two families stopped en route at a waffle house for their much anticipated hot breakfast. This would probably be the last time they would sit around a table together for a long time, if ever again. Barclay and Jean remembered the fabulous Thanksgiving Dinner they had shared with them in their home just a few weeks earlier in November. "You are a long way from home and family, and we want you to eat this meal with us," was Ken and Brenda's invitation.

Ken and Brenda's two children were too small to be very hungry for pancakes or waffles, and the Newman girls were too excited. They left more syrup-soaked pancakes and whipped butter than they ate. It would be only partially true not to admit to the excitement Barclay and Jean also felt. None of them had ever flown from New York to San Francisco, and this was the highlight of anticipation at the moment. When the last bite had been eaten on some of their plates, they began to put layers of clothes on the young ones – sweaters, coats, raincoats, scarves, mittens, and boots. It was still raining and sleeting hard, and the highway at regular intervals was flooding enough to make them wonder if they would get to the airport without drowning the car and all its occupants.

The Newman family and their friends did get there only to find that the scheduled plane had not arrived in Hartford, and if it should be able to land there, it probably would not fly to New York that day, where they were scheduled to fly on to the west coast. The runways were six inches deep in rain, slush, and melted snow.

After Barclay checked and rechecked, they were told that they would fly on to New York as scheduled. Barclay and Jean hugged and again thanked their friends for all the good times their family had shared with them in Manchester those last four months. Jean recalled the wonderful meals Brenda and Ken had prepared and shared with their family also on Christmas day. Once again they did not want the Newmans to feel alone. The Eastons made their unfamiliar town, unfamiliar church, and almost unfamiliar state feel like a second home to the Newmans. From then on whenever Jean heard anyone say "northern" people are not friendly and are inhospitable, she assured them they were dead wrong and would always tell them about one "angel" family in New England.

Finally, the time came for the four Newmans to board their plane. They waded through six inches of falling precipitation to board. Barclay's and Jean's feet were wet to the bone and so very cold when they stepped into the plane. Tina and Dana faired better with their boots on.

The Newmans were off at last. Jean's mother, Leora Butler, had planned to join them on this trip to the Philippines for a short visit. She flew from Jackson, Tennessee to arrive at the airport in San Francisco just minutes before they did, and after two fun days in San Francisco, the family of now five boarded the President Cleveland. They went aboard the ship on the last day of December, so the New Year's Party was festive and lasted most of the night. Not many were able to sleep much that first night. The approaching storms at sea gave the lucky passengers an apprehensive feeling, and the unlucky ones entered into the beginning throes of violent seasickness.

There were only 128 people registered in Economy Class, which was far below normal, so they all sort of rattled around with lots of lounging space. There were 152 people in First Class, but all of them were served by 400 crewmembers. So most every request was met promptly and with a smile.

One evening after the dinner meal, Barclay and Jean were strolling along the decks and came to where the dance band was playing. There were not many people sitting around and no one dancing. After fulfilling several requests, the band members stopped playing and were chatting.

Barclay walked over to the group to get a closer look at the snare drums being used. He casually mentioned that he played the drums all through his high school days. The band leader asked him to play when they began again, and Barclay played the drums. He enjoyed reminiscing about days long gone. Sometime after the first Sunday on board, Barclay was asked to lead the next Sunday morning worship service for Protestants.

Tina and Dana fared well. There were all kinds of organized activities for all the children to participate in – from games to crafts, singing, and storytelling.

During the three-week long voyage, the Newman's ship also embarked at Japan, Taiwan, and Hong Kong. The Newmans and Jean's mother took full advantage of every stop and saw everything that time allowed. Then after three fun-filled weeks, one very HOT, muggy morning, their ship docked at Manila Bay, Philippines. This family was to begin a very new and different life.

Chapter VI

Philippines and Beyond

The Newman family had moved and was pretty well settled in the house that the Philippine Bible Society had selected for them in a beautiful residential area of Makati, just outside Manila. Not long after their move, Rosario Yu, the heart and soul of the Philippine Bible Society, suggested that Barclay go to a Province south of Manila to interview a prospective Bible translator. Jean was graciously invited to go along to see a bit of the rural area.

Jean's mother, Leora Butler, had sailed on the President Cleveland out of San Francisco along with them and had planned to stay in the Philippines for a few months before returning to her job in the States. Rosario extended the same invitation to her to go along on this trip to the countryside, for the ride and for the opportunity to see the beautiful terrain along the way.

With plans all settled for the four of them to drive to a southern Province, Jean wasn't sure where they would be able to have lunch, so after conferring with Barclay, it was decided she should play it safe and take along some sandwiches. She prepared two thick tuna fish sandwiches for each of them, thinking this would suffice until they could return to Manila and back home. Soft drinks should be available. Even with her limited experience in traveling in rural areas outside Manila, she had certainly recalled seeing many "soft drink" signs along the hot, dusty roadsides.

As hoped, this day turned out to be a bright, sunny day, because most days in the Philippines are sunny and beautiful. The day was actually hot, and everywhere the countryside was lush with palm trees, date palms, poinsettias (they were big enough to be trees), frangipani trees, and on and on. The countryside was truly lush and beautiful.

The meeting and interview which Barclay conducted went very well with the prospective translator, and eventually lunchtime approached. The four had begun their trip back to Manila when their Filipino colleague and already dear friend, Rosario Yu (later known as Rose) suggested they all stop along the road and get something to eat. This sounded great to Barclay and Jean, because Jean was always ready to eat, and they were all thirsty by now.

She assured Rosario that she had brought along enough sandwiches for everyone, and all they needed were some cold drinks. Barclay parked the car in front of this very small café and they walked in. The floor was hardened dirt, and Jean wondered if her mother would be shocked. But they all kept following their friend who was headed right inside. Jean looked at her Mom, and she was a picture of serenity, not one trace of worry on her face. Now very early in Jean's life she had learned from her mother the art of worry, and she guessed she had inherited from her the gift of how to worry. You're always supposed to worry – worry if something goes wrong, or worry if nothing is wrong, but might go wrong, if you don't worry.

Just then Jean thought to herself, "I'll bet she's glad I brought along these sandwiches. That's why she's looking so pleased." Everyone sat on rickety chairs at an old wooden table, and Rosario insisted that they needed some more food other than the sandwiches. Jean nudged her Mom under the table and pointed at the sandwiches as she lifted and placed them in the center of the table.

Jean made a lively and big to-do over requesting cold Coca Colas for all of them. She certainly didn't want to offend the very gracious proprietors of the café. Filipinos almost always are the most pleasant, generous, and lovely people in the whole world. They consistently offer the best that they can possibly come up with. There were no Coca Colas, however Pepsis were in abundance, but they would not be cold. But no problem, ice was available. That was fine with Barclay and Jean. Jean was just so glad she could have something from this establishment with which to wash the sandwich down and at the same time not look too picky.

Before the drinks arrived, Jean made what she thought was her biggest mistake of the day when she asked where the restroom was. "The toilet is right over there," someone politely pointed – no, not pointed, instructed. The Newmans learned right away that pointing with your finger in the Philippines is rude. The designated spot was within a few feet of where they were seated, right in the middle of the room. When you entered, only a thin door with big cracks separated you from the rest of the world.

Americans are so finicky and modest about going to a public restroom. Jean's mother went along with her, but only one could go in the tiny room at the time. She insisted Jean go first. Jean wished she had never asked. It was not as sanitary as what the Newmans were used to, but then there comes a time when some things are absolutely necessary, and they won't wait. The two of them managed to endure the inconvenience.

The café food which was hot and delicious looking had now come to the table, and Barclay heartily ate some. Jean just dived into her sandwich with exaggerated gusto, and her Mother did the same. Jean was terribly thirsty, and she drank her Pepsi dry through a straw in just a few long draws, contentedly thinking, "Here is something clean and refreshing." But oh my, not really, she learned later – a strange sense drew her eyes to the now almost empty bottle, and when it did, she all but lost her breakfast right at the table. At the very bottom of the bottle lay a large glob of black gunk. Jean didn't lose any of her breakfast or lunch, but later wished she had. Discretely, she got her Mom's attention and pointed to the bottom of her bottle. She looked a bit disturbed, but whispered, "It's probably nothing. When you think you're going to get sick, you almost always never do."

Four weeks passed, and Jean began to feel a bit lifeless. Her voracious appetite went away, and she attributed these ill feelings to homesickness or deep concern and pity for all the poor people living around them.

Six weeks passed, and Jean began to feel very sick. She made an appointment with a doctor near where they lived in Makati, a booming commercial suburb of Manila. The doctor asked for specimens, and Jean obliged, never once thinking to tell her about the recent bad experience she had had on her trip to the countryside.

The doctor asked Jean to return to her office a week later. The first thing this caring young lady doctor said was, "Where have you been? You have contracted every parasite known to man." It was then that Jean remembered to give her an account of the horrible Pepsi. The doctor at once began a long regimen of prescribing various strong antibiotics.

After many weeks and 467 doses of different, strong antibiotics the doctor finally said, "You have had more than enough antibiotics to kill any normal person, but if this last round of antibiotics doesn't clear you up completely, I will be forced to put you in the American Hospital in Manila." By now Jean was very thin and lethargic. She could only eat a very little by lying flat on her stomach on the bed. Most days she stayed in her room all day, and got up only to bathe and sew, her only activities. She made dresses for Tina and Dana, their two girls, for her Mom, and for herself.

This last strong dosage prescribed by the doctor didn't complete the job as hoped, so off to the American Hospital in nearby Manila Jean went. She took along a copy of every medication and dosage that had been prescribed over the past weeks. When the American doctor looked at the thick stack of prescriptions, he said, "You have had enough medicine to kill a Filipino carabao. I'm going to give you the only thing I know of that you haven't had, and if this doesn't work, I don't know what we'll do."

Barclay and Jean both in high hopes left the hospital, and in about four days, Jean actually began to feel better. In two or three more days Jean was ravenously hungry. She just couldn't get enough to eat. And oh, how grateful she was that her mother had joined them even for a short time on this move to the Philippines.

And of course, as Jean began to recover from her ordeal, the wonderful people at the Philippine Bible Society sent all four of the Newmans on a flight to Baguio City where the mountains are gorgeous, the weather is cool, and American hamburgers were available at the Air Force base. Once again life was good and God was good!

Another one of Barclay's early adventures after moving to the Philippines was a trip in mid-March of 1967 to Ponape, an island in the U. S. Trust Territory of the South Pacific. He and Gene Nida were going there to meet with a Ponapean Bible translation team and several other teams from nearby islands. Barclay flew from Manila in the Philippines to Guam, the largest of the Mariana Islands in the South Pacific, where he had planned to meet Gene and Althea Nida.

The three of them would spend one night in the only hotel on Guam, and then proceed the next day to Truk Island, also in the U. S. Territory of the South Pacific. However, President Lyndon Johnson and his entourage were scheduled to come to Guam and had reserved the entire hotel, so Barclay and the two Nidas had to stay in a makeshift "hotel" with a thatched roof and a foundation on stilts.

During the brief time that Barclay was on Guam he met a very special person, Sam Koperberg. Barclay wrote a letter on March 18th to Jean, the girls, and Jean's mother, Leora Butler:

> This surely has been an unusual day for me… I was invited to attend a breakfast this morning at 6:30. It was good, but I had much rather have slept this morning, since I did not sleep too well last night. Anyway, after eating and coming back to the hotel, I met this man, Sam Koperberg, a Dutchman about my age, who was born and raised in Indonesia… We have spent the entire day together, at first we just walked about and then I got my fishing gear and he went down to the beach with me to fish… It is almost midnight now, and Sam and I have spent most of the time talking about philosophical and religious...
>
> …Tomorrow I preach at least twice and maybe more. At nine in the morning I will speak to the people on the island from Palau through an interpreter and then at ten thirty there is another service strictly for the English speakers of the congregation. It should be interesting.

> By the way, the island (Guam) is crowded with newspaper men, TV men, etc. in preparation for President Johnson's arrival Monday morning. Why didn't he wait a week; I planned to be here first!

On March the 20th Barclay again wrote:

> …Tomorrow we have to be at the airport at 5:30 a.m. for our 6:30 flight to Truk Island. From there we go by Catalina, an amphibian plane, to Ponape. I have been told that Ponape is one of the most beautiful islands in the Pacific. The Japanese called it their garden spot before World War II. It even has mountains with some snow, and some people ski there! But there is one drawback – it rains *every day* of the year. In the mountains the rainfall averages about 365 inches a year… Guam is one of the main stations from which bombers fly to Vietnam, and do they make noise as they take off in a path that seems right over my hotel room.

Following a noisy and sleepless night at the makeshift hotel, the trio flew the next day to Truk Island, hoping to make connections with a somewhat smaller amphibious plane on to Ponape. But when they arrived on Truk, their flight to Ponape had been cancelled because of mechanical problems with the plane, and the spare part to repair it would not be flown into Truk for another week.

The Nidas and Barclay were disappointed, since the translation workshop was to last only three weeks, and they needed to get there to help get the workshop off to a good start.

In the meantime, Hermann Pegal, director of the Liebenzeller Mission (an international Christian organization ministering to youth), approached Barclay and said, "There's no need to just sit around for several days or even a week. Come with me, and we'll go fishing." Barclay was grateful for the diversion and after conferring with Gene, it was decided that he should take the week and go fishing with his new friend. The friend assured Barclay that if the plane were somehow miraculously repaired and ready to go before the week was up, they would radio him, and he would have Barclay back at the airport in only a short time by way of his small speedboat.

Again on March the 21st Barclay wrote while still on Truk Island:

> Well, here I am. Don't ask how or why; I just am. The plane that was to take us from here to Ponape is required by Pan Am to carry a certain spare part, which the plane that brought us from Guam

> must bring to it, but it failed to do so, and will not bring it now for *one week.* I have met some very fine young men who are missionaries here and they have asked me to stay the week with them on the island of Toll… So I'll have a week's vacation there, fishing, swimming, etc. Their boat is going to leave here in less than an hour...
>
> …There is certainly no news, but I did want you to know that all is well, except for the minor rearrangement in schedule. But we'll just have to work a little harder and later when we arrive on Ponape…
>
> The island here is really beautiful and not a single snake. There are several hulls of ships which the Americans sank during the last war – they sank an entire fleet of Japanese ships here; and the concrete pill boxes, called bunkers, are scattered all over the place. But it is hot! …

This was Barclay's first workshop in the Micronesian Islands, and now he and the Nidas would be a week late. Barclay went with the young men to Toll Island, with the assurance that their plane would not fly for another week. But it did! The plane had been unexpectedly repaired overnight and had flown out the next morning, leaving Barclay with no choice now but to go back to Hermann's home and wait for the next flight to Ponape, which would be just short of a week away.

Barclay was feeling pretty low. When the missionaries had received the news that the plane would leave, they rushed Barclay back to the airport, but it was too late. The plane had flown without him. What could he do? He stayed out with his new friends in the ocean water all day with only his swimming trunks on. The sky was heavily overcast, and for this reason he had no fear of sunburn.

Within hours the blisters on his body became numerous and large. He was badly burned with nothing to put on his skin. Even after the week on Truk Island was up, and he arrived in Ponape, the blisters festered and burst. His clothes stuck to him, and although he worked hard at the workshop (Institute), he spent many almost unbearable days and nights.

Barclay has always made a strict habit of being on time for any gathering and so missing the plane made him literally sick. But in the meantime he was able to serve in several capacities on the island of Truk. He spoke at the mission church for two services. He also shared with the students at the mission school, the pastors, and missionaries about the need for Bible translations and translation techniques. He wrote on March 27th, "I have been able to work with the man who is to translate the Old Testament into Trukese. He was supposed to have been at the Bible Translation Workshop, but was unable to go because he was leaving the next day for a month's trip on business to Hawaii."

Then on March the 28th Barclay wrote:

> Well, I finally am on the plane ... The airplane has 16 seats, 8 of which are occupied with mail and other cargo. On this flight the mail has priority over the passengers ... We left (behind) at least six passengers this morning. So, if I'm late... you'll understand why; but I have hopes of getting back on schedule!
>
> I'm looking forward to the Institute (in Baguio City). I'll have to work hard and long while there, but that will be better than the suspense of waiting for the plane...
>
> On Ponape they (the nationals) have big feasts. There are wild pigs, deer, and carabao there ... and the people sometimes fix a whole pig (small one) for each guest. Hope I have one tonight.

On the 28th of March Barclay wrote more enthusiastically:

> ...Actually things seem to have worked out much better than they could have done otherwise. I suppose God is able to bring good out of all situations, if we will only let him. As it worked out, I not only had opportunity to work with the translator of the Trukese Old Testament, but I had the chance to make good relations for the Bible Societies with the German Liebenzeller Mission in the Truk Islands...

Barclay, from the very beginning of his heavy travel schedule as a translations consultant, wrote home almost every day. Over the years he never lagged in this practice. Two days later Barclay again wrote from Ponape:

> It just started raining; here it rains more often than the sun shines. There are thousands and thousands of frogs here. The Japanese brought them to the island to eat the snails and centipedes, and since the frogs have no natural enemies here – there are no snakes, and there are no big birds to eat them – they just grow fat...

Barclay did not write again until April the 4th. The mail was so slow going out he waited a few days in between his letters:

> ... last night was the first night since I have been here that it hasn't rained... From my room upstairs I can look out over the

> Pacific Ocean, and the sight is beautiful with the sun shining on the water. All around the islands is a coral reef, which separates the lagoon from the ocean itself; the reef is about fifty feet across…
>
> My time here has been very full. Besides having to plan my lectures for each day -- I had three yesterday, including one from seven until eight in the evening. I work with translators almost three hours every day. Besides this, I attend Nida's lectures and, of course, he attends my lectures as well. All of this makes for a busy schedule… Tonight we have been invited to attend a Ponapaean feast, which will be put on especially for our group. The people from the village are coming here to prepare it … they will also present some of their regular tribal dramas and dances in acting out their legends… Our institute ends Saturday night, and on Sunday we are going to stay here for worship.

When Barclay returned to Manila after three weeks, his skin continued to peel in large layers. To this day Barclay can barely stand the thought of going to the beach and almost always wears a hat, if he is to be in the sun for only a short period of time.

Barclay and his family had been living in the Philippines for only a short time, when he had a request from a Wycliffe missionary translator to come to a tribal group of people living in the interior hill country near Baguio in the Philippines. The translator knew the language and was working on a translation of the New Testament for this group of people who had never had even a part of the Bible translated into their language.

Barclay recalls that late in the afternoon, after a full day's work with the translator, he was standing outside, watching a tribal man cooking something on a small fire. The Wycliffe translator was also watching, and as she and Barclay conversed about the days' translation questions, Barclay asked her, "How did you translate Acts 1.12 where the Scripture says, 'The Mount of Olives that was about a Sabbath Day's journey from Jerusalem?'"

The translator explained to Barclay that she and her colleague had translated this as, "The Mount of Olives that is as far from Jerusalem as you can walk on a day of rest."

Barclay looked intently at the translator, who then asked, "That doesn't get it, does it?"

He explained, "The phrase goes back to the time of Moses, when the Israelites were living in the desert. In New Testament times it had come to be used as a measurement of distance." Then Barclay asked the translator how the people of this tribe measured distance? "Do they use miles or kilometers? If so, you could translate either 'about half a mile' or 'about a kilometer.' Or if they use time to measure distance, you could say 'about a twenty or thirty-minute walk.'"

The old squatting gentleman – more naked than not – continued to cook his meat on the small fire. The translator discussed the problem in the old man's language and finally decided to translate the verse as, "The Mount of Olives that is as far from Jerusalem as you can walk in the time that it takes a pot of bananas to cook."

Barclay wanted to be very exacting and correct before he agreed to this method of measuring distance, so he asked the translator to inquire of the old tribal man if he meant a big pot of bananas or a small pot of bananas? She repeated Barclay's question, and the old man's brown, shriveled up face broke into a wide grin. Then he replied, "Any fool – even a white man – ought to know that if you have a big bunch of bananas to cook, you build a big fire and use a big pot, and if you have a small amount of bananas to cook, you build a small fire and use a small pot. It always takes the same amount of time to cook a pot of bananas. Anyone should know that."

The translator confirmed that this was true, because she and the other missionary lady who lived and worked with her in the village would go out for a walk each evening while the bananas were cooking, and it always took about the same amount of time, whether it was a big pot or a small pot.

Barclay's first trip to the Micronesian Islands in March and April got off to a slow start, and now it was early June and time to return to Truk Island again to continue working with prospective translators. He wrote his first letter from Guam on June 4th:

> Well, yesterday was a crazy day. I spent a good deal of the time at the ticket office. You have to go through the process of letting the Trust Territory Airlines rewrite your tickets when you get here and that requires a lot of time. My ticket for traveling from here (Guam) to Truk, Kwajalein, Majuro and back to Guam is about three feet long. The plane schedule had been changed for only one flight, and that is because the college on Guam has graduation tonight and the airline is setting the schedule up a day so the students can go home in the morning, rather than wait until Tuesday.
>
> … I should have next Monday to get some work done, since the conference is over on Saturday. But there will be a lot of follow up correspondence to the conference, so I don't know how much I will be able to get done on the dictionary (the Concise Greek-English).

I have just noticed on my ticket that the baggage limit is 30 pounds for the Trust Territory...

Barclay wrote home again on June 7th from Truk Island:

... Our meeting got off to a good start, though we did not have as many here as it was thought we might; however, we had enough to do a good job in the lecture and we should have a few more today. Yesterday I lectured for more than six hours, so it was a full day for me. We met in the morning, afternoon and night. Today I plan to have them do some translating, and from today on, we will actually spend most of the time guiding them in translating and reviewing their translation work, so they will learn by doing.

... I have found out that there has been a quarantine on Kwajalein and on Majuro, though I think it has been lifted now. The deal was that you could go into one of these islands... Most of the people there are Christians, and many of them with their Ph.D. I have to spend the night there on my way to Majuro because Majuro has no lights at the airport. Majuro is like the rest of the islands though – not much of a place as far as being modern is concerned...

It's about time to have class now, so I'd better get this finished. Unless I forget, the building the school is in is one built by the Japanese before World War II (around 1938), and the ceilings are six feet thick with steel reinforcements throughout. The Americans scored a direct hit on the building, and it only made a dent in the ceiling. The people still find bombs here that did not explode; they take the powder and make dynamite to blast in the ocean along the reef to kill fish. There are also a number of caves on the island built by the Japanese...

On June 12th, 1967 Barclay once more wrote home:

The Conference (Bible Translation) was completed Saturday at noon and it was much more successful than I could possibly have imagined. Counting myself we had 23 people participating, and we were able to get the best persons involved in the Trukese translation committee. I spent the rest of my time on Saturday, after walking along the shore for a while, getting my letters started...

In his letter above Barclay mentioned "getting his letters started." From his first initiation as a United Bible Society translations consultant,

Barclay made it a practice to write a personal letter to every individual participant at a workshop that he had either worked with or conferred with on translation matters. These letters served to help answer questions or help make decisions.

One day in early 1967 Barclay came home with a pleasant surprise. He had received his first ever royalty check from Broadman Press in Nashville, Tennessee. Nearly 1500 copies of Barclay's first book, *The Meaning of the New Testament*, had been sold in the States, and Broadman Press had simply mailed the check for $1,000 to the Philippine Bible Society in care of Barclay Newman.

More good things by far happened to the Newmans in the Philippines than did bad things. But before they had gotten a car in Manila, Barclay was returning home from the Bible Society Office by bus. He was seated near the front of the bus and in a side seat facing the door. As he sat there he suddenly realized that there was no small pressure from his billfold which he always carried in his back pocket which could be buttoned. A young Filipino man had entered the bus and was sitting very close to him. Barclay never carried large amounts of money with him but he did have important information in his billfold. Barclay said in a rather loud voice to the young man, "Give me my billfold." The young man made no attempt to retrieve the billfold and sat there looking quite innocent. But when Barclay said again for all on the bus to hear him, "Give me my billfold now!" the young man sheepishly pulled out Barclay's billfold and handed it to him. He had managed to cut the button from the back pocket and slip the billfold out without Barclay even noticing it. Then the thief got off quickly at the next stop.

The Newmans had several live-in helpers to clean and do the laundry, but none of them proved to be very satisfactory until Nene came along. She was a lovely Filipino helper who enjoyed chatting with Jean at the end of the day. She also asked if she could do some of the cooking when Jean's mother went back to the States. Nene thought Tina and Dana were just great because her previous employer, who happened to be Lutheran missionaries, had four lively and "naughty" boys, as she put it.

Jean wrote home on September 11th:

> Last night Barclay and I went to bed in the living room since our very close next door neighbors had their stereo turned up to the highest volume, and at about 2:00 o'clock in the morning we heard a terrible noise. We both sat straight up, almost falling off the sofa bed. I said, "Barclay, it sounded like someone violently shook the dining room outside door, which was a 12-foot ornamental iron gate separating the room from the outdoors."

> Barclay added, "The front windows rattled, and I felt the whole house shake." As it turned out, this morning, we were told it was an earthquake…

Barclay wrote on December 1, 1967:

> It is now a few days past Thanksgiving and the Christmas season is rapidly approaching. Last year at Christmas time we were in Connecticut, the year before that we were in Missouri, this year we are in the Philippines, and next year at Christmas we should be in Indonesia. But we have discovered that wherever we are at this season of the year, our thoughts inevitably turn towards our many friends….
>
> Around our house one would think Christmas had already come because of the latest addition to our family, a puppy named Smaks (the girls said because he smacks when he eats)…

When Barclay was in Bangkok, Thailand, he met Father Walter Abbott for the first time. A conversation between the two of them led Barclay to realize that Father Abbott was serious about the Catholic Church wanting to join with the Philippine Bible Society to make Scriptures available for all Filipinos. After attending a gathering of Roman Catholic bishops and priests, Barclay stated that it was quite a thrilling experience for them to say to him, "We want *you* to come work with us, so that we can also share in the translation of the Scriptures."

In early December Barclay was very happy and excited to report in a newsletter to friends and family back in the States something about the important development in Bible translation work in the Philippines. The Roman Catholic bishops in the Philippines, largely under the influence of Father Walter Abbott, a special emissary of the Pope, have whole-heartedly requested that they be permitted to cooperate with the Philippine Bible Society in the translation of the Bible into the major Philippine languages. And knowing now something about the Protestant-Roman Catholic relationship in the Philippines, Barclay felt this decision to be no less a miracle than the Incarnation itself.

In December of 1967 Barclay discovered that his and Jean's Philippine visas would soon expire and would not be renewed for another year unless the Newman family flew out of the Philippines and re-entered the country. They would then ask for visas for the family of four for another twelve months. The year had been a good one and a busy one, but Jean kept having a strange, almost crippling obsession that she might never be able to leave the Philippines again.

A few days before Christmas, she had come down with a debilitating sinus infection and through the holidays her voice had become a mere whisper. The Newman's second Christmas in the Philippines in their new house had been a real delight. The first house the Newman family had lived in was literally being eaten away by termites.

By January 1, 1968 plans had been made and tickets purchased by the Philippine Bible Society for the Newmans to fly to Hong Kong. Jean was more excited about the trip than anyone, but she worried about her infection and if she would even be able to fly. But they all did! Barclay had to answer any questions directed to Jean, which made her feel real stupid. Her voice by now was completely gone.

When their plane reached Hong Kong the pilot could not land for about 30 minutes. During that holding period Jean's ears were hurting so badly she could do nothing but let the tears roll down her face uncontrollably. This again embarrassed her to no end, but once the plane landed the horrific pain subsided.

A Bible Society staff member from the Hong Kong Bible Society, Rev. Vincent, met them at the airport. The Newmans were welcomed heartily, and their host drove them in his car on the left side of the road up the steep and winding roads to his home. They reached an area near the top of the famous tram where he had a lovely apartment almost adjacent to the tram. The Newman womenfolk could hardly eat the refreshing lunch he had prepared for them for looking out his large windows at a spectacular view of almost all of Hong Kong and in particular the port area. Barclay and Jean clearly remembered making that trip up the incline by way of the tram with Jean's mother almost one year before when all the family were all on their way to Manila.

The next day Rev. Vincent took the Newmans on a drive to the New Territories where they looked into mainland China. Rev. Vincent, with the aid of his helper, had prepared a wonderful picnic lunch to be enjoyed on top of a rocky mountain-like hill. Jean had trouble containing her joy at having made the trip, and suddenly after lunch, having her voice to come back – full volume.

The Newmans had many experiences in the Philippines during their short stay of 18 months before going on to Indonesia. One not so happy event took place one early afternoon when Dana, the younger daughter, was playing with a little neighborhood friend in the Makati area where both girls lived. The two little girls were walking down a sidewalk when the friends' dog came running up to them. Dana naturally and instinctively reached out her hand to pat the dog on the head. When she did this, the dog apparently misjudged her action and jumped up and bit her on her lower lip. The other child ran to get her helper and the three of them came rushing through the Newman's door to relate what had happened.

It was one day after the Newmans had returned to Manila from Hong Kong. Jean was thinking about what a wonderful time all of them had had there. And at the same time she had just laid down her pen and was putting a roast in the oven for dinner guests, when Dana appeared with blood streaming down her chin. Dana had always loved every dog she ever saw, and her big sad eyes mirrored pain and betrayal.

Jean dropped everything, found out from the maid (helper) who had brought Dana home whose dog it was, and what she could learn about the dog's shots. Then she quickly telephoned the doctor. The doctor informed Jean that when a person is bitten in the mouth or anywhere on the head, rabies shots are immediately mandatory, even if the dog has had all its shots.

For a change Barclay had not yet gone out of the country, but he had driven their car to the downtown Bible Society office on United Nations Street in Manila, so Jean called a taxi. There were lots of taxis rushing up and down the main thoroughfare one block away from their house. One came quickly, for which Jean was grateful. She instructed the driver to take them to the American Hospital in downtown Manila.

From the beginning, Jean was moving quickly but at the same time trying to stay calm and to act matter-of-factly so as not to cause Dana to panic or become unduly frightened. Now Jean and Dana had just settled into the back seat of the taxi, when the driver casually turned around and took one long look at her. This is when Jean made her first big mistake. She thought if she told him what had happened, he would start the car up and get them on their way quickly.

Instead, he didn't even start the ignition until he related to them the occasion when his cousin's nephew was bitten by a dog. The dog had not had any shots. He verbally painted a terrible picture of how the boy had contacted rabies, suffered, and eventually died a horrible death.

Dana was only eight years old, and her already big eyes got even bigger and bigger as the story unfolded. The more Jean tried to encourage the driver to stop talking and start driving, the more he stared back at Dana in horror. Jean finally demanded, "Drive us to the hospital right now!" After a few more long seconds, they were off. It was by now getting late in the afternoon, and the traffic into Manila from Makati was horrendous. Jean thought they would never get there.

Well, things didn't get a lot better when they arrived at the hospital. The wait in the reception room to get in to see the doctor wasn't bad, but when Jean saw the needle the doctor was going to put into her small back, she thought she would scream. The small, but efficient Filipino physician saw the concern in Jean's eyes. He glanced at her, sorta halfway hid the huge needle behind his back, and said, "Don't let your daughter see this big needle. I apologize for its size. But it's all we have at the moment."

When you tell an eight-year-old not to look, guess what? If they are normal, they will look or die trying. Jean knew there was no way she could prevent Dana from seeing that fat, six-inch needle. As it turned out, Dana was a real trooper. No tears and no wails. She just took it without a word and not so much as a whimper. After ten such shots with somewhat smaller needles over a period of weeks, information came that the dog was not rabid, and Dana wouldn't need to take the next four shots as had originally been prescribed.

When Barclay returned home from the Bible Society office, the helper told him what had happened, and he immediately left the house to drive to the Hospital to bring the two of them home. This gave Jean a good chance to tell Barclay how brave Dana had been through it all. Dad and Mom were able to assure her that everything would be all right.

Most people would by this time, be afraid of dogs – but not Dana. She was bitten once or twice more after the family eventually moved back to the States. But today she still remains a great lover of her four-legged friends.

In early February Barclay held a Bible Society Translators Conference at the "Four-Houses" (a favorite tourist spot) at Tagaytay in the Philippines. Here he was first introduced to one of the most beautiful spots in the world. The Conference site overlooked Lake Taal and the old volcano. The first chance Barclay got during the meeting, he returned to Manila in order to take Jean and some church friends back to see the erupting volcano.

The group decided to drive down a steep winding incline about 12 miles in all leading down to the edge of the lake. The volcano rises up and is located out in the lake. After a wonderful day Jean and their friends left Barclay at the Conference, which would run through the next Saturday morning. When Barclay returned to Makati, the first thing he said was, "We must go back to Lake Taal tonight and see the volcano erupting at night. Jean later wrote to her mother, "...it was a beautiful sight at night. You could see the lava just spilling out and rocks flying up 600 and 700 feet into the air. It is safe there on the tip top of the cliff unless, of course, it does get worse. The people are still on the island (near the volcano) and won't leave, although the government has encouraged them to do so.

They keep saying it won't get big." Some years ago several hundred people were killed when this same volcano erupted.

It seemed to Barclay and Jean that water surrounded the Philippines, and of course it did. On another occasion Jean's bravery was put to the ultimate test. The Newman's time was to be limited in the Philippines. Barclay's job there was to set up translation projects in eight of the major Filipino languages and then move on to Djarkata, Indonesia, where he would set up the project for the translation of an everyday Indonesian Bible. So it was decided between Barclay and Jean that it would be good for the four of them to see firsthand more of the places that held a particular historical interest to all Americans who knew anything about World War II. One such place was Corregidor, a small island of only about two square miles at the entrance to Manila Bay.

It was here General Douglas MacArthur had planned to defend the Philippines from an invasion by the Japanese during the Second World War. Heavy artillery – impossible to turn inland – was pointed westward, where it was expected the enemy would approach with its naval vessels. However, the Japanese were able to come overland from the east, and under the cover of night, their ships easily captured the island from that direction. MacArthur was soon asked to leave the Philippines but with the affirmation, "I shall return!" And, of course, he did return.

Many years later Barclay and Jean were privileged to sit in the chair that Douglas McArthur had used when he worked and served in Brisbane, Australia during the Second World War.

There were several ways that tourists could reach this island, including a variety of fancy – and very expensive – hydrofoils and other speedboats designed to attract adventurous sightseers. But on arriving along the coastal road south and west of Manila, the Newmans happened to see several motorized outrigger canoes on the beach with bright colored signs announcing these could be rented for travel to Corregidor Island. Fortunately, Barclay had by now learned enough of the language to hire a "captain." The sole crewmember cordially welcomed them aboard, then he "shoved off" and headed across the bay in this vessel without amenities or life jackets of any description. Jean was frozen with fear, but was determined not to spoil the adventure for the rest of the family. When it was all over, she said, "God certainly does take care of fools."

Barclay and the girls took this trip as lightly as crawling out of bed in the morning. Jean sat very near to the one and only blown up rubber tube aboard, and prayed that she would not need it. After they had gone many yards out into the already rough sea, one of the girls gleefully called out, "Look, Mom, at that big ship in the distance crossing our path." This was not new information to Jean or to Barclay, but it was something they hoped would simply go away, if they just didn't talk about it. The very large ocean vessel did in fact go away, but only after depositing enormous waves in its wake, sending their minuscule outrigger into convulsions, which seemed to last for an eternity.

Their captain-steersman observed the horror stricken mother and said reassuringly, "Mum, not to worry, we don't always turn over." Barclay and Jean took him to mean his boat had never before turned over, and they could consider themselves absolutely safe. Their visit to the island was celebrated by shedding numerous tears for those who had suffered and died there – both Filipino and American – and by imbibing numerous soft drinks, so they would survive the oppressive heat. Ultimately, the testimony of their captain proved prophetic – as soon as they returned back across the bay to the golden sand and stepped out on the white sandy beach, Barclay and Jean began "not to worry."

From the last of February until March the 19th of 1968 Barclay traveled to Indonesia, visiting different islands where he lectured on Bible Translation. During this particular time span he traveled a total of 8,000 miles from the time he left the Philippines until he returned again. Besides visiting Djakarta, he went to Makasar, Surabaja, Medan, and Bandung.

May the 5th was upon Barclay much too quickly. He was scheduled to hold his first big month-long Bible Society Translations Institute in Baguio City in the mountainous region some 135 odd miles north of Manila. Baguio is about 5,000 feet above sea level, and the air was cool and crisp during most of the day. Barclay first drove Jean and the girls to Baguio on the 3rd of May. He left the next morning to return alone to Manila, and on Monday the 6th he returned with two busloads of delegates who had met in Manila.

The men and women with some of their families flew to Manila from many countries, literally all around the world – Australia, Borneo, England, Indonesia, Japan, Korea, the Marshall Islands, the Micronesian Islands, New Guinea, North America, Taiwan, Thailand, Vietnam, and from various places all over the Philippines.

One couple from Borneo with two small children walked for two days and took bankas (small boats) for three days to make connections in order to get to Manila. Their plane had failed to pick them up as scheduled. Many denominations were represented at the Institute. There were 15 Roman Catholic priests from several of the countries mentioned. The total enrollment for delegates was about 100 men and women. This number did not include the children.

Gene Nida and Barclay lectured many hours a day for four weeks helping translators and prospective translators of the Bible to understand how to produce better and more easily understood translations. Jean reported that she was rightfully proud to sit in and hear some of Barclay's lectures. One day a priest from the jungles of Borneo said to her, "… your husband (Barclay) is the greatest man living." And Jean wrote home, "… that might be debatable with some, but I agreed …"

Everyone attending the Institute worked very hard. Each day began with a devotional period following breakfast, then there were lectures from 8:00 to 12:00. Workshops followed after lunch where the delegates actually translated portions of the Scriptures. After dinner there were lectures by other Bible Society men working in various parts of the world. To close the day there was a staff meeting each evening from 8:00 to 10:00. Barclay presented most of the New Testament lectures, and Gene Nida lectured on the theory and practice of translation. Three or four others gave the lectures on the Old Testament.

There was only one major problem at the Institute. The Conference was held at the Southern Baptist Theological Seminary, and with that many attendees the water flow was inadequate, and a new pump had to be installed. The food was plentiful and well prepared, although salad greens were perhaps not washed thoroughly.

Dana became very ill with dysentery sometime about the last of the first week of the Institute. Jean did what she could to control the diarrhea, but Dana spent her nights rolling and tossing around in bed, groaning in her sleep as the stomach pains became worse. The medicine available to them was just not working.

During the day, however, Dana kept up a good front and was quite active playing with the other children. One day while Jean was in their room on the Seminary campus mending someone's garment, Dana came running all out of breath into the room, and she was speaking very fast. She said that one of the little boys had fallen off a balcony onto concrete steps down below. Jean remembers grabbing clean towels from the bathroom rack and running as fast as she could to where the child lay. She put the towels under his head and hurried to the meeting room to get the boy's mother.

The frightened mother cradled the boy's head in her lap while Jean drove at great speed to the hospital. She was not real sure how to get to the Hospital in Baguio City, but she did make it there with no wrong turns. The little boy had literally cracked his skull on the edge of the concrete steps.

This Bible Society family had come to the Institute from Vietnam when the fighting was in full rage. The whole family had to be airlifted out of Vietnam by helicopter just as fighting came near to where they were living. They barely escaped with their lives, and everything they owned, except for a few changes of clothes for the family of four, had to be left behind. A few years later, Barclay and Jean heard that the child had not suffered any long-term ill effects from the fall and injury.

Dana continued to get thinner as she endured the bouts of diarrhea, but she mustered enough energy to keep going all day and seemed normal to the other participants. Barclay and Rosario Yu had planned something special for each Saturday for the entire group. On one Saturday the group was loaded on to two large buses and taken on a tour of Baguio City. The Japanese had bombed Baguio City on the same day that Pearl Harbor was attacked. The group saw a few remnants of buildings where the bombs had made direct hits. On their tour they also saw President Marcos playing golf at the famous U. S. Air Force base.

During the strenuous month-long Translation Workshop at Baguio (May, 1968) in the mountains north of Manila, a large group of the participants drove west on another Saturday to the South China Sea for a day of picnicking on the beach (where the Newmans feasted on sea weed and many other good foods to which they were not yet accustomed). Before their meal was adequately digested, some of the picnickers decided to take a small fishing boat out to sea, where most of them enjoyed swimming and diving for coral. Jean had never in her life been exposed to water as Barclay had all his life, and she was as much afraid of water as he felt at home in water.

Fortunately, Barclay had taught their daughters to swim when he was teaching at William Jewell College in Liberty, Missouri. And that day Jean learned just what good swimmers they really were. The young Filipino man took the small boat out in the ocean farther and farther from the shore, until the water was as clear as crystal and only about fifteen feet deep. When he had anchored the boat, both Tina and Dana dived in like porpoises and began to swim happily. Jean became very frightened for them, when the boat seemed to be drifting in one direction and they were swimming as fast as they could in the opposite direction.

The other missionary ladies were swimming joyfully when one of them swam up to the boat and said to Barclay, "While diving I lost my gold metal rimmed glasses, and I can't read a thing without them."

Barclay jumped over the side of the boat, and after listening to her directions as to about where they had fallen off, he dived to the bottom and began the search. All the while the missionary lady was extremely worried and felt utterly helpless. After a few minutes, Barclay came up with the glasses in tow, and everybody aboard the small craft, and all the other divers clapped for the find.

Jean again noticed that the girls were swimming away from the shore and away from the boat. She grabbed Barclay's arm, and said, "Honey, you've got to go get them or they'll both drown. They are not used to swimming in the ocean." By now Barclay was pretty winded, because he had not been well from the mononucleosis virus for very long and had not entirely gained his strength back. Barclay once again dived into the water to retrieve the girls, and Jean was calling them to come in towards the boat.

When Barclay came into arm's reach of them, in fun and not knowing how weak their father was, both at once grabbed hold of him, and they all three started down momentarily. Barclay's strength was depleted, but forcing himself to regain his energy, they resurfaced quickly, and he began "dragging" Dana back to the boat while the older one swam merrily on her own.

On the first Sunday afternoon Gene Nida spent about 3 hours with Barclay and Jean helping them to finalize their plans for their move to Djakarta, which was scheduled for early July. Gene recommended that while their furniture was en route to Djakarta that they spend one week in Hong Kong and perhaps one week in Singapore (what actually happened was that the Newmans spent two weeks in Singapore going back and forth to the Seventh Day Adventist Hospital trying to find a solution to Dana's worsening diarrhea).

Since the Newman's household belongings might possibly take up to two months to arrive by ship at the port in Djakarta, Gene suggested that Barclay and Jean purchase inexpensive cooking utensils, dishes, and mattresses to make do until their shipment could come from the Philippines.

Barclay and Gene Nida had learned that the house in Djakarta did not even have ceiling fans so Gene suggested that Barclay purchase two air conditioners as household furnishings. Gene was also sure the Newmans would need a car, and he said they *must* hire as part of their rental expense a night watchman. Gene assured them that living in Djakarta would be relatively safe, but they would in all likelihood be robbed. This bit of news came from him as well as missionaries already living there, "...and if you are robbed, let the perpetrators have whatever they are after, and don't resist." With this information Barclay and Jean decided to mail home a few of their more precious possessions such as wedding gifts, which they had brought to the Philippines.

Before the Translators Institute was underway, and when Barclay had returned to Manila to meet the group of delegates who were flying in to Manila, Jean and the girls were left to entertain themselves. Jean had learned that north of Baguio City about 9 hours one way by car were the

4,000-year-old Banaua Rice Terraces in the Central Cordillera mountain range on the island of Luzon. The Ifugao Indians are given credit for creating these intricate rice beds going all the way up the sides of the mountains.

They were over 2,000 years in the making. Some people refer to them as the eighth wonder of the world. The Ifugao tribes people farmed the terraces in order to supply their staple crop of rice and at the same time have left behind an architectural masterpiece. Jean knew that Barclay would not agree to her taking even a few of the delegates away from the daily lectures and going on such an extended car trip.

But Jean made further inquires and learned that to fly there and back would take only a short time. A missionary pilot could be hired for 100 Pecos to fly them over the Terraces. Jean waited for Barclay to give consent and one morning, she and three of the men delegates made this flight. Their pilot was Dave Steiger with the Missionary Aviation Fellowship. Jean could just see herself sitting with her camera ready in the front seat next to the pilot, where she would certainly have advantageous picture opportunities. But as it turned out, Philip Stine, one of the delegates and a new recruit for the United Bible Societies asked if he could sit in front so he would not get airsick.

Jean and the other two passengers willingly let Phil sit in the coveted front seat. The sights were breathtaking as the group flew over the jungles, but when they approached the Terraces, the sight was unbelievable – more gorgeous than words can describe. Four cameras were clicking hard and fast.

The pilot explained how he dropped mail to missionaries in that area. He also informed them that he was not allowed to land on the tiny thumb-size airstrip they were about to fly over, but he would do the next best thing. He would approach the critical airstrip as though he were preparing to land and then lift up just before touch down. Jean absolutely loved it even from one of the four center and back seats. And guess what? Phil got airsick and made good use of the paper bag provided. Jean declared that the only thing that made her sick was not getting to sit in the front.

Jean wrote home, "… Look at your middle finger and you get an idea as to what that airstrip looked like to us when we flew over it, and at that it rested on top of a mountain." The pilot showed them three other such strips where he lands 3 or 4 times a week. The pilot went on to say that his job was to land with missionaries who were going into these mountainous places, to deliver missionaries' supplies, and to pick up critically ill people who were in need of proper medical attention. He would fly them to the airport in Baguio City where they could get transportation to the Hospital in Baguio City.

The next day Jean's activities were not so thrilling but indeed interesting. Barclay had asked her to drive to the airport some miles outside Baguio City to pick up a late arrival for the Institute. Rosario Yu, Barclay's dear Bible Society colleague and beloved friend of the Newman "girls" would accompany her. The new arrival was Chow Lein Hwa, who at the time, along with many other responsibilities, was chaplain to Chiang Kai-shek in Taiwan. After collecting Chow Lein Hwa, the three left the airport and began making their way back up the mountain heading in the direction of the City and the Seminary campus, Barclay's car just died. Jean tried numerous times to restart the car, but it finally refused to budge.

The plane had been late arriving and now Jean thought that she was making the new arrival even later. She had been told that a photographer would be on hand to make a group picture of everyone as soon as he arrived.

Jean had an idea, so she said to these two distinguished Chinese, "I'm going to get this car as far off the road as is possible, and the next car which comes around that bend in this road will surely take us to town where we can then get a ride to the Seminary." Before Jean finished addressing the two, there was the car coming right at them. Jean, very unladylike, stuck her thumb up signaling them to stop for three frustrated hitchhikers. Rosario Yu and Chow Lein Hwa had the exact same expression, "Should she be doing that?"

But Jean simply did not know what else to do. If memory serves her correctly, she uttered a desperate plea to God for their safety. She honestly believed that her two companions would rather have walked, but Jean thought this was near impossible. They were miles from the Seminary and the Institute. A great deal of the way would be a steep incline, the temperature hovered in the low eighties by then, and besides Jean had, without thinking, been foolish enough to wear two-inch high heels.

She had already turned down an offer to ride *alone* in a passing taxi occupied by four unwholesome looking Filipino men. And on top of that a Filipino soldier had refused to push the car farther after he broke out the car's tail light reflector.

The third car was just what the three needed. The old car was already occupied with several men and women, but they graciously moved over quickly and with smiles and greetings agreed to take them all the way to the Seminary campus – just in time for the somewhat late photographer.

Mario, a man at the Philippine Bible Society had borrowed Barclay's car and had evidently put a cheaper grade of gasoline in it, and the fuel line had clogged up.

For Barclay and Jean, meeting and working with so many wonderful people at the Translators Institute was truly a blessing. Jean recalls meeting there for the first time Dr. William Wonderly, a man who for many years was invaluable to the Bible Society cause. This was Bill's first time to attend a workshop or work outside his region. He and his wife lived in Mexico, and Bill was responsible for the everyday Spanish Bible, which later served as a model for the *Good News Translation*.

Outside of Dana's illness, the Newmans would never forget the good experiences they had for those four weeks. Gene Nida said there was no doubt but that it was the best Institute the Bible Societies had ever had. He also told Barclay that he would have to slow down or he wouldn't be able to have many more. Barclay and Rosario Yu had done a great job in organizing and bringing together so many translators and prospective translators from so many places around the world. Barclay and Rosario had tremendous support and cooperation from all the staff members at the Philippine Bible Society.

On June 6th, after the Newmans had returned to Manila from Baguio, Jean wrote that Dana's situation with diarrhea had not improved significantly. On the 3rd of June she began to dehydrate, so Jean rushed her to the American Hospital in Manila where they gave her glucose for 15 hours. The doctor there said she had acute gastro enteritis. Her appetite had improved slightly and Barclay and Jean thought she was getting better. Dana had lost so much weight that she looked like "two enormous sad eyes." Jean shared with her mother that she had made Dana a new dress using a size 5 pattern, which was small for a nine-year-old.

Chapter VII

Indonesia, Birth of CEV, To Far Away Places

Indonesia

In June Barclay returned to Indonesia one more time between the Translators Institute in Baguio and the date for all the family to move to Djakarta in July. He held another Bible Society Conference on Translation at Tjipayung, Indonesia. Barclay wrote on June 17th, "… This morning they were mowing the lawn at the Bible Conference. Guess how! They tied two goats and five deer with ropes in various parts of the lawn and they eat the grass." Actually the animals eat the grass very evenly so it is cropped meticulously.

Before the Newmans flew to Djakarta on July 19th 1968 Jean was kept busy in Manila purchasing items such as canned goods and items of clothing, which would not be available in Djakarta.

Djakarta is the capital city of Indonesia where their new home (new to them) was waiting.

Jean wrote home on July 25th:

> …When I got my first glimpse of Djakarta many of my fears were dispelled. I was afraid all the terrible things we had heard about this country would be so depressing. All the red clay tile roofs looked so pretty from the air, and every home, barn, and shed has red tile roofs. It was good to at last be here … There is much poverty here but Manila was truly a good introduction for us, and now I am so grateful that the Lord has let me see gradually the distressed of this part of the world. I could not have taken Djakarta as a first course.
>
> I only hope I don't become too calloused to see and feel the needs of other people. It's something like being a nurse, I guess, you simply have to harden your heart just a little and look up from the street or your heart would literally break from seeing the deprivations. The crippled and diseased people are truly pathetic…
>
> Although we were the last to get through the customs' line, we paid no customs unless, as we suspect, the secretary from the In-

> donesian Bible Society paid the men a fee not to charge us. A few days later the customs agents wanted to charge us 96,000 rupiahs for the Philips three-burner kerosene stove we had flown in with us from Singapore. We suspect another 'pay off' took place because suddenly they came down to 50,000 rupiahs. Consequently, I have the most beautiful expensive apartment size kerosene stove you ever saw – a total of $325.00 U.S. What will the customs be on our car coming from Singapore? The Bible Societies surely have a lot tied up in 'us consultants'! My what it cost Christians back home to bring Christ to a few more people of the world!
>
> ... Missionary friends of ours in Manila moved to Djakarta at the same time we did. They had lived in Indonesia once before. Betty and I find comfort in comparing our frustrations. They have also been much help to us. The other morning Basil dropped by for a minute when I was desperately looking for the right words to say to the garbage man. Basil arrived just in the nick of time to act as my interpreter, and we got the job done with the aid of some money.
>
> When we arrived here on the 19th, our house was not vacated although we had been assured by letter that it would be ready on the 15th. There were people and chickens and dogs occupying the premises...With pressure they all moved out in three days, and we moved in – 13 pieces of luggage, a camera, a stereo, a typewriter, and a tape recorder – all our earthly possessions if the ship goes down or the inspectors or consorts help themselves to our crates coming from the Philippines.

Since the Newmans had spent two weeks in Singapore, they were able to purchase a kerosene stove for the kitchen. The salesperson recommended they buy two extra sets (four in all) of metal rods needed for this particular stove. These rods most likely would wear out long before any other part to the stove would need replacing. The stove and rods had flown along with the Newman's luggage on their way to Djakarta.

Philip Sigar of the Indonesian Bible Society met Barclay and his family at the airport. He took the four of them to their new home. And as reported earlier, the outside of the house was very beautiful. It was located on a corner lot with a wrought iron fence all around. The roof was covered with red clay tiles, the outside of the house was white ornamented with black and black-gray rocks and bricks in front. There were plants of every imaginable description, thick green grass grew in the small yard, and the porch and patio were laid with white marble-like tile – all of which was situated right in the middle of a garbage pile and a sewage ditch running all around the lot. Pedi cabs were parked in the street to one side of the front and a pitiful fruit stand alongside the cabs. And when the Newmans first entered the house, there were whitewashed walls with big dirty smudges everywhere, bare white marble-like tile floors covered with muddy tracks left by animals and the previous renters, and naked electric bulbs hanging by long cords from the high ceilings.

There was a lavatory in the dining area for brushing their teeth, that is, if someone remembered to pump water from a well up into the tanks out in back of the house. The occupants could get water two ways – city water only and only on some days from 3:00 in the afternoon through the night and well water the rest of the time in the two lavatories in the house, neither of which were in a bathroom and one of which never worked. They were supposed to toss their garbage over a pretty white fence to the side of the house, and the garbage man would pick some of it up once a week, if there was any left when the flies and the poor people got through going through it.

The driver of the Bible Society car offered to take Barclay and Jean to a furniture stall where they could purchase four single mattresses to put on the floors as temporary bedding until their furniture could arrive from the Philippines.

A few pots and pans and just enough dishes and flatware were also selected to make do for the coming days. The Newmans later didn't remember what they did for that first evening meal, but they all remember their first night at the new house. Since everything was so new to them they decided to let Tina and Dana share what would later become Barclay's study, which was adjacent to their very small bedroom. They felt the girls would feel more secure with this arrangement for the first few nights in this strange new place.

At 10:00 or shortly after, the four of them prepared for the night. All lay down on their four lumpy single mattresses, and for a few minutes stared up at the single light bulb hanging high above them. Tina and Dana finally fell asleep after what seemed a longer time than usual.

But Barclay and Jean just couldn't get to sleep. Roosters nearby were crowing from every direction, and vendors were hooting, howling, gonging, whistling, ringing bells, and knocking as they paraded up and down the street. They were saying, "We are selling fish, meat, bananas, chicken, baskets, brooms, straw mats, furniture and already cooked food" way past midnight. These young, and oftentimes old men, walked miles and miles everyday and made only a meager daily wage. The muscles on their legs looked like steel. On some, the veins in their arms and legs looked like they would burst. Since the Newman's house was on a corner, they received double benefit from the hoots and howls. And on top of this, they were not warned that the city would come alive at 4:30 each morning when the Muslim prayers would come to the whole city by way of microphones. These loud prayers carried a sad and mournful cadence, and at first sounded weird and depressing to the inexperienced western ears.

Then when those night noises subsided, Barclay and Jean lay in bed listening to the boisterous talking of a small group of men on the street right outside their house. Finally, around two o'clock, everything became silent, and the two of them were very near to falling into a deep sleep. Just as sleep had almost overcome them, the front door burst open. (Evidently they had failed to lock the door. Barclay and Jean jumped straight up in perfect synchronization, and Barclay headed for the living room and the front door. Jean grabbed all four metal stove rods, one for each of their two hands. They had been left on the floor by the open suitcases in the bedroom. She came running right behind Barclay. They rushed to face the intruders (just what they had been told not to do).

Barclay roared like a she-bear and used every Indonesian word he knew and some he didn't know to tell them to leave at once and ask what were they doing in this house? Three of the men nearly trampled each other to death trying to escape the fury. One poor soul tried to quickly explain as he headed for the door why they had come in, but Barclay didn't give him time to finish his explanation.

Tina and Dana jumped up and screamed. Barclay called the police, and in one hour a whole truck of soldiers came. Now the Newmans went back to their lumpy beds again and finally fell asleep just before daylight.

It was not until some time later that Barclay learned that these men were probably night watchmen for the neighborhood and had grown tired of walking and standing around. They simply repeated what they had being accustomed to doing each night – just slipping through the front door and taking a short nap on the floor before canvassing the neighborhood again – or perhaps to sleep until dawn.

The next hurdle the Newman family faced was to hire household help. American and European families were urged and, in fact, were expected to hire help because the people were so very poor and needed any employment they could get. The Newman's first helper was a dear, tiny Indonesian lady. She couldn't speak a word of English, but was anxious to learn and always anxious to please. Soon she was joined by Sue, a much younger Indonesian lady.

Barclay and Jean, with their limited knowledge of the language, recalled the difficulty they had at first trying to explain that it was absolutely necessary for all drinking and tooth-brushing water to be boiled at a full rolling boil for thirty minutes. They had to instruct them not to wash dirty potatoes in the dishpan. They did not know how to make a bed the way westerners make beds, and one day when the young German shepherd dog wet the floor, one of the helpers proceeded to spray the floor on that spot with insect spray.

The Newmans were warned that the helpers in their home would steal anything they could get their hands on, and they should for that reason keep everything under lock and key. Barclay and Jean just couldn't believe this about their helpers, so everything was left out just as they had done in the Philippines. Small change was left on the dresser initially, until they tired of the two helpers picking it all up and handing each coin to them every morning.

One small room with bunk beds in a corner of the garage served as the helpers' quarters. The first night the two new helpers, Ya and Sue were to sleep in the room, Barclay and Jean were awakened by shrieks of anguish coming from the garage. Barclay grabbed a flashlight and ran out to the garage to see what the problem was. Bedbugs were everywhere and had bitten them soon after they lay down. Jean really knew then for the first time what her grandmother had meant when she used to tease, before tucking her in at night, "...sleep tight, and don't let the bedbugs bite."

The next day Barclay gave the helpers permission to scrub their whole room, every inch from top to bottom, after he had purchased and sprayed the entire room with a strong bug killer. He then put their mattresses out by the side of the street to be hauled away and bought them new ones. Barclay had certainly won their hearts.

The older lady named Ya carried Dana around on her back whenever she found time. By now Dana who was still losing weight didn't seem very heavy, and this filled a gap in Ya's life as she thought of her own little ones back home.

After a short time in Djakarta, Barclay arranged for himself and Jean to begin language study with a private tutor, who came each day to their house. Barclay picked up the language more quickly than Jean. Jean was very proud of him, but had a big laugh on the evening when she had invited Ollie Woewoegan and his wife for dinner. As Barclay greeted them at the door, he welcomed them into their home and commented that he was happy to have them come for the evening. He added something about Ollie's lovely wife, and Jean noticed a puzzled look on both their faces. Suddenly, Ollie burst out laughing, realizing Barclay had said the opposite of what he intended to say. He had actually said, "You have a lovely wife, and I want her (physically)."

Barclay had prearranged to have memberships at the American Club where Barclay and Jean took the girls swimming every day before school started.

They had not lived in the new house very long until a big rainstorm came. The beautiful red-tile roof couldn't keep the rain out. In every room the rain poured down. Buckets and pans were placed everywhere and soon overflowed. The owner of the house explained to the Bible Society that this was to be expected, because even when a cat walks across the roof, tiles can be moved, allowing rain to pour in.

Out in the garage was a fuse box with a 20-amp fuse for this four-bedroom, two-story house. And consequently only one electric powered appliance could be used at a time without blowing the fuse. And in order to replace the blown fuse, armed guards had to be called to break the seal and put in a new fuse and then replace the seal. So about all that could be used were the electric refrigerator and one or two overhead light bulbs at certain times of the day. To run the air-conditioner in Barclay's study, you had to unplug or turn off the refrigerator or else run it only between certain hours of the day. If you were planning not to be at home during those increments of time, the helpers couldn't understand that they were supposed to unplug the refrigerator or fan or whatever might blow the precious fuse.

Then school started. It was a smaller school than the one the girls had attended in the Philippines. Tina seemed content, but Dana, because of her lingering debilitating illness, could not seem to accept one more new situation. She would leave school on her own and try to find her way home. She was only in the fourth grade. One day she slipped out of the house, got on her bike, and tried to ride to the seaport in order to board a ship that would take her back to the Philippines or the States.

The Newmans had not been living in the Philippines long, when Tina, the oldest daughter, was fitted with braces by a Filipino lady orthodontist. Tina's teeth did not protrude badly but certainly needed a little straightening to make them perfectly straight. In a short time, her teeth were moving into place nicely, but she would need to be fitted with a retainer before the family made their move to Djakarta.

This was done in Singapore right on schedule, just prior to their planned move to Indonesia. The orthodontist warned Tina to faithfully wear the retainer every night while she slept to keep her teeth from going back to their original state. Tina tried to remember to sleep with the retainer each night, but one Sunday night about bedtime, she came to the room where Barclay and Jean were reading. She looked pretty forlorn and stated that she had lost her retainer and couldn't find it anywhere.

She added that she had already told the Indonesian helper who swept out their entire house every day about the lost retainer. Tina had asked her to help her look for it. They had both been unsuccessful, and Tina feared her teeth would go back to being crooked as the orthodontist had said they would.

Barclay looked at Jean, and she knew there was only one thing to do; get up and start looking in every square inch of the house. She really didn't know where to start, but she knew moving in any direction would be better than just sitting and worrying about it. Barclay added that there were no orthodontists in Djakarta that he knew of, and Jean hated to think they'd have to buy two tickets from Djakarta to Singapore, fly there, and have a new retainer made. Jean had always been pretty good at finding lost items. Barclay had given her good practice over the years. Like any "absent-minded" professor, he often misplaced things, and Jean, declaring herself an experienced "detective," nearly always took on the challenge to try and find the lost article.

First Jean went upstairs to Tina's room with her following close behind. She looked in every inch of the room. She repeated the same in the kitchen, bathroom, living room, and dining room. No retainer. Jean stopped for a minute and thought, "Where could that little metal retainer have gotten to?"

Their garbage had not gone for the week. It would be collected and carried away first thing Monday morning – that is, what was left of it. The very poor Indonesians continued to go through their trash hoping to find something that had been thrown away they could use. When the really ragged, skinny, diseased ones went through the rusted out container for scraps of food, it broke Tina and Dana's hearts – a worry that always weighed heavily on their minds, especially on Dana's.

A light suddenly came on in Jean's head. Maybe the retainer got swept up and thrown into the trash. She went outside in the pitch dark night carrying their big flashlight. She spotted a good sturdy stick, dumped the contents of the container on the ground at her feet, and began inch by inch to paw through each tiny and not so tiny item in search of the retainer. She was so intent on looking she hadn't noticed a woman and a girl come up and stand at her backside. Then they began to giggle! "What's so funny?" Jean thought. "This is serious business. I'm looking for something important." Then it dawned on her, "Here I am an American lady so hungry that I had resorted to searching someone's trash for food."

Jean smiled and said with her expression, "Sorry, I got here first." After sometime there beneath all the mess appeared the tiny retainer – a bit nasty, but there it was. Jean took it inside, smiling as she went, and assured Tina that all would be fine.

Tina wailed, "I'm not ever going to put that back in my mouth." But after several washings in Clorox, Jean convinced her otherwise. Scalding hot water and soap followed, and the retainer was as good as new.

Dana continued to lose weight, and the two American Embassy doctors in Djakarta and one doctor in Singapore advised Barclay and Jean to take her back to the States. One doctor said, "You have two choices. Either you take her back to the States or you can plan to bury her in Djakarta." Her physical sickness had lasted so long it had definitely affected her emotionally. She literally couldn't go to school. And Dana was a child who had always thrived on being with other children her age.

Fortunately, the missionary family who had come from the Philippines to Djakarta at the same time as the Newmans and had packed their household goods with the Newman's shipment were sympathetic with Dana's problems. Betty Costerisan volunteered to tutor Dana at home until the Newmans could make arrangements to move back to the States. The house had been rented in advance for three years, and the Indonesian Bible Society would have to find another renter who would reimburse them. This was taken care of right away, but so much time and effort had gone into the moving process, it would take time for the Newmans to move again and find a place in the States where they could immediately settle in.

Barclay and Jean recall many gracious and helpful people at the Indonesian Bible Society, but several stand out in their minds as being special: W. J. Rumambi and his wife, Liem Sediaji who later worked for the United Bible Societies and was stationed in the Philippines, and Perry Katoppo who was an avid chess player. He once commented to Barclay that he had not found an electronic chess game at any level that could beat him.

Barclay set up the translation project for the Common Indonesian Translation of the Bible, and he stated that women nearly always make the best translators. So he appointed for the team three members who were all outstanding Indonesian Christian ladies – Mrs. A. Susiladyia, Sister Gunanto, and Mrs. Sigar, the wife of a Baptist minister.

Heber and Edith Peacock had a furnished house at Ridgecrest, North Carolina – just out from Black Mountain. They graciously offered their house to the Newman family until other arrangements could be made. It was December before the move could be finalized. Jean remembered going to a department store in Djakarta to buy material to make Dana a winter coat because she had long outgrown the coat she had had two years before when they moved to the Philippines. Three layers of interlining had to be sewn into the coat since there was no woolen material in the stores in Djakarta. Tina would have to make do with one of her mom's old coats until they could buy her a new one in Asheville, North Carolina.

The doctors with the American Embassy in Djakarta recommended that Barclay and Jean take Dana to a doctor immediately when they returned to the States. She had become afraid of everything. This was a child who was never afraid of anything! Once when she was three years old Jean was taking her to their family doctor, Richard Bowles in Liberty, Missouri. She stood up on the backseat of the car and declared, "I'm not afraid of lions, tigers or bears. Why would I be afraid of the doctor?" Now a ceiling fan whirring over Dana's head in Singapore, when Jean had taken her there to the doctor, frightened her beyond reason. She just knew the fan would fall on the two of them and cut them to pieces. Dana had simply become too physically drained to cope with the frustrations of their new home in Djakarta.

When the Newmans started their trip back to the States, they took a few days going through Europe, and then they flew into Asheville, North Carolina. Black Mountain would be home from late December 1968 until August 1971.

As soon as the holidays ended in January and classes were scheduled to resume, Dana again showed an aversion for school. Barclay and Jean took her to a child psychologist in Asheville who assured the Newmans he could help her overcome her "school phobia" and her other fears and anxieties.

Dana improved rapidly with a minimum amount of medication and short counseling sessions with the doctor. After a short time, she quickly learned what the doctor wanted to hear, so she gave him the proper answers. The only phobia she exhibited soon after consultation had begun with the doctor, concerned her bunk bed at the Peacocks' house. She could not sleep on the bottom bunk for fear the top one might fall in on her.

In the early spring Barclay was asked to speak about Bible translation at the Fruitland Baptist Bible Institute in Fruitland, North Carolina, a small town south and slightly west of Black Mountain and about 25 to 30 miles away. The Bible Institute was founded in 1899 and claimed the motto, "Where Preaching is our Passion."

Barclay and Jean started out fairly early in the morning so as to allow plenty of time for them to travel to and find the unfamiliar college campus and its chapel. The morning was still seasonably cool, but the sun was shining brightly, promising a pleasant drive after a cold and icy winter in the mountains. The highway leading to the college soon became unexpectedly curvy but seemed to be clear of all visible ice and snow. They had not been in the curves long until Barclay approached an area on the narrow blacktop road completely shaded by a high rock bluff when his car went into an uncontrollable skid. The car jerked backwards and sent them straight into the rock bluff, sliding furiously on the black ice.

Barclay quickly and frantically said to Jean, "Brace yourself!" There wasn't time for more. The car sped hood first into the bluff, and when it was a few inches from a full force collision, the car jerked backwards again and made a complete 45-degree plunge and sent the car in the opposite direction, the direction they had just come from and exactly in the center of the right lane.

Visibly shaken, frightened, and extremely thankful, Barclay turned the car around and continued slowly on the road to Fruitland. They had driven only a few yards when they spotted a pale-faced old man who had lingered on the edge of a nearby bridge. He looked completely amazed and just stood there shaking his head in absolute disbelief. He had witnessed the whole near disaster.

Barclay and Jean never in their entire lives felt God's protective hand more close to them than they did that morning in the mountains of North Carolina.

In early April of 1969 Barclay wrote a letter to Jean's mother, telling her about the Translators Workshop in India that extended from March 29th to April 11th:

> Greetings from the beautiful land of (Ootacamund) India! Today is the last day of the first week of our Translators Institute. We have more than a hundred people here from all parts of India; and it is our job to teach them (the participants) how to translate and what the various passages in the Bible mean, so they can get the right idea when they translate. This is a unique gathering, because we have people from many denominations (actually more Roman Catholics than any others) representing a large number of languages. Some of these people have come a long way. Two of the young men who came from Nagaland in northern India have had to travel ten days to get here, including two days of walking down from their mountainous region before they could get to any mode of transportation. In that one region of 90,000 people there are at least fourteen major languages spoken, and these are not mutually understandable. Of course all of those who came here, come to work, and we do work from daybreak to late at night…

While at Ootacamund Barclay roomed with his good friend and colleague Bill Smalley. At this Institute there was always a shortage of water. A small pitcher sat high up on a fireplace mantel each day, and many of the participants had gotten very sick with dysentery. Barclay said at times he felt he would dry up completely for lack of drinking water, but he hated to take it when there was so little. His unrelenting thirst grew worse everyday until he and Bill Smalley discovered there was a Chinese Restaurant with a dirt floor in a near-by village. So he and Bill went there several times and just sat there drinking cold Coca Colas.

In May of the same year Barclay attended and participated in the United Bible Society's Triennial Translations Workshop in El Escorial, Spain. Barclay wrote to Jean's mother:

> Greetings from Spain! This is quite a bit different from where I was last month. The hotel is comfortable, and the food is surely the best I have ever had. The main reason for our meeting being in Spain (it is a workshop that the Bible Society staff has once every three years) is because of the expense. Spain is pretty much central and the costs here are low – the hotel charges $4.50 per day for our room and board …
>
> I'm mighty proud of your daughter – she writes me more often than any of the other men's wives write them. My roommate … has been gone (from his home) for six weeks and has received only three letters. That is pretty tough!

It was here that Barclay received a call from the American Bible Society in New York, informing him of his father's death. Barclay had not seen his biological father after he and his mother moved from their apartment in New York City back to Greenwood, Mississippi. It had been some 35 years. Now he returned to the States to attend his father's funeral in While Plains, New York.

Barclay, Sr. had for the first time after so many years made connections with Barclay, and the two had made plans to reunite in Black Mountain, North Carolina in the following summer.

Birth of the CEV

In 1966 the *Today's English Version* (later entitled *Good News Translation*) of the New Testament had been published by the American Bible Society. This translation proved to be well accepted, and soon people from around the country were directing these kinds of questions to the

Bible Society, "Are you planning to publish the Old Testament in the *Today's English Version*?" and "How about both Testaments in a language everybody can understand?"

So because of this wide acceptance, the Bible Society was led to plan a similar translation of the Old Testament. The work was begun in the late 1960's. It was in Black Mountain, North Carolina that Barclay was invited to serve as a translator of the Old Testament for the *Good News Translation*. The translation team projected that the entire Bible would become available in 1975. Actually the entire Bible came on the market in the fall of 1976.

The principal translator of the TEV New Testament was Robert Bratcher, living at that time in Setauket, Long Island, New York. He headed the team of scholars working on the Old Testament. The members were Roger Bullard, Keith Crim, Heber Peacock, Barclay Newman, Eugene Nida who served as a consultant, and Herbert Grether who joined the group a short time after the translation had begun. Each of these men had had previous experience in preparing translations in other languages. Six of the seven had served in some capacity as missionaries overseas.

Each man on the Old Testament Committee worked independently on one or more of the Old Testament books. After a first draft was prepared, copies were circulated among the six members. Comments and suggestions were then correlated by the original drafter. At the week-long (sometimes much longer) meetings of the committee, generally scheduled four or five times a year, the draft was scrutinized by the group. Incorporating and circulating these decisions made during the often lively sessions was again the drafter's responsibility. A draft was again submitted at the next meeting for final approval of the committee, and eventually for submission to the American Bible Society's Board of Trustees.

During the committee meeting in the summer of 1970, Dr. Roger Bullard was asked to write a short summary statement of each committee member. He wrote about Barclay:

> Barclay M. Newman, one of the younger members, joined the committee not long after the work began. Though red of hair, he had a rather quiet and understated presence, but also possessed a wit that was almost frightening. A few humorously honed words from Barclay could slice you into bits so quickly and cleanly that you did not at first realize what had happened. None of us could climb too far up on a pedestal before some remark from Barclay would bring him down.
>
> A most unpretentious person, Barclay made a habit of dressing and acting in a way that would call no attention to himself. He could

be visibly uncomfortable in some situations, but he would make no show of it. He would go out of his way to help you, even at considerable inconvenience to himself and his family.

Because of his work with the American Bible Society in the Orient, Barclay was not always at committee meetings, but when he was not there he was missed. The atmosphere around the table was not the same. A good bit of the ease with which the committee was able to work was due to Barclay's irenic influence and sometimes pastoral concern. Were it not for Barclay's words behind the scenes, the committee might well not have stayed together as a working unit as it did.

Barclay's scholarly abilities were impressive, but like anything else, he did not flaunt them. He was capable of writing up informed and technical notes on points he felt needed elaboration, but they never had the slightest tone of patronization. He worked confident of the scholarship and professional acumen of his colleagues. He revealed his own scholarship with the same ease and confidence in his own abilities, without advertising them.

Barclay was very much the family man. His wife and two daughters were the center of his concern, and it was his desire that their home life be what the home life of a Christian living in 20th century America should be. The Newmans knew the world about them, and memorabilia of their travels were prominent in their house, not by way of ostentation, but as tokens that these far-flung places had been a part of their lives together.

Barclay was the draft translator of the books of Deuteronomy and Jeremiah. They were translated under pressure of heavy duties and other adverse circumstances, but they were well done. When Barclay commented on the material of other committee members, his annotations were well chosen. He did not attempt to rewrite material at length, but he was one of the most creative on the committee when it came to finding some way to restructure a sentence or paragraph in a radically different manner, so as to yield a more concisely stated and immediately apparent meaning.

At committee sessions it sometimes seemed that Barclay was not intent on the work, but the comments he could make during those times when it seemed like his mind was in neutral proved that he could be concentrating on the material and indulging in a bit of nonsense at the same time. While the rest of us droned on, Barclay might start laughing to himself in a kind of under-the-breath hoot. If we were lucky, he might tell us what he thought was funny. And if he was laughing at something we had let slip by, it was a more pleasant way to bring up the matter than someone else might choose.

Barclay was a good friend to us all. He was deeply concerned with what it meant to live as a Christian. Once on the porch of Lee Hall at Blue Ridge Assembly (near Black Mountain, North Carolina), he wrestled with these concerns, trying to put them in words. But that was for his benefit, not ours. Barclay's style of life and deportment was a lesson in Christian living to us all.

To Far Away Places

In April of 1970 Barclay again flew to Kuching, Sarawak (East Malaysia on the Island of Borneo), where he worked with Phyliss Webster and Marge Britzer on the Penan translation of the New Testament. On the 4th of April Barclay wrote Jean's mother:

> Greetings from Borneo! I've not seen any "wild men," but so far I've not gone out into the "jungle" either. Actually the town of Kuching where I am now is a beautiful place, and modern in every respect. There is a museum here which is perhaps the finest in all of Southeast Asia, and there are plenty of other things to do for the people who live here. The weather is a bit humid now, but that's one of those things you have to put up with.
>
> I'm leaving tomorrow about noon for Brunei which the Shell Oil Company has made one of the richest little countries in the world. From there I will spend some time in the "out back." One group, the Penan, still live by what they can find in the forest – they can track down a wild pig by sniffing on the ground, and that's some accomplishment!

And again on April the 11th Barclay wrote home:

> … right now I'm in Borneo with the Penan tribe. They have always been jungle nomads, but the government is making them settle in villages, and this is the first of their villages. …To get here we had to fly over a lot of jungle area, and then land on a small strip made by the Borneo Evangelical mission. These missionaries, by the way, live right along with the natives in the jungle and in their village. After we landed it was a two-hour hike (these people often walk for a week at a time to get to another village) to get here. As we were coming up the trail, a couple of the men shot katydids from the trees with their blow guns – it was fantastic! They pointed

> out animal tracks and birds that took me forever to see. When they hunt the wild pigs, they can sniff its trail through the jungle…
>
> I have just returned from my bath in the river, and from washing my clothes there – at least the water is clear and relatively clean.

Barclay wrote a short article a few years later in which he described a conversation he had with two missionary translators and a married couple, who were also translators, all working in Sarawak at the time:

> During the 1970's I was the United Bible Societies Translation Consultant for the language projects of Borneo and Sarawak that were served by missionaries from the Borneo Evangelical Mission.
>
> During one of my visits to Sarawak, I was approached separately by the two single missionary ladies who worked with the Penan project and by a married couple who worked with another project in that area. They each said, "Before we were appointed by the BEM, we had to sign a statement affirming that the Bible is inerrant and must be interpreted literally. After attempting to translate portions of the Bible, we can no longer hold to this belief, and you are the only person we can talk to about it."
>
> I have often wondered what might have been the outcome, if someone had not been there to listen to the concerns of these devout translators and to share with them the conviction that much of the Bible was not to be interpreted literally…

Barclay in this same year began to write the *Acts Handbook* to be used by translators around the world. In May he attended a Bible Society Translations Workshop in San Jose, Costa Rica. Here Barclay met for the first time Alfredo Tepox who was living in Mexico. They became great friends.

In January 1971 with his many travels, writing, and translation responsibilities, Barclay still found time to teach the January Bible Study at the First Baptist Church in Asheville, North Carolina. It was during this time that he became acquainted with Cecil Sherman, the pastor, and Dr. Claude Frazier, an allergy specialist with his office in Asheville. This same month Barclay traveled to Nairobi, Africa where he worked for a week with translators there, and in late January extending to the end of February Barclay attended the United Bible Societies Triennial Translation Workshop (TTW) in Banglamung, Thailand.

At the Banglamung Workshop Barclay recalls confronting a 12-inch lizard starring him in the face when he put his hand on the light switch in his small bathroom. Jean later asked him, "What did you do?"

Barclay's answer was, "What could I do?"

Jean persisted, "Weren't you afraid it might get in your bed"?

Again Barclay answered, "What could I have done about that"?

During this year Barclay's *Concise Greek-English Dictionary* was at last published by the United Bible Societies.

In 1971 Barclay worked with the Old Testament Translation Committee for the *Good News Bible* for ten days in early July, and again from July 16th to August 7th. The first ten days the Committee members met together with their families and worked at the Blue Ridge WMCA Assembly near Black Mountain, North Carolina, close to where the Newman family had built a new home and was living there at the time. The second Committee meeting was held at an American Baptist Assembly in Green Lake, Wisconsin.

In the months of June and July, Barclay and Jean were at the same time in the process of selling their house and car in Black Mountain, packing up for the temporary stay at Green Lake, and after the Committee meeting moving halfway around the world again. The family seemed stable enough for another move, so Barclay accepted the challenge of working in West Malaysia where a new translation of the Malay Bible was sorely needed.

Not long after Barclay had been invited to participate as a translator for the Old Testament *Good News Bible*, he was asked to move to West Malaysia where he worked as a United Bible Societies Translations Consultant for a number of Asian countries. When he began the task of translating his assigned books, his time was now divided between his consultant work in Southeast Asia, which required a great amount of travel, and his visits to translation projects, writing Bible Society Handbooks, and anticipating his family's move to Malaysia, where he would initiate the Malay Bible project. But before the Newmans could claim West Malaysia as home, they first had to spend a month in Singapore.

Barclay and family had once again sold their home and most of their household furnishings of only eighteen months in Black Mountain, North Carolina, and moved to Singapore with only suitcases filled with clothes, a few of Barclay's books, and some small items for their girls. Now the Newmans had no place to call home. They were told by the Bible Society in Singapore that probably the best thing for them to do would be to live in the YWCA located on Channing Road near the Singapore Bible Society, until visas could be obtained from either: Singapore, Malaysia, Thailand, or Iran. And whichever one offered visas first for their family would be where they would live for as long as that country's government allowed them to live and work with the Bible Societies.

Chapter VIII

Striking Out on Faith

On August 7, 1971 Jean and Barclay wrote to Jean's mother, "Well, we are surely 'striking out on faith' but we are almost certain one of these places (Thailand, Malaysia, Singapore, Iran) will open up. We have asked Allied Movers to ship our household goods (only a few) to Singapore." There the family would wait for visas.

So for four weeks the Newmans lived, ate (if they brought their food in), and slept at the YWCA, and prayed. Their lives were utterly consumed by not knowing where home would eventually be. Jean had always said that Barclay's biggest weakness, if you could say he had one, was not being able to patiently wait for something, not knowing what lay in the future.

Their daughters must have taken after their Dad in this respect. They wanted to get somewhere, anywhere so they could enroll in school before the last minute and know whether or not they would be required to wear school uniforms and have them made. Secretly the whole family favored living in Singapore, but this visa did not come through.

The Executive Secretary, Peter Hsieh, of the Singapore Bible Society contacted Barclay as the fourth week approached and suggested that the family fly on the weekend to Penang, a beautiful Island in the northern part of West Malaysia. Barclay bought tickets and they flew from Singapore to Penang.

This was a welcome diversion for Jean, Tina, and Dana. Barclay flew there with them and helped them settle in, but almost immediately, he had to leave in order to attend a meeting, and Jean and the girls were left on their own to explore the beautiful white sandy shore just beyond where the Rest House was located. In the past the British had built Rest Houses throughout Malaysia where guests could stay for rest or recreation at very reasonable prices.

Without transport to get around the city, Jean and the girls entertained themselves in various ways. With Tina, there was not much of a problem – just give her a book, and she could read for hours. Reading for Dana, on the other hand, was a short order thing you did if you couldn't do anything else. With energy enough for two, Dana and her Mom still remember taking each other for a long walk on the beach, pretending to look for treasures that perchance had washed ashore since the time Marco Polo had sailed along these very same shores.

In fact, they had already found fragments of Ming pottery that had been washed ashore like so many colorful blue shells made smooth by the pounding of the waves. But that day they had hoped for something special. After a few yards walking and splashing with their left feet on the sand and their right feet in the ocean water, another wave came in and something grabbed their attention like a flash, and as they both darted for the object they collided. But one of them came up with a tiny, shellacked, wooden, carved bowl with a lid on top and right in the center was a tiny knob for lifting the lid.

Excitement and curiosity got the better of them. They had to open the box. When one of them pried the lid off, all they saw was a small amount of soggy white rice. What in the world? – not big enough for someone's lunch. A bird couldn't live on so little. The two of them looked up and saw some old fishermen dragging in their fishing nets, and although Jean and Dana could speak very little Malay, they thought they would ask and hope to understand what the old men said.

So they held out the little box with a questioning look, and one of the men understood immediately. In his broken English, he explained that a lot of fishermen going out to sea early in the mornings would throw out the tiny container of rice as an offering to the gods of the sea, hoping to be blessed with a large haul of fish for the day. The Newmans still have the little wooden box in a prominent place in a curio cabinet. After a couple of days, Barclay returned to his waiting family to hear the stories each had to share.

Only a few days after returning to Singapore from Penang, the West Malaysia government came through with visas for the Newman family. Now at last they knew where they would be living for the next three years. Now the girls could be measured for school uniforms and have them made. Tina and Dana would experience going to the International School housed in an old palace, which once belonged to the Sultan of Selangor, West Malaysia. There were approximately 350 students enrolled from many nationalities. The old house was well landscaped with sloping green turf, graceful clumps of bamboo and beautiful old rain trees. On the sharp hills rising behind, the thick Malaysian jungle grew – green, dark, and magnificent.

Barclay arranged for tickets and on a Sunday afternoon they flew from Singapore to Kuala Lumpur, after first booking a room at the modest

Malaysia Hotel. Tina and Dana were terribly anxious to see their new school and get enrolled. They were apprehensive, because they had already missed the first week of classes, and they were without mandatory school uniforms. The girls were so restless and cross that Barclay decided to try to get their minds off the approaching Monday morning. He discovered he could take them to a nearby amusement park in Kuala Lumpur, with hopes that the excitement and exercise would wear off some of their nervous energy.

Monday morning finally came after a night of little sleep. Barclay and Jean went by taxi to the school with the girls, enrolled them, and assured the administration that the girls would be fitted for uniforms as soon as possible.

Barclay and Jean now had the task of finding a house to rent and buying a car. They went first to see the pastor, Lloyd de Run, of the First Baptist Church in Petaling Jaya, where they would later decide to live. Petaling Jaya was an industrial town adjacent to Kuala Lumpur.

Lloyd gave Barclay the name of a car dealer, and almost within the hour, he had bought a Ford Escort demonstration car. It was a small car, but it was adequate and almost never failed them. A gallon of gasoline in Malaysia at that time was approximately two and a half times more than what Americans were paying, so for this reason, a small car proved to be more economical.

The same morning a Chinese lady, Mrs. Yuen, was contacted, and Barclay and Jean agreed on the house she showed them in Petaling Jaya. This house would be home for the next six years. The house had two stories and five bedrooms, one of which became Barclay's office/study. The house had many large windows in every room, none of which had screens. The windows closed with louvered glass slats. Hoards of mosquitoes came in and out at will. Large cockroaches were sometimes seen flying from the outside in, especially after a hard rain. Unlike many houses, this house had a fair sized yard with a monsoon drain around the entire house.

Lloyd de Run and his wife, Irene, soon became two of the Newman's best friends. Lloyd's father was Dutch, and his mother was from old Ceylon (now Sri Lanka). Irene was a beautiful Chinese lady who had the energy of three people and just as much enthusiasm. They were then in their fifties. Lloyd had been a successful business man in lumber until a year or so before, when he was asked to take over the pastorate of the First Baptist Church in Petaling Jaya, where the Newmans transferred their church memberships soon after moving to Malaysia.

Jean wrote home, "There is only one other American family in this church at the present besides us, and they (Kathy and Ray Fry) pastor a mission church in Klang… The de Runs had four children of their own and had raised 18 other children, who didn't have parents or else parents who didn't want them. One of their daughters, Claire de Run, was Miss Malaysia in the nineteen sixties."

The de Runs invited the Newmans out for Chinese food at least once a week. Tina and Dana once said, "… they help to take the place of relatives for us." The de Runs never forgot birthdays for all the Newmans, and on one Christmas, Jean recalls having twelve varieties of orchids throughout the entire house, thanks to Irene who ran a flourishing florist.

Jean and Barclay wrote to their family in Tennessee to share their new circumstances and address:

> On top of all our activities, we had a birthday party for Dana – one she will likely never forget. This lady, Carol Tomkins, we had just met and mentioned earlier, heard Dana say she was going to be 12 on September 25th, so Carol said to Jean, "Dana ought to have a birthday party." I hesitated – then I explained to her that I didn't have cake pans or anything to cook with. (Our shipment did not arrive in Kuala Lumpur until sometime in November). So Carol offered to loan me everything I needed. She offered to make sandwiches, deviled eggs, and then buy all 8 children (she would invite) a ticket to see *South Pacific*. Four of the children she planned to invite were her son and three youngsters he had met from Australia who were new here (Petaling Jaya) and quite lonely. In all we had Tina and Dana, Carol's son Roger, two children from Arabia and the three from Australia…

Barclay continued his travels to various places in Southeast Asia in the fall of 1971. In October he went back to Singapore for planning meetings, and in November he went again to Sarawak (Borneo), where he once more worked with Phyliss Webster and Marge Britzer on the Penan translation of the New Testament.

Barclay later shared with Jean what the pilot of the small plane he was flying in told him as their plane was approaching the airstrip where Barclay had traveled to work on the Penan New Testament: Just about the time for the plane to land, the pilot radioed to learn if any other plane was in the area. A notorious pilot known as "The Red Baron" radioed back to say he was aware of them and for them to continue with their approach to the airstrip.

Barclay also recalled the thrill of landing on this airstrip, which was situated in the mountains. The runway, handmade with primitive tools by the nationals, was very short and narrow and was curved alongside the curve in the river.

When Barclay returned home, he recounted another event that happened one day when the Penan tribal men invited him to go with them in their dugout canoe down the river near their village. The rapids were swift and fast-moving. Large ragged boulders bordered the sides of the wide river, and often these boulders cropped up in the middle of the water. Barclay has always been an exceptionally good swimmer, but he had never swam in swirling rapids. In spite of this, he felt safe because there were a number of the Penan men along for the thrilling ride, and he was confident they would certainly rescue him if the canoe tipped over and they were all thrown into the rapids. It was not until later that he learned the truth. Phyllis and Marge shared with him that the Penan men had never learned to swim in any kind of water, and they would sink like a pile of rocks.

After the Newman family had been settled in Petaling Jaya, West Malaysia, a town just outside the capital city of Kuala Lumpur, it was only a short time before Kuala Lumpur was declared the Federal Territory of Malaysia.

Thousands of Malays, Chinese, Indians, Europeans, and others witnessed the gala occasion. The fireworks displayed were a spectacular sight, glittering and bursting against the dark night with palm trees swaying all around and brilliant, prize winning hibiscus bushes of many colors in full bloom. The vegetation in this tropical country was always green and lush.

Jean wrote home on the 12th of April:

> We were putting in too many hours (working in the office) … so we decided to take off for about 11 days and see the country … the girls had a 2 and ½ week spring vacation … On April the 4th we began our trek across the country. We drove across the peninsula of Malaysia (West) to the east coast and spent our first night away on a beautiful beach. Here we had planned to meet our friends, a psychology professor, David Catron from North Carolina, his wife and three children (who also lived in Petaling Jaya).
>
> We all worked our way up the east coast of the country until we were not far from the northern part of the peninsula. We stopped along the way and shopped, took pictures, and one of us was dumb enough to climb to the top of a cocoanut tree. Yes, you guessed it. It was Dana. I (quickly) took her picture and called a halt to further climbing … The beach was very beautiful all along the way, and we held our breath each day as we saw the sun setting. At one point where the highway went more inland, we were driving casually along the highway (not a very large highway) where dense forests

flanked us on both sides, when a huge tiger bound across the road several yards in front of us (the car). That was a sight I will *never forget.* Most Malaysians never see a wild tiger in their entire life time, and they told us that tigers are becoming extinct in Malaysia.

When we had driven a good way up the east coast going north we parked our cars, rented a fishing boat, and went out 12 miles to an island where we stayed for two days. Just hiring a boat … was a real experience. No one in the little fishing village seemed to be able to speak a word of English so Barclay's Malay sure came in handy. The whole village turned out to hear the transaction. Brownie (little Chihuahua) was the chief attraction and the girls' hair is always a source of fascination for these people. We had to take all our food onto the island. It was fun cooking on a two burner oil stove. One night Barclay cooked fish native style. I just wish you could have seen this sight. He took a certain length of cane split open (lengthwise), placed his fish (the tails) in the slit and tied the cane at the open end with some cane stripping and placed them over the open fire. …They were delicious.

After we left the island we drove on north when we reached the most northern tip of Malaysia where Thailand borders. We then turned west and drove south to a small town where the next morning we loaded our cars on the train and went by rail right down the middle of the country. It took us 8 hours to go 128 miles through the jungle. … The track was very winding and mountainous with the jungle on both sides. We took peanut butter and jelly sandwiches and oranges and bananas with us and the nine of us, 5 children and 4 adults, had a great time chatting and eating most of the way. When we arrived at Kuala Limpis we drove through beautiful mountains on back to our homes in Petaling Jaya (next to Kuala Lumpur).

His first goal was to establish a translation project in which the whole Bible would be translated into contemporary Malay. A few years prior to Barclay's moving to Malaysia, Dr. Bill Smalley had spoken to him about the need for an up to date Malay Bible, since the only one that was in existence had been translated many years prior and was now very old and archaic. Malaysia, of course, was a Muslim nation and Christians were not allowed to witness in any way to Muslims. However, since there was a large and financially influential constituency of Chinese Christians in Malaysia, the government agreed that a Bible could be translated into Malay for their use, but not for general distribution.

It was late November, when he completed the initial writing. Jean, his wife and secretary recalls typing the handbook 7 to 8 hours a day on week days and 2 to 3 hours on Saturdays and some Sundays.

In February of 1972 Barclay traveled to Sarawak (Borneo) where he worked with the translators of the Penan New Testament translation. In March he began searching for a translator or translators for the proposed Malay Bible. A workshop was held in Singapore from March 9th to 15th to search for the right persons to do the work. Barclay wrote an article entitled "A Translation in Search of Translators,"

> **"Wanted: two translators for the Malay Bible."** By correspondence and by word of mouth, the news was circulated throughout the Christian communities of Singapore and Malaysia that the Bible Society was sponsoring a new translation of the Bible into Malay and that two qualified persons were needed to do the work. There are many who can write creatively and express themselves in Malay, but to find two people with Christian commitment and motivation and with the ability to translate the Word of God into language that is easily understood would be a "miracle" indeed. Practically all Malays are nominally Muslims; and though many of them may be creative writers, few are motivated by a desire to produce a good translation of the Christian Scriptures!
>
> Half A Miracle Is Better Than None! The situation looked dim and hopeless when the workshop for prospective translators was held in Singapore. All present had the proper motivation, but only one spoke Malay as a first language, and it was obvious that he had no creative writing skills. However, the Rev. Peter Hsieh, General Secretary of the Bible Society of Singapore, Malaysia and Brunei, had received a letter from a young man who had assisted in the translation of a Methodist hymnal into Malay, and for several years had prayed that somehow he could have a part in translating the Bible into Malay, since the older Malay version was most difficult to understand. The Rev. Elkanah Suwito had heard about the workshop too late to attend all of the sessions, but was eager to come for an interview. The "interview" lasted for three days! This young man had both the motivation and the skills. The Bible Society requested that he be released from pastoral responsibilities to work full-time on the translation.
>
> **Two Halves Make A Complete Miracle.** "Faithfulness to the meaning of the Biblical text and naturalness in the language into which you are translating" were the goals set before Elkanah and

almost a hundred other translators from various countries of southeast Asia during a month of intensive training at the Translator's Institute in South Thailand. Attending the Institute was Mr. Samuel Lewis of Singapore, an English missionary who had been working among Malays since 1957. He had even been awarded prizes in national competition for his creative skills in Malay. Moreover, Sam had a special interest in all aspects of Malay culture and religion and had worked on a translation of the Gospel of Luke into Malay for persons with a traditional background. Sam and Elkanah became friends and finally colleagues. Although Sam could not serve as a translator, he agreed to review Elkanah's translation and make comments, which could be valuable in light of his own knowledge of Malay language and culture. Sam could also put Elkanah's translation to the test by getting reactions from Malay readers and from Malays who heard him reading and preaching from it. Even though Elkanah remained the sole translator, the combination of skill and experience the two men brought to the project was enough to constitute one complete "miracle"!

A Miracle and A Half. Mr. Shamdin Ahmad is a specialist in Malay style. For 20 years he served as a journalist for the Utusan *Melayu*, the largest and most influential Malay newspaper. In 1971, he became a freelance writer. His interests extend to Malay music and dancing, and he has written the words and music for a number of Malay songs, which have been recorded by top vocalists. But how does he fit into the translation?

These three men – Elkanah, the translator; Sam, the consultant; and Shamdin, the stylist – are currently working on Scripture Portions which are checked by a United Bible Societies Translations Consultant for this area (Barclay M. Newman) for faithfulness to the original Greek text before they are circulated in trial editions to elicit responses from Christians and non-Christians alike. The first of these trial editions was the Gospel of John, entitled "Marilah Lihat," meaning, "Come and See." To date, almost half of the 10,000 copies printed have been sold, suggesting that many people in Malaysia are eager for this message.

The Bible Society of Singapore, Malaysia and Brunei had hoped for a miracle – two translators. Instead, the Society witnessed a miracle and a half, or possible three miracles, depending upon how one counts miracles.

"Yes, that is clear," replied Elkanah (once at a meeting), "but it is not nice," suggesting that the translation of a passage of Scripture could be said in a better way. The Malay committee will keep on looking for that better way to express the meaning – for the way that is "nice."

Throughout the translating process of the entire Malay Bible, Elkanah Suwito, who was an Indonesian Chinese Methodist Minister, living in Melaka, West Malaysia, did the original drafts, and his wife Hannah typed his materials before Barclay checked them against first the Greek text and later the Hebrew text. In their committee meetings Barclay answered questions about exegesis, always making sure nothing was left out of the text and nothing was added to it.

On his own, Barclay had already been studying the Malay language even before the Newmans had arrived in Kuala Lumpur. At this same time, Barclay continued to have responsibility for the Dani translation project in Irian Jaya (Indonesian New Guinea), the Dusun translation project in Brunei on the island of Borneo (East Malaysia), the Burmese Old Testament project in Myanmar (at the time Burma), the Patani Malay project in Yala, southern Thailand, the Common Indonesia translation (Java and Sumatra), the Penan translation project in Sarawak, the Sinhala Old Testament translation project in Sri Lanka (originally called Ceylon), the Tagal, Murut, Sengoi, Kayan, Iban, Lun Bawang, Kenya, and Sambungan Tagal translation projects also in East Malaysia, the Malay and Muslim Malay in West Malaysia, the Trukese project on Truk Island, the Ponape project on the Ponape Islands, and the Marshallese project on the Marshall Islands.

Barclay recalled a funny but embarrassing experience he had when working once on the Tagal project in East Malaysia. He had gone there to work on this translation project and so had Jean Davis. When room assignments were made the wife of their hostess assigned Jean and Barclay to the same room. Barclay and Jean looked at each other as if to say, "There has to be a better solution than this." That evening the host returned and straightened out the dilemma. To their great relief, they each were given separate rooms.

Periodically he visited each of these projects, where he participated in workshops where he sat down with the translator or translators, and answered questions that had arisen while in the process of putting God's Word into their own language. Barclay in turn asked the translation team members many questions about key and difficult passages and how they had rendered these passages of Scriptures for the understanding of their own intended readers. Translation principles were often discussed.

In May of 1972 Barclay attended and participated in the four-week United Bible Societies Triennial Translation Workshop (TTW) in Ruschlikon, Switzerland. In August he traveled back to North Carolina for a two-week meeting of the *Good News Bible* (GNT) Old Testament Translation Committee. The later part of August he returned to Indonesia to work with Bible translators there.

In December Barclay wrote the Newman's Christmas letter:

> Malaysia is a multi-racial and multi-religious community; and this is clearly evident toward the end of the old year and at the beginning of the new year. The Malays, all of whom are Muslim (except for a very few Christians), recently observed their month of fasting, climaxing it with great festivities on *Hari Raya*, the day on which the fast was broken. In early November, the Indians celebrated *Deepavali*, which is primarily a family celebration, and is a day of great festivities, including the giving of gifts to the children. And in January crowds of Indians will gather at Batu Caves to observe *Thaipusam*, a day of penance when people fulfill vows by carrying *kavadis* (a heavy wooden or steel frame supported by sharp spikes that enter the body) up to the cave. In February the Chinese will begin their New Year's celebration, which is the most important Chinese festival in Malaysia. Throughout the year the Chinese have a number of special days, but none can compare with the events that surround the coming of the Chinese New Year. We ourselves are looking forward to Christmas with all that it means to us.

One family in particular stands out as both helpful to and supportive of the Newmans – it is the Hugh and Kathryn Smith family, who lived nearby in Kuala Lumpur. On one occasion they became profoundly and sadly involved with the Hugh Smiths. It was a warm August morning sometime after breakfast, when the telephone rang. It took Jean a minute or two to get to the phone, which was half way across their long rambling house and up a set of steps. When she answered, she felt suddenly very weak. It was someone from the hospital – the University of Malaysia Hospital in Kuala Lumpur, not far from their house in Petaling Jaya.

A staff member had secured the Newman's name and telephone number from the American Embassy. Hugh and Kathryn, along with their daughter Kendra, had left the information with them before the three of them left for a much needed holiday. Kathryn had asked Jean if they would keep in touch with their fifteen-year-old son Scott, while they were away.

So just the night before the sad event, Barclay and Jean had invited Scott over to their house for dinner and games with Tina and Dana. Barclay and Jean can still clearly remember hearing the laughter and good-natured banter between the three of them.

Never before had the Malay government allowed western teenagers to work during their school holidays in the summer months. But this year was a first, and the Newman's younger daughter, Dana, had secured a job at an A & W root beer restaurant not far from their home. She felt very proud, carrying eight to ten large mugs of root beer in one trip. Scott Smith was hired by the Colgate-Palmolive Company and was assigned to work in various departments.

At about the same time, Hugh and Kathryn and family were scheduled to attend and participate in the annual meeting of the Southern Baptist missionaries living and working in that area. Scott and his sister Kendra had always attended these meetings with their parents, but this year Scott wanted to stay home and continue working, since they had only a few weeks in which they were allowed to have a job. Hugh insisted that he should stay home with Scott, while Kendra and her mother attended the meeting. But with Scott's six-foot frame and convincing appeal, it was finally decided that Hugh would attend the meeting as he had in the past. Scott joined them on the weekend, and everything seemed to be running smoothly.

When the mission meeting came to a conclusion, Hugh, Kathryn, and Kendra were invited by friends to travel north of Kuala Lumpur to the Cameron Highlands. This was a unique and beautiful, lush mountainous area, very cool and refreshing after living all year in hot, tropical Kuala Lumpur. And since Scott was doing so well both with his job and his personal needs, they decided to go with their friends, after first spending a few days with him at home, washing clothes and preparing meals for him to have available for the next few days.

Jean replaced the receiver, dressed quickly, and headed for the hospital, leaving Barclay behind to tend to the needs of Tina and Dana. She sat by Scott's bedside and talked to him, assuring him that his parents were on their way, all the while not knowing if he could hear a word of what she was saying. The only response she got was the hissing sound of the respirator, which he was hooked up to. On his way to work, a car had struck him, breaking many bones and inflicting severe head trauma. The hospital was very near where the accident occurred, and he was put on a respirator within minutes of his accident. Some hours later, Hugh and Kathryn with Kendra arrived at the hospital, and the doctors' prognosis was not good.

After a few long hours the doctors recommended that the respirator be removed, and with much pain and agony his parents agreed to allow them to do so.

At the beginning of the school year, one of Tina's classmates had already died from the effects of a bite by a monkey. The Newman girls experienced constant loss of their friends – from either sickness or more often with the transfer of their parents to another country.

On December 19th Barclay and Jean wrote her mother:

> This Christmas is a little different from all others. The girls are big girls now so they know everything they are getting (for Christmas) and in fact, picked out most every item. I (Jean) felt kinda bad about it so Barclay and I decided to get each of them one thing that would be a complete surprise to them – an alarm clock for their bedrooms (Tina will certainly need one in College). I wrapped them up downtown so they could not possibly know what they were. I put them under the tree and felt quite safe until that night one of the alarms went off, and Barclay and I jumped (fortunately both girls were away for the night)!

One day, after Barclay and Jean had lived in Malaysia long enough to feel at home and at ease with their surroundings, they decided to have lunch at a nearby restaurant, do some necessary shopping for office supplies, and then go to an open-air market to stock up on fresh fruits and vegetables.

They returned home sometime after 1:00 o'clock in the afternoon and planned to work in their offices until dinnertime. When they went into the kitchen to put away the groceries, Jean noticed that Ainun (pronounced "i noon"), their helper, very quietly stepped through the door of the kitchen from a back room where she had been ironing, and whispered something in Malay to Barclay. He joined her, and in a very low voice, she described to him in her language, which Barclay understood well by now, that while she was ironing, a cobra slithered through the open outside backdoor just feet away from her and continued to crawl across the tile floor. She explained how she tried to "shoo" it away, but it wouldn't shoo.

When Jean had finished putting everything away in the kitchen, she realized that the whispering had aroused her curiosity, and she joined the two of them. When entering through the backdoor from the outside, you first entered the washroom, and from there you could go through one door to the kitchen or through another door into a large, very well lighted room. There was a sliding glass door going completely across the far end of the room, which opened out into a side yard.

On most days Ainun set up her ironing board there. Now she was describing to Barclay how the snake crawled across the full length of the room and had wedged itself, its entire length all stretched out, in the tracks of the large sliding door. She didn't seem to be afraid, but I guess she thought Jean would be more than a little frightened.

When the Newmans had first moved into this house, there was a palm oil grove in their neighborhood, situated at the back of both their lot and the short row of houses directly behind them. A construction company bought the land with the palm oil trees and had bulldozed the trees, clearing out all growth to prepare for building a large housing complex.

Barclay was later told that cobras lived in and among the trees in order to feast on the rats that like to eat the clusters of palm oil nuts. When the trees came down, the cobras started looking for new homes. So more than one cobra tried to get in their house, as well as in some of their neighbors' homes.

Barclay and Jean made a quick decision. They had no choice but to kill the snake, if they expected their older daughter Tina to ever come near that part of the house again. Then too, they had no guarantee where the snake would go, if it decided to move from the door track.

Barclay didn't have a garden hoe or anything else to use for a proper weapon. So they reasoned that they could take a large butcher knife and wire it to the end of the one long handled broom they owned. Their plan was for Barclay to stab the snake in the track from inside the room, and Jean, in the meantime, would go outside with a short handled hatchet and stand by the sliding glass door. Jean would actually not have a hand in this execution, unless Barclay missed, and he assured her that he would not miss.

Jean was fully confident that Barclay would stab the snake on his first try, but if just by some fluke he didn't make direct contact, she would be ready. She would come up close and chop off his head with the hatchet.

Both Barclay and Jean were positioned. Barclay came down hard, but he missed! The cobra quickly spread his head and began to slither out the door right towards Jean. She lost her courage, screamed, threw the hatchet in the air, and ran. Barclay felt awful and came running fast out to the side yard and succeeded in hacking off the snake's head.

One outing recommended by Bob Wakefield, a missionary with the Southern Baptist Convention, in particular stands out in the Newman's memory. When the right time came on a Friday afternoon, the Newmans drove to the east coast of Malaysia. After eating they made camp by spreading out a couple of blankets on a sandy beach and waited for the sun to go down. They had been told that the very large female turtles come every year to this same area and lay their eggs. The plan was for the Newmans to hire a small Malay boy to be their "lookout" while they either dozed or fell asleep on the blankets and waited for the boy to come for them when he spotted a big turtle coming out of the ocean. Barclay stayed awake keeping an eye on his family, but Jean who could never sleep even in a different bed from her own fell sound asleep on the soft sand. The girls denied it but they slept a bit as well.

At a little after eleven o'clock the Malay boy came running in the Newman's direction and motioned for all the family to follow him. It was hard going having just come out of a deep sleep and running in the loose sand. But not far away was a huge mother turtle, which had just begun to lay her eggs after first digging a shallow but broad hole in the wet sand. Although encouraged not to, Jean took a few really quick snaps as the mother labored. Tears seemed to stream down her face, and although the Newmans had been told that several grown men could sit or stand on the mother's back not even Dana ventured to sit on the shell of the mother turtle.

Barclay and Jean and the girls had many experiences while living in Malaysia. Some things happened right out of the blue, and some things happened because of what one or the other of them might imagine they could get away with. But if something went wrong in the household, you could stake your life on the fact that Barclay would be out of the country checking Bible translations with some of his translators. And when this next incident occurred Barclay was away, and Jean was left in charge of the children and the household.

It all started when a few days before Barclay was scheduled to be traveling. Dana, their youngest, presented her Mom with a tiny energetic monkey for her Mother's Day present. Three members of the family had planned to go out for dinner one evening with their pastor Lloyd de Run and his family, but Dana had begged off, because she had something already planned with a friend.

Barclay, Jean, and Tina returned early in the evening to be greeted by a grinning Dana and a big-eyed, squealing, miniature monkey. "Happy Mother's Day," Dana fairly shouted and presented her Mom with this runt of a monkey. What could Jean say? At first, she was secretly and silently annoyed. She never really had time or temperament for pets or even appreciated them. She only tolerated their only pet, a small brown Chihuahua, because he was supposed to be a stabilizing factor for the girls in this new and strange country where they were now living.

As time passed, Jean grew to love this helpless little creature. Dana had rescued it from the pet shop in Kuala Lumpur and had hoped her Mom would give it a good home. The tiny monkey with enormous eyes and long spindly tail sat on Jean's shoulder, eating bananas and then wiping its tiny hands on her blouse. Each morning Barclay secured her outside on a long, light weight chain near the shade of a tree during the day, where she could climb on the lower branches. At night one of the girls put her in a cage under an overhang on the open patio.

Since living in Malaysia, it had become a daily ritual that early in the afternoon, Jean removed the dried laundry from the clothesline in the back yard. The Indian helper washed clothes the first thing every morning and hung them out to dry in the hot sun. Then she would clean the house, and leave about lunchtime.

On this particular day, as Jean flung the warm, fresh, sweet smelling clothes across her left arm, she surely felt something staring at her. Big, squinting eyes literally pulled hers up. And she looked straight into the shifty eyes of a rather healthy-sized ape, which was perched on the limb of a small tree in the neighbors' yard just a few feet from her head. He had a wicked look, made more prominent by big tusk-like appendages protruding from the corners of his mouth. And it didn't help any when Jean saw how large he was, especially when compared to her tiny monkey.

Where had this thing come from and what would he do? Why this thought dawned on her, she didn't know, but thankfully it did. She moved fast! After throwing the clothes down on the ground, she loosened the baby monkey from her chain, grabbed her up, and rushed her to the cage on the patio. She put her inside and wired the small door shut. Thinking the newly acquired pet would be safe, she went back to retrieve the clean clothes now in a heap beneath the clothesline.

No sooner had she picked up the wash, than the big, brazen ape went straight to the cage and began to shake it violently. Barclay had made a good-sized cage out of thin wood and chicken wire and had put the cage on tall legs which were not too sturdy, but certainly sturdy enough for this tiny monkey. The question rushed through Jean's mind, "What can I do?" The girls would be coming home from school soon. Her better judgment warned her not to tangle with an erratic ape.

But she had to do something and do it quickly. She reached for a nearby metal and plastic lawn chair and hoisted it over her head and face like a shield. Then she grabbed her broom and yelled furiously at the ape – hoping to scare him away. He didn't scare very easily, and he simply leaped up on the edge of the roof just above the cage. All he wanted to do was to reach the baby monkey and kill her, and he would wait until his chance came.

Jean took the little female out of her wobbly cage and rushed her inside the house, where she could secure her in a small storage room with no windows and only one door.

All the Newman's windows – and there were many in their rambling, two storied house – were closed by rotating a handle that brought the louvered glass slats together – no screens on any windows. Jean ran from room to room, securing the downstairs windows first, and then flew up the stairs to close the second floor windows.

Jean began making calls. First, she called the police to come and kill the big ape or at least carry it away to the zoo or back to the jungle – any place would do. A young Malay policeman responded at once, and he and Jean went outside, where he could take careful aim and shoot the intruder. The policeman in his perfectly pressed uniform, slowly raised his pistol and aimed.

Jean blinked her eyes and plugged her ears with her fingers to give protection from the big "bang," but no bang came. The unperturbed ape stared bored and innocent into the officer's eyes. Clutching the weapon now in both hands, his arms came slowly down. He couldn't pull the trigger. All the young man said to Jean was, "I can't kill him. He's somebody's pet gotten loose." Then the officer left as quickly as he had come. The ape stared triumphant at Jean, and she stared back.

Jean's thoughts by now ran amok. Couldn't this Malay man see her predicament? Here she was – a helpless woman with two children and a baby monkey being held hostage in their own home by a stranger's pet ape.

No sooner than he was gone, Jean rallied. Maybe this big guy would get tired of waiting and just wander off. He didn't. He sat perched on their roof, patiently watching for another chance to slaughter the little female monkey. The ape actually looked content as he patiently watched and blinked his evil eyes -- he could outwit this family, and he held his position.

Jean went back inside the house and found, she didn't remember how, the telephone number of an animal control officer, and again the response was swift. She led him to the side yard and pointed up to the roof. She repeated the whole story a second time in her broken Malay. The man understood when he sighted the ugly animal. He raised his shiny rifle high and aimed, but he too, didn't have the heart to kill the beast. Down came his gun, and he was off.

It is always hot in Malaysia, especially late afternoon, and by now the house was getting really warm. Overhead ceiling fans just stirred the hot air around. The girls returned from school. The big stubborn ape was still perched on the edge of the roof just above the monkey's cage. Jean explained to Tina and Dana what had happened; at the same time, she warned them to stay away from their intruder and not to dare leave any windows or doors open where he could come in.

Dana had an idea, and that was what Jean was afraid of. Dana quickly changed from her school uniform into her long pants, got her Dad's bow (she said it was hers by now) and arrows, and climbed onto the roof on the far side of the house by way of an upper story balcony.

Jean was yelling, "Be careful, Dana, you'll fall off and break your neck." This girl was always a climber, and there was no stopping her. She had rescued this little animal once from a horrible life in the pet shop, and she was going to protect it now. Ever since the Newman family had moved overseas, it seemed that Dana on her own sensed that she should become the "man" of the house whenever Barclay was out of the country.

By this time, all the Newman's neighbors saw and heard the commotion and began to stroll one by one into the street, which was positioned slightly above their lot. The pavement was about even with their roof. The house was built on a slope that gradually went down. From the neighbors point of view, this made the house and yard a perfect amphitheater.

They were all lined up to see Dana armed with her big bow and a good supply of arrows, and the big monkey nonchalantly glued to his perch. Dana raised the bow and arrow and aimed, while Jean watched from the ground below and prayed. Dana missed the ape only by inches, and the arrow flew over Jean's head into the yard of their back door neighbor.

Jean saw immediately that she had to stop this exercise, but not until Dana had sent one more arrow whizzing past the ape, just barely missing a second time. Jean feared someone in the yard directly behind them would be injured by flying arrows. So she implored Dana to stop shooting with the bow and arrows.

It was by now late in the afternoon and the Malay, Chinese, and Indian household servants of the Newman's neighbors, having come outside after a full day's work, witnessed the whole drama and had a big laugh. Something exciting had happened that day to break the everlasting boredom of their mundane lives. Dana and Jean went inside, but they checked often to see if the intruder had gone away. He hadn't. Their windows stayed closed, and the house got very hot. Jean had visions of three people roasting in the night, but they didn't, and they survived until morning. They had no choice but to protect their little monkey and themselves as well. This old rascal was determined to wear them down.

After another day, Barclay returned home to a hot house, a squealing female monkey, a worn-out wife, and two excited daughters. When they had finished telling him every detail of their harrowing experience, they led him out to see the big ape still perched on the edge of the roof. Barclay thought for a minute, and then reminded them that their family was scheduled to leave on a trip to the States in just a little over a week, and there seemed to be only one solution to their problem.

Give the monkey to a little boy who had told his mom he wanted one and who lived in Kuala Lumpur, the city next to theirs. They had learned from a friend that he had begged his parents for one, and the Newmans now knew they couldn't leave to travel to the States and hope that their Malay helper would protect their "baby." A phone call was made, and Jean's Mother's Day gift took a ride across town to live in yet another home.

After Barclay and Jean and the girls returned from North Carolina several weeks later to their home in Petaling Jaya, their Chinese neighbors Eng Kiat and Kim Koh reported that for almost the whole time they were away, the stray ape stayed on his perch constantly day and night, leaving only long enough to scavenge for something to eat. The whole neighborhood feared he would never leave. Eventually he did.

Over the years Barclay shared many stories of his time spent with Bible translators in Southeast Asia. One of these is a "fish story" – not exaggerating the length of the fish but another unique turn of events as the fish were being prepared to eat:

> Anne Wilding – a long time resident of Thailand and brilliant (Bible) translator – was not as adept at meal preparation. But the most frustrated I ever saw her happened when someone brought her a red plastic bucket full of lively six-inch catfish of the variety that could crawl from pond to pond. That evening, I watched as she dropped three of them into a skillet of hot water, and I continued to stare as they immediately jumped out of the skillet and crawled out of the house through the open kitchen door. We had pimento cheese sandwiches for supper.

Barclay had gone on another occasion to the Pacific island of Ponape, and he later wrote of his experiences there:

> Sometimes it's not what you eat as much as the way in which the dish is served – or better, a combination of both. While the guest of honor at a feast on Ponape, I sat on the floor in a large circle with the other participants, as we listened to the rhythmic pounding of the kava plants on stones in two of the four corners of the building.
>
> When the pounding ceased, the thick, slimy-green liquid was poured into coconut shells and passed around for each of us to take a swallow (which I faked!). However, the places where the sub-

stance came into contact with my lips immediately felt numb, as though injected with Novocain. Ponapaean men will occasionally sit around and drink this stuff for days at a time, but I wouldn't be able to even sit around, much less drink more than a fictitious swallow, before keeling over. The servers then placed some large banana leaves in front of each of us and began piling them high with all sorts of fish and tropical fruits, as well as rice and other delicious delicacies. Although the pile in front of me was more than a foot high and with a diameter of two feet at the bottom, this would have been considered small in comparison to what a chief would have been offered. Apparently, a person of truly "high" status would be treated with a majestic mound of morsels seven feet tall or more. I wondered what would be done with my "leftovers," until I looked around the room behind me and saw the men of the village, sitting patiently with their wives, children, and (not too patient) dogs. As soon as we finished devouring more than our share, and even before we were completely on our feet, these people were sitting where we had been and hastily stuffing down the massive remains of this gourmet meal.

I had occasion to recall this event a few years later, while with my friend Ollie Woewoegan, dining at a "restaurant" in Surabaya, Indonesia. Once again I was eating from a banana leaf, but this time two beggars were standing just outside the unenclosed front of the building, starring at us. As soon as we stood up and walked over to pay for our food, these two men – slowly but deliberately – came over and scooped up the scraps in the banana leaves and quietly departed. They would not go hungry tonight, because we had intentionally left a large amount behind.

The concept of a buffet is not universally understood, and sometimes the result can be disastrous, as happened in Pyramid, Iran Jaya (the Indonesian half of New Guinea) during a Bible translation workshop. This is a "stuff and starve" society, where people are accustomed to eating what food is available at the time, because food is always an uncertainty, and whatever is left over will either quickly spoil or be eaten by uninvited guests of the insect world.

Counting the staff, there were more than twenty attendees at this particular gathering, when it was decided a buffet would be substituted for the usual passing the food around the table, which was difficult in itself. This was difficult because – as the sweet potatoes were passed around the table – each person would carefully dig through the dish to choose the largest potato with the most colorful meat. On this buffet occasion, the first six men actually wiped out the entire amount of food, except for a few scrawny, undesirable pale potatoes.

These Irian Jaya workshops were always concluded with a feast of pigs, sponsored by the local people. Pigs are prized commodities and in a sense the backbone of the social order – an outstanding pig can sometimes be bartered for two or more wives. We of the Western World are known for experiencing culture shock, and it did me good to see the reverse happen during one of these celebrations.

I was there with Ollie Woewoegan and Mrs. Susilaradyia (Susi for short), both of whom were from Djakarta, Indonesia and had never before been to Irian Jaya, although I had on several occasions. To understand their shock, you have to realize that men of the Dani tribe (our hosts) wear only a penis sheath made of a gourd, with the cup of the gourd fastened to the testicles and the tip fastened around the waist. The elevation of the terrain stretches more than a mile high (glaciers are found there), and to keep warm the men mix pig fat with dirt and smear it on their bodies, then sit in a squatting position with their arms crossed over their chests.

Pigs are slaughtered, cut up into small pieces and placed into a pit with corn, cabbage, and sweet potatoes. Then the pit is covered over with banana leaves, hot stones are put on top of the leaves, and water is poured over the stones, steaming the contents of the pit. When it's serving time, the men (whose fingernails are lengthy and caked with dirt!), dig out the food (with their not too clean fingers) and serve it on banana leaves to the guests. The shock experienced by my two Djakarta friends is best revealed through Mrs. Susi's comment to Ollie, "Did you see where he scratched himself before he served us?" Then both of them turned a deep shade of green.

Several of the tribes in Borneo have the custom of serving food in a bowl without a serving spoon. You dip your own spoon into the dish and put the food on your plate, then eat off the spoon, before dipping again to get more of whatever you want. For the most part, these dishes contain a lot of sauce, and I have actually seen food fall off a person's spoon, when dipped back into the serving bowl. On one occasion, I'm certain there was more food in a certain dish at the end of the meal than at the first. My remedy – eye what attracts you, dip deep and fast, and never return for seconds, especially not for seconds deposited there by someone else's spoon.

As a means of causing fermentation of food, several tribes in Sarawak, East Malaysia bury pork, vegetables, and rice in bamboo containers (made from large hollowed out sections of the bamboo tree). Then – when the time is right – the bamboo is dug up and the ingredients emptied into a bowl. Although the taste is somewhat pungent – much like sour pickle juice – the dish is enjoyable when served with boiled rice. I was glad that when this tasty morsel was first served to me, I was not informed of its origin.

At this same meal in the interior of the jungle, shish kebabs were served, and I – as the guest of honor – was handed the choice kebab, consisting of four two inch cubes of pig fat barely warm on a bamboo skewer. I deferred, which seemed rather to please than to offend the host, who apparently had hoped this would be my response. "Arm of orangutan" – I never in my life expected this as a main course. But when the Penan villagers of Sarawak went out to hunt wild boars, none were available, and this was the only major source of meat they were able to bring back. What disturbed me most was not the skinned shoulder and arm that the hunters presented to my host to cook for me, but the sight of the whole orangutan hanging on a post in the middle of the village before it was butchered – this animal whose hair was almost exactly the color of mine and whose facial expression mirrored what I remembered of my cousin some years ago. Or was that me whose image I remembered in the mirror?

During a conference at a secluded site some distance from Taipei, the capital of Taiwan, I was plagued by a sore throat and decided early one morning to go to the dining room, to see if I could get a glass of orange juice. As I walked into the room, it seemed to be empty, but I spied the metal pitchers with long thin spouts from which the waiters always poured the juice; so I proceeded in that direction. As I approached, a strange sight appeared in the mirror behind the counter. It was the image of our waiter, slurping down juice with the spout stuck deep in his mouth. I decided against any orange juice.

During that same conference, we were seated at noon around a table with a Lazy Susan in the middle, when a platter containing a beautiful tropical fish settled directly in front of me. I noticed something strange – evidently, someone had cut out a piece of the fish with a serving knife, leaving the front half of a roach stuck to the remaining piece and struggling for dear life. As I sat there amazed, one of the other participants asked, "What are you looking at?"

"The fish!" I replied. "I've never seen a fish exactly like this one before!"

> Some years later – while en route from Djakarta, Indonesia across to Surabaya by train .... This train ride to Surabaya was overnight, and I was lucky enough to have obtained a sleeper berth – Spartan though it was. The hour was late when I boarded, and I was very tired, so I went directly to my upper cubbyhole and prepared myself for a good night's rest. To my surprise, this was the quietest and most relaxing train ride I had ever experienced, and when I crawled out of my quarters early the next morning, the reason for the smooth journey became obvious – the train had never departed from the Djakarta station.

On at least one occasion Barclay was forced to walk for an hour in the jungle before he could reach the Penan village where he was scheduled to work with a couple of Bible translators living in this remote area. He recalled some of the apprehension that an American not accustomed to such a trek might naturally feel:

> From the airstrip, we had an hour's trek through the dense jungle to reach the Penan village, during which time the men would demonstrate their skills with their blowguns by shooting beetles and other eatable insects that were grasping the bark of the massive trees. But my primary concern was with snakes, not insects, and I always walked along with my eyes glued to the ground in front of me. Whack! Keplunk! It was the horrendous head and heavy green body of a huge (deadly) green snake striking the ground in front of me. The man walking behind me had seen this venomous viper dangling over my head and had quietly severed its head with his machete.

Barclay had a number of encounters with airplane flights in Southeast Asia, and he shared some of these with his family:

> My first encounter with the reality of a plane crash happened early in my professional career while waiting in Bombay for a connecting flight to Bangalore in the south of India. After waiting and walking back and forth through the departure lounge for several hours, I finally became both impatient and agitated and barged my way through the anxious mob to ask someone at the check-in desk why the plane was so late. He explained, "It crashed on the way here, and we're having some difficulty finding other equipment to take its place."
>
> Once my flight from the coast to Pyramid in the interior of Iran Jaya (West New Guinea) was overbooked and required two of the

Canadian-manufactured "Otters"' instead of the usual one. I was assigned a seat on the second plane, and we took off soon after the departure of the first. About halfway to Pyramid, the pilot announced, "Please look out the windows on both sides for the other plane. It went down somewhere along here, and we need to radio its exact location to the rescue helicopter, if at all possible".

We never did spot the wreckage, though a search plane later did.

In the meantime, Jean recalls the Sunday when she awoke to a bright sunny Sunday morning in Petaling Jaya, Malaysia, then she proceeded immediately out to the front driveway to pick up the Kuala Lumpur paper. She rarely scanned the front page first, but this morning her eyes were drawn to a small article only one column in width and less than two inches long. The article stated how a small aircraft flying to Pyramid in the interior of Iran Jaya (Indonesian New Guinea) had gone down in the jungle, with no word from the pilot or any survivors. Since the flight was identified by both number and destination, and knowing this plane had left for Pyramid at almost the exact same time as Barclay's plane was scheduled to depart, her assumption was, "That was Barclay's plane!"

She couldn't think straight at first, but then decided not to share this news with Tina and Dana just yet. They always worried about their dad flying on those small planes going into jungle areas. She decided that she would fix breakfast as usual on Sunday morning, hurry the girls to get ready for church, and they would go as usual.

Jean was tormented with worry, but she decided not to share this news with their pastor for fear someone might get the word back to the girls. So she reasoned that if by ten o'clock on Monday morning, she had not heard from the Indonesian Bible Society in Djakarta that all would be well with Barclay. She didn't know how, but reasoning and hope were better than the alternative.

In her mind she played out how she would have to sell all or most of their household furnishings and take care of a thousand things to prepare the three of them to return to the States without Barclay. Jean still recalls those terribly anxious moments and hours that dragged by, and how at the same time, she felt buoyed and comforted by God. When ten o'clock on Monday morning finally came, and she had not heard from the Indonesian Bible Society, her complete being rejoiced, as she thanked God, and shared her story with Lloyd de Run, pastor of the Petaling Jaya First Baptist Church. She also received a good tongue lashing for keeping to herself for almost twenty-seven hours the agony of having read that article without sharing it with him.

Barclay related to his family and friends a series of two humorous events that happened in Bangladesh, New Guinea, and Malaysia:

> Some years ago, I was in Dacca, the capital of Bangladesh, visiting a team of Bible translators, when one of them invited me to "tour the city" with him in his ancient VW "bug." People were thronging all around the plodding vehicle, and we were experiencing difficulty, wriggling our way through the maddening mass of humanity that constantly surrounded us.
>
> Particularly troublesome was a gentleman who was less than sober, and when our car came crawling to a sudden halt, he quickly volunteered to help us get it started again. So we got out and allowed him to open the hood. Where was the engine? He'd never seen a car without an engine, and I said, "The engine was here when we started. What have you done with it?" He immediately disappeared into the crowd, and nobody bothered us after that.
>
> … Biak is an island off the northwest coast of New Guinea, and it used to be necessary to overnight there before proceeding into the interior of the mainland… From there you could ride into the town in a local "taxi" – a small, Japanese-built pickup truck with boards along the side of the bed for seating and a roof overhead for protection from the sun and rain.
>
> I stepped in and sat where the board that paralleled the back of the cabin joined the longer board that reached from the front to the rear on the right side. As we traveled down the road, frequent stops were made, until each of the three boards was jam-packed with passengers, including the almost naked gentleman with hog tusks in his nose, who had squeezed in beside me. Then the passengers started getting off at their intended destinations, until only he and I remained on the seat. And he remained there motionless, squashing me up against the wall of the vehicle for the final miles of our ride, without making any attempt to move away from close bodily contact with me.
>
> Suddenly I remembered – the men of the Dani tribe have a house in each village where only men are permitted, and the way they keep warm while sleeping there at night is to "pile up" around the fire. This preference for closeness of bodily contact – that has no homosexual implications – is also carried over into other phases of their lives, and it's not uncommon for two warriors to be seen walking along side by side holding hands.

The third incident which took place in Malaysia will be included in a following chapter.

In early June of 1973 Barclay flew to New York where he continued working with the *Good News Bible* (GNT) Old Testament Committee members. It was planned in advance that Jean and the girls would follow him towards the last of June to either New York or Black Mountain, North Carolina, where the committee members would continue their work.

On June 14th Jean wrote home, "I'll be having the two ladies (from Sarawak, Borneo who will be living in our house while we're away) come in here four days before I leave … So I know the time will be busily spent orienting these ladies and trying to get away (to the States)…"

These two ladies mentioned in Jean's letter were Phyliss Webster and Marge Britzer of the Borneo Evangelical Mission. Barclay had been traveling for several years to this remote village in Sarawak, Borneo to assist the two lady translators as they continued translating the Penan New Testament.

Phyliss had gone to live with the Penan people in Sarawak, Borneo when she was still a young lady. Her native home was Australia, but she had left everything behind and gone to live with these people. The Penan had no written language when she first arrived, so she began the arduous task of writing down their oral language and then later teaching them to read the written language. Her goal was to translate the New Testament into their language so they could have Scriptures in their church services.

Phyliss had shared with Barclay on one of his trips to work with her that when she initially joined the Penan, they did not live in huts or houses. They lived in trees and moved constantly through the jungle, hunting wild animals and gathering anything edible. The government had forced them to settle in one place by the time Barclay had gone there to work with Phyliss on the New Testament translation.

Phyliss talked about how hard it was for her to learn to sleep in a tree without the fear of falling out. Wild animals roamed the jungle, and this mode of bedding down each night was a safety precaution for the Penan. Phyliss told how all night long the men would, from tree to tree, call out in a loud voice to each other as a means of checking on each other.

Now some years later, Phyliss would be coming to Petaling Jaya in West Malaysia, bringing with her the Penan New Testament manuscripts. The entire New Testament had been completed, typed, and was now ready for the printers to finish the work. Barclay had spent many sessions with Phyliss and her colleague Marge Britzer in Sarawak answering their questions and giving exegetical help as they continued the arduous task of putting God's Word into the Penan language for the very first time.

Jean looked forward to their coming. Phyliss was to arrive first. Jean planned a special meal, using her best china and linens for Phyliss. But before her arrival, Jean told her daughters Tina and Dana not to be surprised if Phyliss didn't have the proper table manners that she had tried to teach them over the years. She explained that Phyliss had been living for a number of years in the jungle with a tribal people. Jean didn't want the girls to giggle or show any signs of astonishment.

But Jean vividly recalls that evening meal. Phyliss put everyone to shame with her impeccable table manners. It was a lesson for all the Newman "girls."

Throughout the entire evening all three of the Newmans listened with absolute eagerness to Phyliss as she shared with them the story of her trip from Sarawak, Borneo to the airport in Kuala Lumpur, West Malaysia. Jean took careful notes as the story unfolded, and she later wrote Phyliss' account (with Barclay serving as her meticulous editor) which was later published in the ABS *Record*:

> "THE MISSION PLANE IS GROUNDED. Repeat. The mission plane is grounded." These words reached Phyliss Webster by radio at her home at Long Lamai, a small village in the interior of (East) Malaysian Borneo near the Indonesian border. There were other words, which followed, but these had little significance as Phyliss wondered what her next move would be. Sure, the voice on the other end had added that a part for the plane would be ordered tomorrow from somewhere in Europe, and that it would possibly arrive within a week's time.
>
> But from long experience Phyliss knew that a week would almost certainly grow into a month, and she had to be in (Petaling Jaya) near Kuala Lumpur some 1,300 miles away with the Penan New Testament manuscript long before that time. (Jean was to pick her up at the airport, bring her to their home, and then she and the girls would be leaving in only four days to travel to the States).
>
> There was only one other alternative – she would walk out of the jungle – a seven-day journey by foot – to the town of Bario, where she could catch a commercial flight to Lawas, the mission headquarters. Over the years Phyliss had heard similar messages, but none had carried so much meaning as on this occasion.
>
> More than 20 years ago Phyliss had left her native Australia, and her job as a secretary, to work among the Penan people in Borneo. At that time, the Penan were still jungle nomads who lived in remote places deep in the jungle, seldom staying in any one locale for more

than a month at a time. They built very temporary shelters in the trees and hunted the wild game with their expertly made blowguns. In recent years many of the Penan people have become semi-settled, living in small communities and raising some rice. Along with this, many of the Penan continue to carry on a partially nomadic existence, and they remain the country's best hunters, skilled with blowguns.

Phyliss was the first white person to live among the Penan, and she recalled her earlier days when she had traveled through the jungle with them. She had not made such a trek of this distance for several years. The distance itself, when measured in miles, was not so long; but it would involve crossing four major mountain ranges exceeding 6,000 feet in elevation and numerous smaller ranges. There would be rivers to cross, and they would encounter wild animals and dangerous snakes in the course of the seven days it would take to reach Bario.

Phyliss turned her thoughts to the preparation for leaving. The time was short. She must quickly pack and then select men and women from the village to accompany her. Many decisions had to be made; the Penan men would never agree to let her take this trip, unless all possible precautions were made to insure her safety, as well as that of her colleague, Marge Britzer, and of Thelma (a missionary), who was visiting Phyliss at the time.

Since everything would be carried on the backs of the men, the little mementos she had collected over the years would have to be left behind. Every article would have to be packed in kerosene tins lined with plastic to keep out the tropical rain and dampness; each tin would have to be carefully weighed, so that the load could be equally distributed among the men. Rice and some dried meat would have to be taken along. Blankets would be needed during the cold, wet nights.

Phyliss had thought long in advance about what final words she would say to the villagers. She had prayed that she could leave with them a sense of urgency for distributing the Scriptures to all the Penan people when they were finally typed, printed, and mailed back to them. The effectiveness of her more than 20 years of service depended on their taking over where she had to leave off.

But now, due to this unexpected turn of events, she would have to ask once more for their help before they could have their long awaited Scriptures. She called on the tribal leader and told him the story of the radio message from the beginning, convincing him of his responsibility, and requesting his leadership in choosing the Penan men and women who would accompany her and her two companions. Each person had to be approached individually, and with the right attitude;

each had to be convinced that this was a responsibility worthy of his or her trust. When the 16 villagers were finally chosen, and preparations had been made, a small boy of nine asked to go along with his father – bringing the total number to 20 – ten Penan men, six Penan women, the three missionary ladies, and one small boy.

On June 14, 1973, before daylight, the little party of 20 was ready to go. For one full hour the whole village – men, women with babies, and the children – walked with the group as they began their trek. Then most of the villagers turned back. Goodbyes came hard. Everyone was crying. Old men waved them away after numerous instructions about where to spend each night and what they must protect themselves against – the wind storms, the wild animals, the snakes, the slippery river rocks, and on and on.

By noon the group had reached Long Banga, a Saban village, and a few of the villagers were still walking with them. It was a Christian village they had reached, but some of the people were not strong Christians, and they were in the midst of a pagan funeral. The group had hoped to have lunch there, but instead they spoke words of encouragement to the bereaved, visited with the village chief, and then they went on as far a Kelabit Pulan, a comparatively rich village; and there they spent their first night.

The next morning 15 villagers from Kelabit Pulan accompanied Phyliss and her party for two hours as far as Beuang Village, the home of a very poor Penan tribe. Those who had accompanied them from Long Lamai had now all turned back, except the men and women who had been chosen for guides. At Beuang the villagers cooked sweet potatoes and served the travelers plain boiled water. This was the best they could offer. The group rested for one hour, and just as they were getting ready to leave, the villagers presented them with a pile of walking sticks from which each could choose.

The remaining six days were much the same. The group would arise at about four each morning, cook enough rice for the whole day, pack, and be ready to walk just before daylight. The Penan women would walk, one in front and one in back of each of the white ladies, often pushing and pulling them over the steep places and preventing them from falling forward on the way down the sides of the mountains. The party would walk all day until four in the afternoon, stopping occasionally for a five-minute rest, except at noon, when they would take a "lunch break" of some 15 minutes. The meal consisted of rice cooked early that morning and served on a banana leaf.

Each night the men would find a safe campsite and begin the night's preparation. Half of them would hunt for wild meat, and the other half would prepare a long platform for 20 tired and footsore travelers to sleep on. The hunters would kill, clean, and cook the meat for that night's meal, and smoke the remainder to be carried with them the next day. The sleeping platform was made above the ground in hopes of avoiding snakes and wild animals. The men cut small trees and branches and tied them together to make a quick shelter for the night.

Finally, when everyone had settled down to sleep, the rains came down hard. Everybody was soaked to the bone. Phyliss had the men check the manuscripts, and they were dry. That night there was little sleep. Cold, wet blankets don't encourage sleep, even in weary travelers.

Early in the journey a large river at Baram had to be crossed. The boulders along the sides were huge and jagged, and for two hours the group of 20 walked over the slippery rocks, until eventually the river could be crossed where it was only waist deep.

The seven days went slowly by until Bario was reached, where a plane was waiting for the three ladies. The trip was over, and the people and the manuscripts were safe. The Penan men and women would go back and wait – patiently – for the time when their new Scriptures would be printed and sent back to them.

In the summer of 1973 Barclay and family had been in West Malaysia for three years, and the government refused to renew his family's visas for another three years.

Since the Malay Bible had not been completed, Barclay decided to move with Jean and the girls to Singapore and work with Elkanah Suwito from there with hopes that the Singapore government would grant him visas for at least three years.

Barclay's writing and travel schedule was extremely heavy, so it was decided that Jean could fly to Singapore and look into renting a house and buying a car. Barclay had been told that Bill Wakefield with the Southern Baptist Mission Board would be leaving Singapore, and his house would be available to rent.

Jean was happy to get away from her desk and typing and make the trip. She arranged with the Wakefields to see their house. It would certainly be adequate. With the help of the Singapore Bible Society, she arranged to buy a second-hand car. When she left Singapore she was grateful that everything seemed to have fallen into place, and she could hardly wait to report to Barclay that these two big items had been successfully taken care of. Now to once again apply for visas for the family of four.

As soon as Jean arrived back in Malaysia, Barclay had even better news to share with her. Dr. Asmah Haji Omar, Professor of Malay Linguistics and Dean of the Faculty of Languages and Linguistics at the University of Malaysia, had called him and asked if he would be willing to set up a translation department at the University. Barclay could hardly answer, he was so surprised and thrilled. He had earlier written an article for Bernama, equivalent to the U.S.'s United Press, and she had seen his article.

Barclay quickly regained his voice and told her he would really be happy to take on this challenge, but he couldn't, because his and his family's visas were due to expire in just a short time. He explained that Jean, his wife, was in Singapore at that very hour arranging for housing and transportation. Dr. Omar assured Barclay that if he would accept her offer, there would be no problem in securing his visas for another three years. The University of Malaysia would take care of it for him.

Barclay felt like his prayers had been answered. Now he would be able to stay and work with Elkanah for the duration of the Malay Bible project. Fortunately, Barclay was able, with the help of the Bible Society in Singapore, to cancel renting the house, and they would also take care of selling the car Jean had arranged for.

When Barclay and the family had first settled in Malaysia, he had allowed time each day to study the language. He had obtained some good language study material and had worked hard at learning the Malay language. For practice, he went each afternoon, to a small café near their house, where he would sit and talk to anyone who had time to listen. Usually a young boy would be more than happy to let Barclay practice the Malay language with him, because he in turn, wanted to learn English. Barclay soon began to feel confident that he could manage lecturing in Malay at the University.

But Barclay also knew that setting up a translation department and lecturing in Malay would require more technical terms than he had been using with the young child.

As he began making plans for class lectures on the theory and practice of translation, he realized he could not use any of the religious illustrations he had been accustomed to using at Bible Society Translation Workshops and Seminars. Every illustration had to be based on a secular theme. Most, if not all, his students at the University of Malaysia were Muslim.

Barclay spent the next three years lecturing at the University, while continuing to work with Elkanah on the Malay Bible. When Barclay's travels interfered with scheduled classes, he was allowed to have make-up sessions and meet on Saturdays – whatever it took.

Besides Barclay's involvement in lecturing on the theory and practice of translation and setting up the Translation Department at the University of Malaysia, he also worked in March of 1974 with Bible translators in Bandung, Indonesia; in October he worked with Anne Wilding in Yala, Thailand. Lecturing, traveling, and meeting with translators took up much of his time, but he managed the same year to write four articles, which were published in the United Bible Societies publication *The Bible Translator*.

In the winter of 1974 Barclay and Jean received a long distance call from a doctor at a hospital in Nashville, Tennessee, saying that Tina, their elder daughter, had become quite ill and had been admitted to the Vanderbilt Hospital. She had entered Belmont College in Nashville in the fall of 1973, returned home at the close of the school year, and had returned for her second year the following fall (1974).

Jean had flown to Nashville in March of 1975 to bring Tina back to Malaysia, where she would remain with the family until the four of them returned to the States. She spent her days doing volunteer work. In the summer of 1976 Dana had graduated from high school in Kuala Lumpur just before her 15th birthday, and she was anxious to return to the States.

1975 found Barclay in Indonesia once again working with the Common Indonesian Bible translation team for part of April and again in August. He continued to lecture at the University of Malaysia.

In March of 1976 Barclay returned to Biak, the largest of the Schouten Islands, off the northern coast of West Papua, the Indonesian part of New Guinea. He wrote to Jean and the girls:

> My luggage is less today than yesterday. I left all the grocery items for the Aricheas, and I don't have the Malay New Testaments any more! Yesterday I spent two hours trying to get them through customs, and finally gave up. (he wanted to share the Malay New Testaments with translators in this Indonesian area). So I have only *one* with me now. There is someone traveling from the Bible Society to Biak on Saturday, and perhaps he can bring them, provided the Bible Society is able to get them out of customs. What a mess! By the time I left the airport, all the passengers had long gone.

After spending the night on the island of Biak, Barclay was able to travel to Pyramid and then on to Jaya Pura. He wrote home the 7th of March:

> Well, I finally arrived in Pyramid late on Saturday afternoon. I had to spend the night on Biak, as expected, but the airline did pay for the hotel. Then, we had to get up at four in the morning to catch

> the flight from here to Jaya Pura. When I arrived, no one was there to meet me, so I walked over to the missionary guest home. Finally, I found out that they thought I was coming on a plane in the late afternoon, and so would not be able to go into Pyramid until Tuesday morning, because of immigration regulations requiring me to go to the town of Jaya Pura (one hour away) to register with immigration and the police. I managed to get into town, and with the help of the office boy, I rode on his scooter to immigration, the police (station and to the), photographer (required three passport pictures = $2.50 US). Then back to the mission station. The MAF (Missionary Aviation Fellowship) planes don't generally fly on Saturday, but fortunately one of them was going into the jungle, because the pilot was returning from his medical check-up; so I helped him off load what was (already) on the plane, and then helped him load, so I could get here (Pyramid). After that, the trip was easy!

After much contemplation it had by now become clear to Barclay and Jean that because of illness the family must go back to the States. Springfield, Missouri was chosen. For six months the Newmans lived in the First Baptist Church mission home. Both girls wanted to go back to Missouri. Tina enrolled in Southwest Missouri State University in Springfield (now Missouri State University), and Dana enrolled at William Jewell College in Liberty, Missouri.

Barclay and Jean had planned to return to Southeast Asia and continue to work with the United Bible Societies in that area, but family circumstances made that impossible.

Barclay did, however, go back to Petaling Jaya and Kuala Lumpur in September (1976) and remained there until January 1977. He returned to complete his assignment at the University of Malaysia and also to continue working with Elkanah Suwito on the Malay translation of the Bible. But shortly before he flew back to West Malaysia, Barclay and Jean began looking for a house in Springfield to purchase and settle in. This would give the family a base from which Barclay could continue to travel and would give stability to both their daughters. The two of them drove all over the city of Springfield, searching for the right house, and eventually decided on a four-bedroom (one for Barclay's office) house in Southeast Springfield.

A few weeks later, after Barclay had returned overseas, it became Jean's responsibility to close on the house, write necessary checks, and buy a few pieces of needed furniture. Their shipment from West Malaysia came a few weeks after Jean and the girls moved into the house.

Chapter IX

Back to the States and Off Again

Soon after Barclay returned to Springfield in January 1977, he resumed his travels to Asia and Africa, working once again with Bible translators and continued writing articles. He and Heber Peacock were asked by the Canadian Bible Society to compose a children's book of Scriptures entitled *Good News in Paper*. Barclay also began the exercise of writing song lyrics while traveling overseas – while flying or waiting in airports or during free time at meetings or at night in his hotel room.

Jean believed that this was time well spent in preparing Barclay for the translation of poetry throughout the *Contemporary English Version* of the Bible, which he would begin to translate in the early eighties.

In April 1978 Barclay traveled to Singapore and Kuala Lumpur to work once again with translators. Barclay wrote from Singapore on the 17th of April:

> The good news is that I arrived here safely last night, though the plane was almost two hours late. The problem was the immigration "lines" in Taipei (Taiwan). The room was one pile of people, pushing from all sides to get into the lines. We were so crowded that a few times I let go of my briefcase, and it didn't move! …
>
> Now for the bad news. I kept waiting for my bag and finally asked if they (luggage) had all arrived. The answer was "Yes." I put my bag in bond at Taipei so as not to have to fool with it, as I did when I went through there a few years ago. When you check in to leave, you give them the tag and they put it on the plane direct, though they give you a check number. Somehow they checked out the wrong bag and sent it as mine, so my bag may be in South America. … they are allotting me Singapore $100.00 to buy some clothes until it (my bag) arrives. So I'll go shopping when the stores open. I'll go either to Metro or else to the Japanese store.

And so the saga continued. Barclay further explained on the 18th and 19th of April 1978:

> Well yesterday I received word that my luggage had been sent to Hong Kong and would be forwarded here (Singapore). From what I was told, it is safe and would be only a matter of time, so I'll plan to go on to Kuala Lumpur today. …
>
> Yesterday I did my shopping at Tang's; bought two batik shirts (Indonesian batik) at $12.00 each, two pair pants (not such a bargain); two nice pair socks; and some locally made underwear, which fit (at least before washing). I am to present the receipts at the China Airlines office at the airport before my departure. I have an early afternoon flight, but will perhaps change, so that I can wait on my suitcase.
>
> So far this has been an unbelievable trip. My suitcase arrived in the airport in perfect shape before 4:00, and so I was able to get on the 5:00 flight to Kuala Lumpur (West Malaysia). I cleared customs with no trouble...
>
> Before we got to Petaling Jaya/Kuala Lumpur I asked him (the taxi driver) to stop at the Apex Pharmacy … while there I called Irene de Run (Barclay and Jean's close friend when they lived in Petaling Jaya), and she insisted that I come to her home, since Maylee's (her youngest daughter) room was vacant; she is in the room with Irene. So here I am.
>
> Outside the window are stacks of dogs in cages (Irene's son Edmund raised and trained security dogs to be hired out), so I wondered about sleeping; but they were quiet, and the steady rhythm of the oscillating fan kept the mosquitoes off. I slept really well – my best night so far.
>
> Barclay further elaborated on the 21st of April:
>
> This is Friday, and I had an inspiring early morning concert – 20 German police dogs "singing" in concert with the mosque prayers. I think God must have enjoyed the dogs better than the mosque – at least they were in harmony. …
>
> I took the pants I bought (in Singapore) with airline money to a tailor and got them altered a bit, so they look good. I'll write a book – "How to Travel and Make $5.00 a Day."

It was on this trip and while Barclay was staying at the home of Irene de Run that he broke in half a "root canal" tooth on a small rock or bone in his breakfast rice, which had meat. He was scheduled to fly on to Melaka, West Malaysia from Kuala Lumpur to work with Elkanah

Suwito. By the time he reached Melaka, the pain has become almost unbearable, so Elkanah took him to a Chinese dentist in Melaka.

Barclay wrote from there on April 23rd:

> I put something white in my mouth; it could have been either a bone or a small rock. Anyway I felt a strange sensation, like all the filling was suddenly missing from my lower jaw tooth (farthest back). As soon as I got to Melaka, Elkanah got me in to see a dentist (dental surgeon, and *very* good, so it seems). He showed me that the tooth had split lengthwise all the way and had to be extracted. It took a full 3 and one half hours (his office closed at 4:30; I was there about 4:00, and left his chair at 7:45). Three X-rays, numerous injections, three assistants, antibiotics, pain pills, rinse pills, and a second visit the next day! What would be the cost? Malay dollars 40.00 – can you imagine? He did give a discount, because he knew Elkanah, and I am a minister. But even with a discount, that's still cheap.

On that same day Barclay and Elkanah flew to Bangkok, Thailand for the United Bible Societies Triennial Translations Workshop (TTW). The pain from Barclay's "removed tooth" continued to get worse, so he asked Howard Hatton to take him to a dentist in Bangkok.

Barclay shared with Jean on April 25th:

> Ever since the jaw tooth was extracted, I have had some pain and a lump in the jaw. So I went to a dental clinic (in Bangkok) again today. The dentist saw me at 1:00, referred me to a dental surgeon, and she then made an appointment for 4:00. She extracted the (imbedded) wisdom tooth, then the portion of root that was left from the other tooth. … I am holding an ice pack on my right jaw with my left hand while writing this letter. The pain is not so terrible now, but this is to keep it from bleeding….

The outcome was that Barclay ended up with a dry socket, and the dentist, after seeing him on a total of three occasions, prescribed strong antibiotics.

While at the TTW Workshop in Bangkok Barclay shared with Jean:

> This is the first time I have been without pain in more than a week now. Sometimes the pain has been rather severe; the dentist said the socket was dry, and so she stuffed it with some medicine, and I have no pain at all. The gauze can come out on Monday, she says.

At this Workshop, it was Barclay's privilege to meet Ulrich (Uli) Fick from Stuttgart, Germany for the first time. He was General Secretary of the United Bible Societies, and Barclay described him in a letter to Jean as "a very gracious person." Over the years Barclay had great respect for Uli and for the leadership that he was giving to the UBS.

While in Columbo on this same trip Barclay was robbed. He described the event in his letter to Jean on September 9th:

> As you know, you have to declare all your currency when you arrive here. So I counted my US dollars and placed my wallet back in my briefcase, where I keep it to avoid being pick-pocketed or having it fall out. Well, on Tuesday morning, I woke up early and remembered that I had not checked my wallet along with my other valuables into the hotel deposit box. I looked for it, and it was *gone*! We had a police investigation – that was comical, the sergeant trying to take down my statement, and Celestine Fernando and I had to smile – and I also placed a notice in the paper, offering a reward for the recovery of the wallet and of my air travel card and driver's license. I also had Celestine cable New York (Bible Society office) to notify them of the lost air travel card.
>
> I was careful to place my wallet in the briefcase. But I went to the restroom on the plane (either before or after), and it could have gone then. That is hard to imagine, since no one was sitting beside me on the plane. I did place my briefcase down to pick up my bag at customs, so it could have happened there. Or the hotel is a third possibility. There was a total blackout here on Sunday night, and I was in the restaurant at the time.

From Sri Lanka, Barclay went to a Bible Society translations workshop in Miri, Sarawak in western Borneo to assist in the translation work of Scriptures for the Iban people. Formally the Iban spread along the coast of Sarawak and were engaged in costal piracy. They were always in search of agricultural land, and much of the time they fought to gain this land in aggressive warfare. They were known to be headhunters and practiced enslavement of women and children. Barclay worked with Father Pickler, a Roman Catholic priest, on the Iban New Testament translation. Also in September Barclay worked with translators in Burma.

Barclay told about an incident that took place more than once when he was working in Rangoon, Burma. His colleague, Basil Rebera, confirmed Barclay's account. When the two of them returned by elevator to their rooms at the President Hotel, they had to jump up simultaneously to start the elevator moving, and if any other persons entered the elevator, they sometimes asked at least one of them to jump up together with the two of them to insure the elevator would start going up.

In January 1979, Barclay and Jean's first granddaughter, Christina Lynn Simkins, Dana's first daughter was born. The proud grandparents thought they didn't want grandchildren until they first held that precious little girl. They were blessed again in September of 1980 when their second granddaughter, Malea Ann Simkins was born. It was not until February of 1988 that their third granddaughter, Andrea Jean Simkins was born. Barclay and Jean often kept the girls on Friday or Saturday nights, and they always enjoyed every minute of their stay. Over the years the girls have been a great joy to both Barclay and Jean. It was always a delight to watch them grow up into lovely young ladies.

In August of 1980 Barclay traveled to West Malaysia to work with Elkanah Suwito on the Malay Bible, which was nearing completion. From this trip he returned with a florist box from Irene de Run full of orchids for his elder daughter's wedding. And on August 23rd Tina had fresh flown-in orchids bordering and topping her wedding cake and orchids for both sets of parents.

There was no problem getting the orchids through customs after Barclay arrived back in the States. Irene had taken care of that by including an official certificate declaring them free of insects or diseases. But out of the goodness of her heart she also tucked away something in a clear plastic bag in the bottom of the box – candy, called dodol and made from white sugar and cocoanut milk. The candy was pure white in color and cut into squares. The customs official reached under the orchids into the bottom of the box and brought up the bag. He then looked at it and questioned Barclay at length. Barclay explained that his friend Irene in Malaysia was a generous soul and wanted to send his wife Jean some "sweets." After several tense minutes, Barclay asked him to taste it and explained to the official, "It is good candy and you may keep it and enjoy." The official took the bag of candy and Barclay was free to go. Who knows what happened to the good candy!

In May of 1981, Barclay attended and participated in the United Bible Societies Triennial Translation Workshop (TTW) in Chania, a small town on the Island of Crete. The meeting was held in a Greek Orthodox Monastery right on the Mediterranean Sea – a beautiful setting. The water was a radiant blue, and night and day, the waves crashed relentlessly against the rocky shore. When the men and women Bible Translation Consultants gathered from many countries for these meetings, they worked hard and long. In order to attend a TTW each participant was required to write and present to the group a technical paper on some aspect of translation either on a biblical or linguistic theme or both. These papers were intended to benefit all the participants in their respective field of work.

All Consultants were expected to attend the reading of these many papers; the sessions ran from early morning until late afternoon, and often into the evenings.

With a concentrated program such as this, time off was welcomed at the end of the week, so almost every weekend an excursion was planned for the group.

Jean was fortunate enough to attend several of these workshops with Barclay. She recalls arriving at the Monastery on Crete after a long flight, her invitation to go hiking early on her first morning (there was room for only one more on the van). Barclay insisted that Jean take that one available seat. So before her suitcase was even unpacked that night, and very early the next morning, she joined the group, who hiked on a rough and steep trail going down into a deep gorge and out again.

The trail was rocky, often with huge boulders on both sides. Each step had to be chosen carefully. As the group descended, high bluffs arose on all sides, and they were beautiful with many shades of gray color mixed with the various shades of green. Small streams had to be forged, and Jean recalls taking off her shoes and wading across the icy cold water.

Even after the Crete Workshop had gotten off to a good start, it was learned that a number of the participants required their papers to be copied – one set for each person. Some of them had made stencils ready for copying, but others had simply brought one paper with them. Jean recalls Edith Peacock asking her to work in the office with her. The two of them cut stencils and mimeographed page after page, day after day on a cyclostyle machine. Jean was more than happy to be of help and to feel needed. She and Edith had a great time working together. During the entire workshop, they never quite got the black ink off their fingers and from under their nails.

At these large gatherings of translation consultants, involving so many men and women from so many nationalities, something funny almost always happened. A good number of men attended these meetings without their wives. So at most of the workshops, the staff in charge of the housing and facilities arranged for someone to come every day or so to collect the dirty laundry -- shirts, pants, socks, and underwear of the men and women involved with the sessions. The Monastery staff thought they had secured in advance a Greek man from the small town to wash clothes for the participants.

But when the hired man came the first time to gather the dirty clothes, he left the dirty underwear and socks and took everything else. When questioned about this, he answered, "Who me, wash dirty *underwears*? No, I don't do that."

Because of his travel schedule, Gene Nida had arrived late for the meeting and had not heard the jokes being passed around about "the dirty underwears." So one morning, when Jean went out to the clothesline in back to hang up Barclay's freshly washed underwear and socks along with hers, Gene approached her in whispered tones, "What's this story going around about dirty underwear?"

Barclay had earlier shared with Jean the story, so she explained to Gene Nida, and the two of them had a good laugh.

On the 13th of September 1981 Barclay was invited by the National Avenue Baptist Church in Memphis, Tennessee, his home church, to be the Homecoming guest speaker for the morning worship service. Here Barclay was able to visit with his old friend, William E. Lyles, the friend who had taken him to Union University in Jackson, Tennessee many years earlier. This would be Barclay's last time to reminisce with him. Barclay's former schoolmate, Eugene Gafford, was pastor at National Avenue at this time.

February 28th through March 3rd of 1982 found Barclay teaching the book of *Jeremiah* for adults at the Family Bible Conference at First Baptist Church in Black Mountain, North Carolina, where Edgar Ferrell was pastor.

To Jean's delight Barclay also wrote home often and on the 1st of November he wrote from Rangoon, Burma:

> On the wall of the room where we (translators) are working there is a picture of Jesus (the usual one), below it to the left (is) a picture of Anne Judson and to the right Adoniram Judson. Then a third row has the paintings of his first three converts. Sparrows have built a nest behind the picture of Jesus and have otherwise desecrated it as well.

On the 2nd and 4th he wrote again from Rangoon:

> Our (translator's) Workshop is going well. The people are sharp and interested in learning, which makes work a pleasure. … The workshop has been successful – the Karen participants are convinced of the need for an entirely new translation (common language) rather than of the need for a revision (of the old one). Today the principles and procedures will be worked out …

I'm in the dining room now – it's not too appetizing when the waiter has a mouth full of (very red) beetle nut! Basil (Reberra) and I hope that he doesn't spew when waiting on us …

From Rangoon, Burma Barclay flew on the 7th of November to Dacca, the capital of Bangladesh, and from there he traveled on to Chittagong which is near the Bay of Bengal. Here he was scheduled to work with translation committees and individual Bible translators. He wrote home on the 8th:

> … I will have some discussions tonight with the Bengali Committee. It is an important translation, with ninety million people here in Bangladesh.
>
> … The main Chakma translator is a tall, handsome young man in a wheelchair. He was an outstanding athlete, but was in a motorcycle accident. He attempted or contemplated suicide, but became a Christian finally. The hospital staff has now trained him to be a pathologist's assistant, testing routine things.

So from Rangoon to Bangladesh and on to Bangkok, Barclay worked with translation groups in Bangkok before flying to Melaka, West Malaysia. It had been a tiring two weeks of concentrated work.

Jean received a letter from Barclay written on the 14th of the month, and she was again amazed at what all can go wrong on one of these extended work sessions:

> As I write this it is 7:30 a.m. on a Sunday morning, and I'm in the coffee shop of the Wisma Hotel where I spent the night. I can see them "rinsing" the glasses from the night before…
>
> My MH 83 flight from Bangkok departed almost an hour before the time originally scheduled, the time I had told Elkanah (Suwito), thus getting me into Kuala Lumpur (Malaysia) earlier than I had anticipated. Immigration and customs were swift, and I did not have to wait long for my luggage, so I was out early. I waited for an hour and a half, then decided to phone the Malaysia Hotel, where I sometimes go, and where I had told him (Elkanah) to contact me, if it was not possible to meet me at the airport. The hotel was full, and they had no reservation in my name. Then I called the de Run's (home in Petaling Jaya, a town bordering Kuala Lumpur) knowing that I could find overnight accommodations there. The household helper answered the phone and replied, "Mrs. de Run is in U.K.

(United Kingdom), and so is Edmond and Maylee." Only Margaret (Edmond's wife) was in Kuala Lumpur, and she was not in.

Then I began to attempt a phone call to Elkanah in Melaka, and kept getting a busy signal from the operator. The phone next to me was in the hands of a gentleman who concluded his conversation by saying to the party on the other end of the line that he was going to get a taxi to Melaka.

Immediately I asked him if he were alone, and he said, yes, so we agreed to share a taxi to save expenses. His name was Isa, from Esau, obviously a Muslim. But he knew "Brother Suwito," as he called him, because of Elkanah's connection with the Methodist school. We inquired about a taxi, and the price was $100.00, the set price for airport taxis. Now you pay at the airport desk, and only airport taxis are allowed to take passengers. That was expensive, and we decided to take the taxi down to the city bus stop (where the town to town taxis were available). It is a multi-storied place where you bargain for taxis. We found one, and he wanted $50.00, which we also thought was too much, so he agreed on $13.00 a piece, and he would find two other passengers. None were available, and finally I bargained with another driver who agreed on $12.00 (each, and he would look for one more passenger). Our luggage was quickly taken from the first cab, and I agreed to pay the cost of the third passenger, if we would get on the road right away. Then he (the driver) decided that he had to have a fourth passenger, and ran down to the street below. I went back to the first driver and told him I'd pay $40.00, if he would leave immediately, and he agreed. We were off – it was almost 7:30, and I had arrived at 5:00.

Taxi drivers (here) buy only enough gas to last a trip at a time, so we pulled into a service station, and I heard a thud. A motorcycle had bumped into us. The driver was not hurt, and his cycle was not damaged, so the matter was settled with a few choice words between the two men.

On the highway, with the usual sort of driving – arrived in Melaka at 10:00, and the driver agreed to take me to Elkanah's place. (When we got there it was) Dark, not a light in the house. We drove down to the end of the lane, to the Anglo-Chinese school, where one of the young men said he would be until midnight; he would tell Rev. Suwito that I had gone to the Wisma Hotel. By now the taxi driver was exasperated, and so he went to the taxi/bus station and refused to take me any further. My friend and I got out there, and I tried to bargain with a beja driver or two; got disgusted and decided to walk. When I got here (the hotel) I was informed that every hotel in town was fully booked because of the long weekend. Monday is a holiday (Deepavali, Festival of lights, I think).

… I now have a room, and that is where I am, but I'll continue the story as is.

What to do? Well, nothing I could do except eat supper (now 11:00 p.m.) in the coffee shop. I had kweh tau and a coke … In the coffee shop/hotel lobby is the only T.V. (in the hotel), and it had a video tape running with a Cantonese movie. What else to do? I sat and watched, while having the receptionist phone Elkanah's house every 15 minutes, assuming he would have started back from Kuala Lumpur after not meeting me there. No luck. Seated beside me was a young Chinese man, a fine looking and educated person, who was here with his brother and sister and … friends (ten persons in all). They had booked two rooms, but evidently the hotel was so full that they had been given only one room (actually one room with an anti-room where two roll away beds had been brought in for the boys; the girls (8 of them) would sleep in the other room. He asked me, "Would you like to bathe in our room? The girls are going out for a walk around Melaka" (12:00 p.m.), and I said, "Thanks!" He got an extra towel, and I used my shampoo to wash my hair and to bathe with.

My plans were to spend the night in the hotel coffee shop, but they informed me that it was not allowed, and the shop would close about 1:00 to 1:30 a.m. They then called around and discovered that the Traveleze Hotel had an open (24 hour) shop, and I could sit up there if I purchased a drink. My (Chinese) friend, who had allowed me to shower in his room, then volunteered to drive me (in his Mercedes Benz) the two miles there, so we put my green bag and carpet in his "boot." He said, "I need to inform my sister," and went up to his room. When he returned, he said for me to come wait in his room because the friends had gone to look up the auntie of one of them, and they would stay there (they didn't leave on my account, but felt crowded). They would phone back if they found her (they didn't return and didn't phone, as it turned out). That left *only* the Kim brothers, their four sisters, and the fiancé of one of the brothers, so they offered to let me stay in the room with the two brothers. I agreed.

They offered me one of the 30-inch-wide beds, saying that the two brothers could sleep together, but I refused. There were two wicker chairs there (the anti room was a sitting room), each with a pillow in the seat, so I took the two pillows, placed one under my hips and the other (doubled up), under my head. One of the boys gave me a blanket. We turned out the lights and went to bed. Time: almost 3:00 a.m. At close to 4:00 one of the boys went to the bathroom and apparently had diarrhea. When he finished, he bathed and came in for other clothes (I think – I kept my eyes shut, and I was facing the wall). By 6:30 I was ready to get up, and they were too, since they had hoped to get off by 7:00 (as it worked out, I saw them around until past 8:30, because the three who had gone out had not returned).

After getting up, I started calling Elkanah once again, and finally at about 8:30, his servant answered, "Dia 'dah pegi ke Penang. 'Tak taku bila balik" ("He's gone to Penang. Don't know when he'll return"). So that was that. I had also called and found that one hotel could let me have a room on *Monday*, but that didn't sound too good. Then the girl at the desk said she could shift around the reservations and make a place for me, beginning today sometime. I decided to go walking until I could get into the room (about noon)…

With nothing settled except a room at the Hotel on the 16th of November he wrote:

So far no contact with Elkanah … He must be taking a segment of his "annual leave." … This morning I went to have my Kuala Lumpur to Singapore ticket reconfirmed and at the same time to reserve a seat on the Melaka to Kuala Lumpur flight so as to make connections on the same day. "Sorry the Melaka to Kuala Lumpur sector has been cancelled for two weeks." (Not enough passengers).

As it turned out Barclay once again had to take the suicide drive by taxi back to Kuala Lumpur, and weeks later he learned that Elkanah never received his letter saying he was coming to Melaka to work with him.

After Barclay had moved back to the States in January 1977, he was invited by Dr. Asmah of the University of Malaysia in the eighties to return to the campus as an External Examiner for the Diploma in Conference Interpretation and Diploma in Translation for the academic sessions 1988/89, 1989/90, 1990/91, where he met with the graduate translation students and graded their final examinations. Jean was also able to return to Malaysia with him, and it was good for the two of them to visit with former church members and neighbors.

In April of 1983, Barclay traveled to Legon and Ghana, Africa, Bangkok, Burma, and the Philippines to continue working with various ongoing translation projects in these countries.

On a Sunday evening in July, the First Baptist Church of Springfield, Missouri held a "Service of Songs" when the choir presented a collection of hymns Barclay had written. The words to these hymns were always expressions of his faith, and he had a profound desire to share the messages found in them.

On September 29th Barclay was invited to speak as the American Bible Society representative for "Bible Translation Day" at the Russel Senate Office Building in Washington, D.C. Barclay recalls that Senators Armstrong and Hatfield, among others, were also presenters that day. This was Barclay and Jean's first trip to Washington, D.C., and needless to say, they both enjoyed the experience of seeing for the first time so many places of interest in their nation's Capital.

A year later in November Barclay once again returned to work with translators in Rangoon, Burma. On the 1st he wrote:

> Your letter arrived! Which one? The one you sent last June, of course. The man at the desk checked for me, and finally, in the third batch of roach eaten letter, I saw one that looked like yours, and I was right. Undamaged, and not even nibbled on. So I suppose I got a letter before you did…
>
> The hall boy, room boy, or whoever, then left and soon he came back with a local cigar in his mouth, a smile on his face, and three "Do Not Disturb" signs in his hand! I think I got the message across to him the second time.

Later the same day Barclay wrote:

> The translator I'm working with had his father killed (accidentally or mistakenly shot by a Burmese soldier) and his two uncles killed by communist terrorists. The tribal peoples here, especially on the fringe area, have a very difficult time. They must work 50% of their time for the "State," which means that they are essentially slaves – forced to carry the ammunition or food into the military camps. The translator is working here in Rangoon, but his salary comes to less than half of the minimum expenses. He is a very diligent person. I hope we can get him a raise (in salary).

On November 3rd *The Religious Herald* printed Barclay's new hymn, "God's Word for All Earth's People." This hymn was sung at countless American Bible Society Volunteer meetings across the States and in other countries as well. The words have been included in this account.

In May 1984 Barclay once again attended and participated in the United Bible Societies Triennial Translation Workshop – this time in Stuttgart, Germany. Before the workshop was scheduled to begin, participants were given the opportunity to come early to Stuttgart in order for about 50 of them to take a trip into East Germany. This was before the infamous wall had been torn down. Barclay and Jean were included in this excursion, and today they feel very fortunate to have been on this trip where they saw many famous places.

The group's first stop was at the Castle of Wartburg where Martin Luther had translated the New Testament from the original Greek into German and where there was a copy on display. On this trip they also traveled to Wittenberg and visited the All Saints Church where in 1517, Luther nailed a protest to the door, known as the "The Ninety-Five Theses." Other places of interest were visited, such as Frederick the Great's castle at Potsdam, where the group enjoyed a tour of the lavishly decorated rooms, and later that evening they were treated to a superb concert.

Jean later shared one humorous experience. The large bus with all the Bible Society passengers had arrived at the border between West and East Germany. The driver stopped as he was instructed, and passports were collected from everyone and given to the guard. Most of the guards were big Russian men, and Jean kept thinking they would come aboard and perhaps question each passenger. She thought of every German word she had learned in college and prepared herself for intelligent answers, if they should be demanded.

The group sat and waited for permission to enter East Germany. One hour went by, then two, and finally almost four hours went by before they were allowed to cross into East Germany. But shortly before the bus was allowed to move, a huge Russian guard did indeed enter the bus and looked straight at Jean who was seated next to Barclay on the front row of the long bus. He spoke in heavy, harsh German, and Jean almost forgot her own name.

During their wait, a busload of young people pulled up beside the Bible Society bus. After a while, they became bored and impatient. So the passengers on each bus began to write notes back and forth to each other by way of holding up sheets of typing papers with the words written in large letters. This made the time go faster for both young and old.

Jean had put in her purse cookies, crackers, and cheese from the flight to Stuttgart the night before, and she and Barclay were eager to have a bit of food after a four-hour wait. Crackers and cheese never tasted so good. She only wished there had been enough for everyone. A late dinner had been planned in the event they were held up and also to give them a chance to visit places of interest along their route.

Chapter X

Progress of the Contemporary English Version

It was during the May 1984 United Bible Societies Triennial Workshop in Stuttgart, Germany that Eugene Nida approached Barclay and asked him if he would be willing to serve as the drafter for a Literary Liturgical translation of the Bible for the American Bible Society. Barclay agreed and soon began prayerfully to prepare some sample texts of materials for the Gospels, which he (Nida) agreed to review. Barclay never forgot the statement Gene made that day, "Translators are not made. They are born." Barclay reasoned that this could possibly be true, but not always.

But before Barclay began the process of translating selections for youth, he recognized the definite need of developing some specific guidelines that were later elaborated in a number of articles, one of which was "Translating for Children," published in *The Bible Translator: Practical Papers* (1978).

When the Translation for Early Youth was transformed into the *Bible for Today's Family/Contemporary English Version*, Barclay brought together these translation principles in an article published in *The Bible Cause* in the spring of 1991; he further elaborated on them in *Creating and Crafting the Contemporary English Version*, a book published by the American Bible Society in 1996. In this book the "why" and "how" of the CEV Bible translation are explained, and answers are given to such questions as why was the translation undertaken, and what makes it different from other translations. It also explains how the CEV translation team adhered to the same biblical principles and standards that were used by the King James Version's translators 400 years ago. Before presenting these principles, it is worthwhile to note Barclay's humorous description of the daily routine of those who translated the texts for the TEY (Translation for Early Youth):

> On weekday afternoons: we listen to TV's Sesame Street and Mister Rogers; Saturday mornings: we watch cartoons on TV; Sunday mornings: we check with Second, Third, and Fourth Grade Sunday School classes; Between times: participate in conferences with school and Sunday school teachers; Spare time: we read pop-

> ular children's literature in the proper age level: Other times: we listen to educators in primary schools; Sometimes; we translate. Always: we pray, review, and rewrite; Never: Ending! Always making note of language level and proper syntax for our intended audience.

In the summer of 1984 Barclay was asked by Alice Ball, General Secretary of the American Bible Society, to travel to Honolulu to inquire whether or not the Hawaiian Christians wanted to accept the Bible Society's offer to initiate a new translation of the Bible or for them to continue to use the old translation. It was decided that the old translation should be printed until a new translation could be put into action.

Barclay had already accepted an invitation to come to the Fiji Islands to attend a workshop sponsored by the Bible Society in the South Pacific to work on a Study Bible. While there he had an unusual experience with the "bug" world. He was housed in a compound with hut-like accommodations. His room was on stilts about six to eight feet off the ground. The walls to the room came up about waist high, and the compound lights shown brightly all night right in his face. Barclay has always required a dark room to induce sleep, but he thought he had a good solution for his predicament. He reached into his suitcase, pulled out his swimming trunks, and placed it over his head shutting out the light and at the same time positioning the opening of one leg so that he could breath. Sweet sleep came until he suddenly awoke to something moving in his open mouth. A roach had crawled into his mouth! Jean later asked him what he did then. His answer, "What could I do? I pulled it out and threw it as far as I could."

From Taiwan Barclay was scheduled to fly directly into Pyramid, Irian Jaya by way of Djakarta, Indonesia to secure a visa and to receive police clearance to enter the country. From this workshop he had planned to fly once again to Rangoon, Burma where he would work with Basil Rebera on translation projects.

Barclay arranged to make all five trips in succession – one after the other in order to save on the purchase of overseas tickets. He was away from home and his home office a total of eight weeks.

When Barclay arrived in Honolulu on the 18th of July 1984 he wrote a letter home:

> There was a note for me to call Pat Munford … She has arranged a meeting for us and three of the Hawaiians connected with the proposed project. She has come into this late, but there have evidently been misunderstandings and hurt feelings on the part of the folks here, and the project is apparently at a standstill.

On the 20th Barclay shared more about the Hawaiian project:

> "Mission accomplished!" At least here in Honolulu. Yesterday I met with the people interested in the Hawaiian project. What they really want is a reprint of the already existing (old) translation, and I think it ought to be done, since none are presently available, and there is a real demand for the translation.

Hawaiian Bibles were currently needed and because Barclay's past experience told him that it might take up to 20 years for a new translation team to be set up, the translation completed, the work checked, rechecked, and printed, he agreed with the group to go with the reprinting of the old translation.

On the 23rd after arriving safely in Suva (Fiji) where the workshop was to take place Barclay wrote a short letter home:

> Today went O.K., but (some of) the Samoans are difficult – one complained about the accommodations, quantity and quality of the food, manner of service; and he even complained when the announcement was made that they … would have our clothes washed for us! (he added) "Have never heard of such a conference! A waste of Bible Society money!"

Barclay said he kept real quiet. He reported that the food was wonderful, and he is always grateful not to have to wash his own clothes when at a workshop.

Later Barclay wrote:

> Last night at supper I asked one of the Chinese what a certain dish was, since I was in the process of eating a piece and had another on my plate. He answered "Ears!" Gene Nida (sitting next to Barclay) immediately asked, "Ears of what?" The man stuttered and finally pronounced the word correctly "Eels!" The meat was soft, rather bland, though it was covered in sauce. Today we had whole squid (about 6 inches long), and you could bite from either end!

On the 6th of August Barclay described how his room was cleaned:

> …I had an opportunity to watch them "clean" my room. The woman who did the bathroom had on rubber gloves, so she cleaned the commode, then picked up my drinking glass, held it under the

faucet, and proceeded to clean it by running water over it and rubbing her fingers around the rim! Wow!

After two or three days in Djakarta, Barclay was off to Pyramid, Irian Jaya (Western New Guinea) to work with Bible translators and to attend meetings. In Pyramid, Barclay joined Myron Bromley, who had lived and worked in the jungle with the Dani tribal people for many years. Barclay had flown there on several previous occasions to help with the translation of the Scriptures for the Dani people, who were one of the most interesting groups he had ever had the joy of working with. Barclay reported that low dark clouds always seemed to hover over these people in the highlands of Western New Guinea.

This area is known as the Grand Valley of the Baliem River, sometimes referred to as the "Garden of War" – a reference to the stone-age culture and warrior traditions of its inhabitants. Although it is a lush and picturesque spot, its people have been considered some of the world's most primitive people.

The Indonesian government and missionaries have sought to suppress tribal warfare, cannibalism (never practiced in the Grand Valley), pagan beliefs, polygamy, and the ritual of chopping off young girls' fingertips as a mark of respect to the deceased.

The last major clan fight in the Grand Valley was in 1966. At one time there were 70 Dani clans forming 12 war alliances. Most of the battles were ritual events with the number killed or injured amounting to no more than a dozen men. But in the 1966 uproar 100 men were killed – because steel axes and "parangs" (large knives) were used instead of the traditional ceremonial weapons.

Most Dani couples continue to adhere to their traditional social ways – in which men live apart from their wives and children, with only occasional cohabitation.

On the 22nd of August Barclay wrote, "Each day there is a lecture and then time with translators from this region." After nearly three weeks in the jungle of Pyramid, Barclay was off to yet another country. This trip took him again to Rangoon, Burma where he worked with Basil Rebera, a United Bible Societies Consultant, on translation projects there.

We now go back to the significant events that resulted from Gene Nida's conversation with Barclay in Stuttgart, Germany concerning the possibility of a Literary Liturgical Translation of the Bible. It was on October 9, 1984 that Gene Nida came to Barclay's home/office in Springfield, Missouri, where they reviewed the drafts and made minor changes in the texts Barclay had prepared. Soon after these revised drafts were submit-

Barclay Newman, 4 and 1/2 months old

Barclay, one year old, 2/22/34

Barclay and father, 3 years old, 1934

Barclay M. Newman, Sr.

Barclay, 5 years and 10 months

Barclay, 6 and 1/2 years old with dog

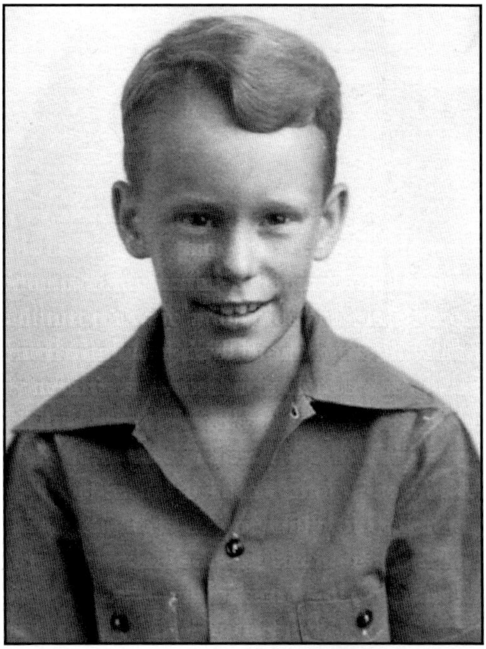

Barclay, 10 years old, 1941

Barclay with mother, 9th birthday, 2/22/40

Barclay, 11 and 1/2 years old

Barclay, 11 and 1/2 years old, with cousin Jimmy Westbrook, 9 and 1/2 years old

Barclay, Treadwell High School, Memphis, TN, 1949

Barclay high school graduation, January, 1949

Barclay at Union University, fall, 1950

Barclay at Southern Baptist Theological Seminary, May 25, 1956

Tina and Dana Newman, 1959

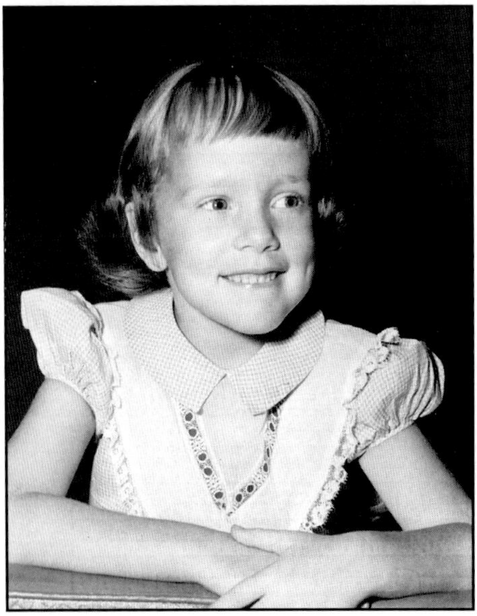

Tina Newman, October 1961

Dana Newman, October 1961

Tina, Jean and Dana Newman, 1970, in Malaysia

Gene Nida, Jean Newman, Tina Newman, Althea Nida, Dana Newman, Fall 1970. Black Mountain, NC

Barclay in Bangladesh, October, 1974

Barclay in Pyramid, New Guinea with Dani Tribe, 1972

Barclay with translation committee, 1991

Barclay honored at Union University Homecoming, February, 1992

Barclay reading final proof of the CEV, July 2, 1994

Barclay receiving first CEV, June 8, 1995, New York

Roger Bullard portrait of Barclay working on GNB

Jean with her woodcarvings, Winter, 1994

Barclay with R. C. Briggs, July 2006

Jean and Barclay Newman, 2008

ted to the American Bible Society's General Officers (Alice Ball, Laton Holmgren, and John Erickson), the officers met behind closed doors to discuss together with Maria Martinez, Vice President of the Scripture Publications Area, the need for such a translation.

On Thursday the 13th of December 1984, when Barclay was in New York for Gene's ABS Board of Manager's appreciation dinner, Maria informed him that the General Officers did not think the time was right or that there was a pressing need for a Literary Liturgical Translation of the Bible. She did, however, ask Barclay if he would be willing instead to work on a translation for early youth. This proposition was very acceptable to Barclay, and he immediately responded, "Yes!"

Barclay's wife, Jean, had accompanied him to New York for the celebration dinner. On Friday, Gene inquired of Barclay, if the two of them could go on Saturday to his home in Greenwich, Connecticut, in order for them to plan for this new translation. Barclay said he could not go because he was scheduled to preach the next day at a small church in Missouri, where the congregation was celebrating Bible Sunday. Jean recalls the two men simultaneously and inquiringly looking straight at her, and she knew what was coming. She somewhat hesitantly agreed to substitute for Barclay as the speaker at the Clever Baptist Church in Clever, Missouri.

Immediately the two Newmans, with Althea and Gene, made plans on Saturday to go to Gene's home in Greenwich, Connecticut. The plan was to put Jean on a late Saturday afternoon flight out of New York, heading for Missouri. But before her departure time, the three of them sat around two card tables placed together in the Nida's living room. There they decided on which texts should go into what would later be called *A Book About Jesus*, the first in the experimental texts for the Early Youth Translation. Barclay returned to Springfield on the 20th, after they had drafted (still at the card tables) some of the texts the two of them had decided upon. Thus was born what would later become known as the *Contemporary English Version* of the Bible.

What had originally been planned for a Literary Liturgical Translation was now evolving into a translation for early youth, later positioned as *Translation for Early Youth* (TEY). From the very beginning of the translation for early youth, Barclay also began to think in terms of (1) Who would be the primary *audience*? (2) What *level* of language would be used? (3) What *goals* are we aiming for? (4) What will be our overall *principles* and *procedures*? (5) How will we conduct our *testing*? (6) How can all these questions be best addressed for this early youth translation?

To quote Barclay, as published January 1989 in the St. Louis Post-Dispatch:

> (In the past) Bibles for children have been merely paraphrases of Bibles for adults. But the Society (ABS) won't settle for mere adaptations. Rather its standards for accuracy demand that the children's Bible be a direct translation from the Hebrew and Greek...
>
> ... Informal surveys of representatives of Christian denominations in the mid-1980's had convinced the Society (ABS) of a need for a "children's English" translation...

It was determined that the primary *audience* would consist of people between the ages of five and nine. But youth of this age come in many different packages and from many different places. Their abilities, experiences, interests, and perspectives differ widely, and yet the *goal* was to reach as many of them as possible.

It was assumed that youth in the five to seven age bracket would for the most part have the Scriptures read to them, whereas those in the eight to nine age bracket would be able to read the Scriptures for themselves. Fortunately, the *audience* may be somewhat narrowed down, by assuming that most of them will probably be church oriented, with at least some background in traditional biblical vocabulary.

Also, it was realized that early youth often lack purchasing power, which means that there is an adult audience that must be considered. It was assumed that for the most part they will be Christian parents, Sunday School and Vacation Bible School teachers, teachers in Christian schools (Protestant and Catholic), and other church oriented adults. The language, which young people appreciate (not necessarily what they themselves might produce) and which some adults assume they appreciate, are not always the same.

The American Bible Society's *goal* was that both young people and adults, whether Protestant or Roman Catholic, Christian or non-Christian, would all discover the early youth translation (TEY/CEV) to be a readable and accurate translation in contemporary English and would use it. Such a text should be especially effective in evangelistic situations (youth and adult), where a translation in present-day English speaks more effectively to both youth and adults than does traditional biblical language. Also this text could well be appreciated in Bible study groups, where early youth Scriptures might serve as an effective "bridge" toward the understanding of more traditional translations.

Barclay noted:

> This is a lesson learned from the Indonesian context, where the Indonesian Children's Bible is now widely used by adult Christians

> (including pastors), even though *Today's Indonesian Version* has for years been well accepted.
>
> ... A set of "Principles and Procedures" is an absolute necessity for any translation project. It keeps translators on track ... the translators must decide where they are going! That is to say, the *audience* must be defined, which in this instance is particularly difficult to do, as will ... become evident.

The drafting of the Translation for Early Youth (TEY) New Testament was done entirely by Barclay with Gene Nida and Jean Newman as the primary reviewers. Early in the process, it seemed wise to involve the Roman Catholic Church. So Archbishop John F. Whealon of Hartford, Connecticut was approached about the project and asked if he would be willing to review these early drafts. He did and later responded in some detail, raising questions and making comments that initially led Newman and Nida to believe that he was not sympathetic with their approach to Bible translation.

So with fear and trembling (Barclay wrote, "In all twenty-five years that I have known Gene Nida, this was the one and only time ... that he was visibly shaken"), Gene and Barclay arranged to visit him on the 25th of February, 1985 to discuss the proposed translation. Barclay later wrote, "Immediately our fears were dispelled, and from the moment we met him, we knew we had a true colleague. And we were correct – no one contributed more to the project than Archbishop John F. Whealon." Ultimately, he was the one who initiated the granting of the highly valued Imprimatur of the New Testament. On February 17, 1991 after reviewing a CEV draft, he wrote Barclay and said, "I have reviewed this draft and find it accurate. It has a freshness that gives new meaning to many verses."

Barclay was already involved with preparing Scripture portions and selections for the American Bible Society and tending to some administrative aspects of the Translations Department. To add to their workload, he and Gene had also been asked by ABS to revise the *Good News Bible*.

In light of their heavy workload, Gene felt this committee work could be best done, if it took place away from their offices in order to avoid all interruptions. So the two of them, accompanied by their wives, spent one session in Ventnor, New Jersey (August, 1985) and five sessions in Fajardo, Puerto Rico (March 1 -- 31, 1985; January 2 – February 1, 1986; January 1 – February 28, 1987; March 1 --31, 1988; January 6 -- 31, 1989), dividing their time between the *Translation for Early Youth* (CEV) and the *Good News Bible* revision.

Jean Newman served as a recorder and typist on a "primitive" laptop computer, while Althea planned, shopped, prepared some of the meals for the four of them, and arranged for other activities on the weekends; for Sunday worship the group usually attended a Lutheran church in San Juan.

On Barclay's birthday 1987, Gene Nida wrote to him:

> Barclay, I have never worked with anyone on anything which I have so much enjoyed. It has been amazingly stimulating, and I have learned so much from you. How fascinating to see how your mind works! You have such a contagious and spontaneous humor and such a keen sense of the ridiculous, two important reasons why you are such a first-rate translator, reviewer, and editor.
>
> Your creative work on the translation for 'early youth' is really impressive …
>
> But the best thing of all has been the genuine pleasure of getting to know you personally, to realize your sincerity, to recognize your sensitivity to the needs and concerns of others, to note your devotion to Christ, and to experience your openness to suggestions.

At the same time Barclay was fully aware that if he and Gene continued to revise the *Good News Bible* (GNT) in the direction the process was moving, the uniqueness of this translation would be completely destroyed. So it was finally agreed that only sensitive and gender inclusive passages would be revised.

In December of 1988, Barclay wrote to all United Bible Societies Translations Consultants worldwide:

> … we solicit your input in the *Good News Bible* "Limited Revision." After considerable research on the matter, we are fully convinced that the word "limited" is the key to the project. In the words of a university professor who for ten years made the GNB required reading in his classes: "We need a revision that is limited to sensitive language and sensitive passages. And we need it quickly! The Bible is the only text we have that uses sexist language."
>
> … As a translation, the GNB (GNT) has its own integrity, as well as a large constituency of dedicated users, who would not be pleased with significant alterations in the existing text. On the other hand, some people have such a negative attitude toward the GNB that no revision, however drastic, could possibly win them over. It is also true that the very thought of a substantial revision has become a source of division among certain Bible societies. We

> must turn this around and make this project a source of healing and unity.
>
> We now ask you to join the ABS in this *limited* revision of the GNB (GNT) ... Remember, the more proposals for change, the more possibilities for division! So please propose only what you think are *absolutely essential* changes.

Barclay had for 12 years served as a United Bible Societies Translation Consultant and lived with his family in the Philippines, Indonesia, Singapore (for weeks at a time), and West Malaysia where he traveled all over Southeast Asia. After returning to the States in 1977 where he took up permanent residence once again, Barclay was given the title of United Bible Societies Research Associate in 1978. His overseas travel resumed as he continued to work with translators around the world, and his writing responsibilities increased each year. But in March of 1987, he began to work full time as the Translations Officer of the American Bible Society while living and working out of his home office in Springfield, Missouri.

Barclay continued to attend the United Bible Societies Triennial Translation Workshops, and in May the three-week long meeting was held at Harper's Ferry, West Virginia. Soon after that, Barclay was requested by the National Conference of Catholic bishops to translate the *Lectionary for Masses with Children*, including the full three-year cycle. New Testament passages were taken from the already completed *Contemporary English Version* of the New Testament, while the Old Testament passages were taken either from those previously published in *A Few Who Dared to Trust God* or else translated especially for the occasion of the lectionary. These same passages were later incorporated into the CEV Old Testament.

For the American Bible Society's fiscal year of 1985/1986, Barclay was away from home a total of 82 days.

The Psalms and those Old Testament passages that were prepared for the *Lectionary for Masses with Children* were not ready for inclusion in the *ad interim imprimatur* process approved by the National Conference of Catholic Bishops in November of 1990, and so the NCCB Administrative Committee was not empowered to grant the *imprimatur* for these texts. However, they were favorably reviewed by the Committee for Pastoral Practices.

On into the eighties Barclay continued to write song lyrics and poems. The following was copyrighted by the United Bible Societies and sung at gatherings around the world to the tune of "Stand Up, Stand Up for Jesus" by Webb.

God's Word for all Earth's People

God's Word for all earth's people, for ev'ryone who reads;
The message is clear and simple. To meet their deepest needs.
God's Word for all earth's people, the truth do not withhold;
Proclaim from roof and steeple, make known to all the world.

God's Word in ev'ry language, our mission and joy.
All people need God's message, for them our strength employ.
God's Word in ev'ry language, the Lord has sent us forth.
With joy, provide God's message for ev'ryone on earth.

God's Word in all its fullness, our calling and our task.
Make known the scripture's greatness, its truth to all who ask.
God's Word in all its fullness, complete in ev'ry hand;
Reveal the Scriptures freshness that all may understand.

Chapter XI

CEV on Mission

Colin Reed, who became one of Barclay's most valued colleagues and close friends, was invited to join the staff of the Bible Society in New Zealand in 1978. Previously he had been a successful businessman involved with specialty food manufacturing and later with property development. Since then, Colin has been a staunch supporter of American Bible Society Bible publications, first the *Good News Translation* and more recently the *Contemporary English Version*. More than any other Bible Society within the United Bible Societies organization, the Bible Society of New Zealand has faithfully and diligently promoted the sale and distribution of these products. A few years later, Colin reported that combined, these two ABS translations sell more in New Zealand than any other translation. Colin also held the position of Global Vice Chair Person of the Asia Pacific Region Board.

Through the years Barclay has frequently composed poetry for Jean. She remembers well one of the many poems he had written. It was dated May 30, 1984 on their 31st wedding anniversary:

If time would only stand still

I've always known that time would not stand still,
nor yet return to where we will …
if time would only obey,
I'd have it return and forever stay
in May, that special day!

He footnoted the poem, "Not really, because each day we share is better than the other."

Earlier that same year on Valentine's Day he typed on bright red paper another poem for Jean:

On Valentine's Day

On valentine's day I think of you
-- especially then,
for I remember when –
... and it was leap year too...
all my love on this day
and on every day
always.

Again in September of 1986 Barclay spent two weeks working with Myron Bromley at Pyramid, Irian Jaya at a Bible translation Workshop, where there were 39 nationals, 11 expatriates, and 29 languages represented. Barclay and Myron lectured on Bible translation and checked translations in their initial stages.

But Barclay had not been there long, when he shared in a letter that Myron had become very ill on a Friday night. He was in terrible pain, but did not know what was causing his excruciating discomfort. His wife was a medical doctor, but nothing she was able to do under the circumstances helped to relieve his severe pain. Miraculously, they were able on Saturday to get him out of the jungle in a small plane and to a hospital.

An American surgeon had just returned three days before from furlough and his colleague, a Dutch surgeon, was preparing to depart for home leave the very next day. Had Myron waited one more day, he would not have survived. His diagnosis was thrombosis (blood clot) of the arteries supplying blood to his intestines, and both surgeons were needed for the procedure. The American doctor operated, while the Dutch doctor administered the anesthesia. Since a section of his intestines had already turned purple, two feet had to be removed. Myron would recover completely, but he would need bed rest for at least six weeks.

Barclay added in his letter:

> The workshop seems to be going well, though I have a few extra responsibilities, now that Myron is no longer working with me. It's raining now, which is a good sign, since the natives get "restless" on clear nights and hoot and howl all night long; they sleep a bit, get up, go back, yelping all the while they are awake, sounding like a pack of wild dogs! Not scary, but sometimes disturbing.

In all, Myron Bromley and his wife Marj spent nearly 40 years working in this remote place called Irian Jaya in the western half of New Guinea. Marj is an Australian by birth, but she gave up her medical practice in her homeland when she answered God's call to serve as a medical missionary. Myron wrote years later in a newsletter:

> … how thankful I was again to have shared my life with her … Yet we have been reminded this year that neither the field where we served nearly forty years, seeing God work in remarkable ways, nor the United States nor Australia, is really home. That is yet to come, when clutter and slowness will be left behind and we see His face.

In November, Barclay once again visited Ghana, Africa, where he spent a week working on Bible translation projects with Gilbert Ansre and others.

In the mid-eighties with Maria Martinez's encouragement, Barclay began to look for some paid "reviewers" for the *Translation for Early Youth/CEV*, who later might possibly become full-time translators. In the meantime, Barclay – who had never been known to move slowly – completed his drafting of the New Testament on August 23, 1988 (Jean's 57th birthday!). This had been accomplished in a period of approximately 18 months.

In the meantime the Catholic Bishops who had requested that Barclay prepare the *Lectionary for Masses with Children* met on November 13 in Washington, D.C. to discuss issues of concern. One of these involved the approval of this new and fresh translation that was presently being developed for the CEV. *The New York Times* reported on their proposals:

> They approved a new translation (*Bible for Today's Family/CEV*) of the Bible for use at children's masses in which Noah builds a "big boat" rather than an ark and swords are pounded into "garden tools" rather than plowshares. But the bishops balked at changing the text of the Gospel (of Luke) to read that Mary laid Jesus "in a feed box."
>
> … (because) Christmas carolers might start singing "Away in a Feed Box," the bishops quickly got permission from the American Bible Society … to reinstate the word "manger."
>
> Once assured that the word "manger" would be restored, the bishops approved the use of the translation (CEV New Testament) by a vote of 209 to 29.

As previously stated, Barclay had completed his initial drafting of the New Testament by August of 1988, but in order to translate the Old Testament and the Deuterocanonical passages for the lectionary, he had

had to put aside his work on the CEV Old Testament. The Lectionary was published in 1993.

In 1988 the United Bible Societies Handbook on *Matthew* (authored by Barclay and Philip Stine) was published. Barclay once again traveled to Asia in April, where he spent time in Singapore and Kuala Lumpur, Malaysia speaking about Bible translation in general and the new *Contemporary English Version* New Testament, which was due to be available in the spring of 1991.

Barclay had begun as early as December 1987 to look for prospective translators for the Old Testament. He wanted to involve the Catholic Church, so in August of 1988 he arranged for a meeting with Robert Hodgson, who was on the teaching staff in the Department of Religious Studies at Missouri State University in Springfield, and the two of them met briefly together. In September Bob began as a paid reviewer on the editorial team of the already drafted New Testament. He had previously helped to circulate *A Book About Jesus* for review by eleventh grade school teachers in the Roman Catholic school system of Springfield. One of these teachers, Sister Regina Schroeder of the Immaculate Conception Church, was extremely helpful. Later she even adopted *Luke Tells the Good News* as the text of choice for the adult Bible class that she taught one evening a week.

On March 2, 1989, Barclay wrote, "Sometime along the way – when it seemed that the translation might be widely received and that a New Testament was inevitable, we realized the need of having some paid reviewers and a stylist to check our translation for accuracy and naturalness." Mrs. Evelyn Ritchie Tower, a Presbyterian from Richmond, Virginia, was selected, and she agreed to become a team member for as long as the project required. Evelyn was also an accomplished, prize-winning poet. After the CEV New Testament had been published and circulated in May, she wrote on July 14, 1991, "… your neat format makes it impossible for the reader to ask himself, 'Now what was I just reading about?' Altogether, a fitting and useful rendition of the Word, all set to go on its mission."

In early May, Barclay expressed his desire to include on the review and translation team a scholar from either the Nazarene or Assemblies of God tradition to begin reviewing the New Testament and then to begin drafting parts of the Old Testament. Donald Johns of the Assemblies of God was recommended. Don held a PhD in Biblical Languages and Literature from St. Louis University and was now in his third year of teaching at the Assemblies of God Theological Seminary in Springfield, Missouri, after having taught three years at Central Bible College. The two of them met for lunch on May 23, and after interviewing him, Barclay felt he was the right person for the job.

That summer Don worked part-time on the editorial team as a reviewer of *A Few Who Dared to Trust God*, and the next summer he worked full-time drafting 1 Samuel. Initially, he indicated that he would not join the American Bible Society as a full-time employee. But when he and his wife were in Jean and Barclay's home for dinner in January of 1990, Barclay asked him to join the team on a full time basis, and the next morning a phone call came from him, signifying that the answer was "Yes." On May 1, 1990 Don Johns became a full-time translator for the American Bible Society.

Barclay first met Steve Berneking while Steve was a student at Missouri State University. At the time of this first meeting, Steve expressed a desire to work as a Bible translator. While he was working on his Bachelor of Divinity degree at the Baptist Theological Seminary in Louisville, Barclay kept in touch with him, and after Steve moved to New York to earn a doctorate at Union Theological Seminary, Barclay asked him to do a project for the ABS. Upon completion of his residency at Union, Steve moved to Springfield, Missouri and attended Campbell Street Methodist Church. Steve and his wife Paula and their children remained close friends with the Newmans.

Bob Hodgson left the CEV team to work with Fern Hagedorn and Andrew T. Seltz in the ABS multimedia program, before actually becoming a drafter, leaving Donald Johns, Steve Berneking, and Barclay to prepare the drafts. Don translated Deuteronomy, Joshua, Judges, 1, 2 Samuel, and Jeremiah; Steve Berneking translated Numbers, 1, 2 Kings, 1, 2 Chronicles, and Ezekiel. Barclay had already translated the New Testament, to which he now added the 27 remaining Old Testament books.

Each of them drafted their texts individually, and then circulated the drafts to the others for comments, before meeting for an oral reading and thorough review of the drafts with Jean present as the secretary. The drafts would then be submitted to the American Bible Society Translations Subcommittee, the Program Committee, and ultimately to the Board of Trustees for final approval.

To help make the TEY/CEV the best possible translation, readers and reviewers were needed. At this time Howard Clark Kee, Chairperson of the ABS Translation Subcommittee, agreed to read and review all drafts. He made the statement to John Erickson, "This is a lively version, which should communicate effectively to both children and their adult readers." Howard Kee recommended Darrell Whiteman, Richard Jeske, and Ann Johnston, also of the Translations Subcommittee, to review drafts and contribute in other ways toward the development of this new translation. Erroll Rhodes made detailed comments on the CEV Old Testament, which were always helpful. In light of the interest being shown by other Bible Societies in this project, Barclay felt that all United Bible Societies Translation Consultants should also be given the opportunity to participate by reviewing the drafts as they were presented to the ABS Subcommittee on Translation – thus making this translation an international project.

Barclay wrote:

> The TEY/CEV … project is now off to a good start, and it has a wonderful potential! But this is only the beginning! There is still a long way to go. And without an extra measure of God's grace and the continued cooperation of the *full* team … the project will never reach its fullest potential.

One question in particular was asked by numerous, interested readers of the Bible, "Will this be a genuine translation, or should we call it a paraphrase?"

Barclay in 1991:

> A paraphrase is the restatement of a text or a passage in the same language, often to clarify meaning by adding explanation, whereas a translation is the communication of a message from one language to another, and it may be structured in either a traditional or a contemporary style. Traditional translations of the Bible retain as much as possible the form of the original text (for example, nouns for nouns and verbs for verbs, word order, and sentence structure). A contemporary translation continues where traditional translations leave off by asking, "What is the most natural way today to express the meaning of the original in an accurate and contemporary style?"
>
> The idea of a contemporary translation has its roots in the New Testament itself, which used the "contemporary" Greek of the first century (Koine) to express the Christian message. The CEV (TEY) is simply following the same pattern for today's readers by using contemporary English to translate the Word of God, which is in itself contemporary to every generation!
>
> The translators of the *King James Version* had similar aims. According to the introduction that was published with the earliest editions of the KJV, the translators realized that a Hebrew or Greek word could not always be translated in the same way every time it appeared. They also knew that in order to make the meaning clear

for their readers, they must often use a form that was different from that of the original languages.

With the experimental texts, *A Book About Jesus*, *Luke Tells the Good News*, and *Good News Travels Fast* published and available, it seemed an opportune time to begin the important task of continuing to test the level of language and style of these books. One member of the team, Jean Newman, was selected to make a detailed analysis of the language and style of school textbooks currently being used by teachers in the second and third grades.

Arrangements were made for her to visit and dialogue with an experienced second/third grade public school teacher, who was now retired, but kept up with the latest textbooks used in the school system by tutoring students in these two grades. Mrs. Mae Hamilton was happy to be of assistance and gladly loaned Jean copies of her currently used textbooks on a variety of subjects, including science, reading, language, and social studies. All these books had copyright dates corresponding with the time that work had begun on the translation for early youth.

After reading a total of 1,400 pages, Jean noted that the word "whom" appeared only one time in the social studies book, and not once in all the other textbooks.

A few years later on February 4, 1992 Ken Waters who is a journalism professor at Pepperdine University wrote to Barclay:

> As a journalism professor at Pepperdine, someone trying to teach college students the fine art of communicating in print, I'm finding your comments fascinating. When I told my introductory journalism class that an expert on the English language suggested that perhaps "whom" was outdated, they let out a cheer. It seems learning the "who" vs. "whom" distinction still eludes most students. A discussion on murky construction, wordiness and the use of jargon took on new meaning when I began to tell them how the *Contemporary English Version* (of the Bible) translation team decided to eliminate words like . . . , "sanctification" and "justification" from its translation. Some students looked aghast, but one student commented: "Gee, perhaps I could read the Bible and understand it for a change."

The words "who" and "which" were used sparingly; throughout the books it was discovered that "and" was used frequently in every book. The third grade social studies book employed "and" 524 times within the 200 plus pages Jean read. Sentence initial "and" was somewhat rare, but it appeared quite often at the beginning of clauses. Other general observations were noted: The words/phrases "Later," "However," "Finally," "For example," "Then," "Next", "First," "Now," and "Even so," when used at the beginning of a sentence, were almost always followed by a comma.

While Barclay and Gene Nida were in the process of developing the book *Act Now* (published as *Good News Travels Fast*), which focuses on evangelism for today's youth, Barclay felt it would be well worth their time to involve some teenagers from First Baptist Church of Springfield, Missouri. Jean prepared a dinner in July of 1985 for six young people and after the meal, they were introduced to *Act Now*. Barclay described to them the intended audience, "We are aiming for a translation into youth's idioms, but at the same time one that avoids slang." These young people were asked for their input, and a second meeting was also planned for them a week later, in which they again actively participated. Their suggestions were taken seriously and incorporated into the nearly completed manuscript before it was submitted to the American Bible Society.

The team received further feedback from elementary teachers, and Don Johns shared with the team relevant testing with his five very articulate children. They often contributed by telling him how their peers at school and outside the classroom would use and understand certain words, what they would appreciate and understand themselves, and words or phrases, which most certainly would seem awkward.

During the translation process, Barclay had spent Sundays, visiting the second and third grade Sunday School classes at the First Baptist Church of Springfield, where he dialogued with the children, the teachers, and especially with Bette Bogart, the superintendent of that department. His objective was to learn whether or not the translations were clear and enjoyable to the youngsters. After Terji Hartberg received and read the two trial publications *Luke Tells the Good News* and *A Book About Jesus* he wrote John Erickson:

> … I have to tell you that it (*Luke Tells the Good News*) is a most interesting publication, as was its predecessor *A Book About Jesus* … All we have seen so far for children are either retelling of stories or use of existing "adult" texts selected for children …

On September 12, 1990 James Marsh, an SIL person, wrote to Basil Rebera after reading and reviewing *Luke Tells the Good News About Jesus*:

> As I stated in the comments, I appreciate this new translation. I think it will prove helpful in training Aborigines and Islanders in becoming more independent in drafting of translations … I think

> this version will be a tool which God is going to use … the critical comments I make below are made in the context of gratitude for this new translation and for even greater usefulness in future editions.

Children's reading and writing specialists also read and commented on the manuscripts and publications. To name a few: (1) June Brown, Professor of Elementary Reading and Special Education at Missouri State University; (2) Peggy Burke, Instructional Specialist in Writing and English Language Arts for the New Jersey State Department of Education. Peggy commented on the book, *A Few Who Dared to Trust God.* She stated, "The text is very readable with a 'sense of story' evident in almost all of the selections …; and (3) Evelyn Ritchie Crim Tower, Special Education Teacher in Richmond, Virginia, and a published poet and author.

As the experimental texts were being more widely shared with adults, many of them began to say that they too would like to have a translation, which was easy to read and understand. One lawyer bought the CEV New Testament as soon as it appeared, and he told Jean, who was also an active Volunteer with ABS, "I work with words all day, and when I come home at night I'm tired. I like to read my Bible before turning in for the night, and with the CEV I can read a few passages, and then the next night I don't have to turn back to find out who the speaker is and who is being spoken to."

Barclay and his family had lived in the Philippines in the sixties, and he observed:

> Tagalog is one of the major languages in the Philippines, but until the Bible was translated into contemporary Tagalog, the Filipino Christians used to say, "We speak two languages: 'Church Tagalog' and 'Tagalog Tagalog.'" Are we English-speaking Christians also bilingual, using one language in church and another outside church? Must unbelievers learn a new language before they can receive the new birth? Is our love of the vocabulary of Zion a stumbling block for non-speakers of our in-group language?

The translators of the *Contemporary English Version* believed that they had a calling and a responsibility to make the Word of God available in a language that everyone in the English speaking world would understand and appreciate. Such a translation is extremely important today, when people from so many diverse cultures are coming to our shores and hoping to learn our language. What better tool of evangelism than a translation of the Bible in contemporary English?

When the CEV New Testament was first published, erroneous information was spread about the translation. Someone said that the actual translating took about six years to complete, and there were one hundred translators. It was true that there may have been 100 people world wide reviewing the texts and mailing comments, but certainly not translating it. Barclay had translated all of the New Testament in approximately 18 months (supported and read by Gene Nida), and later he brought in three translators (ultimately two others) to work with him on translating the Old Testament. Barclay used the New Testament to train Don Johns and Steve Berneking, and consequently they made excellent suggestions for which Barclay was grateful. The translation committee met for their review sessions in Barclay's living room for the duration of the translation of the complete Bible.

Throughout the nineties, Barclay and others on the translation team were asked by the Volunteer Department of the American Bible Society, under the leadership of Faye Flemister, to speak about this new translation at dozens of churches and convention centers in major cities all across the States. Barclay also traveled to England, Scotland, Wales, Canada, Australia, New Zealand, the Philippines, Singapore, Kuala Lumpur (West Malaysia), and several African countries, including Ghana, Nigeria, Tanzania, Uganda, and Kenya, to discuss the uniqueness of the *Contemporary English Version*, which he felt represented the "cutting edge" of Bible translation:

> It is the first among English Bibles, *based upon an entirely new concept of translation*. All other Bibles may be classified as traditional, because they count on the reader's ability to decipher a written text. The CEV differs from these in that it takes seriously the needs of the hearer, as well as that of the reader, who may not be familiar with traditional biblical phrasings. The CEV is unique among English translations of the Holy Bible: It can be read aloud without stumbling, heard without misunderstanding, and enjoyed by children and adults alike, because its contemporary English style is lucid and lyrical.
>
> The *Contemporary English Version* is a fresh and faithful translation, not an adaptation, of the Holy Bible, prepared directly from the original biblical languages by the American Bible Society in cooperation with more than fifty other Bible Societies worldwide. The CEV combines the best of international biblical scholarship with over two hundred years of experience in translating the Word of God into more than 2,000 languages around the globe, including everything from Algonquin to English to Zulu.

By January of 1991, the countdown was approaching for the publication of the New Testament, known at first as *Translation for Early Youth/ Bible for Today's Family* and later as the *Contemporary English Version*. Proof pages were carefully made ready by a committee of three in New York: Ester Vargas-Manchuca, Anne Schabert, and Liisa Sobottka, all of the ABS Scripture Publication Department. Proofreading of an entire New Testament requires a lot of checking and rechecking. When they had finished their labors, Barclay then reviewed the text for errors that may have crept in, introducing minor changes, and making certain that all footnote references were correct and corresponded with the "letter" designating them. Barclay recalls that on at least two occasions, he and Jean worked for 19 hours straight – stopping only for meals and toilet breaks. They worked 15 hours on many days, and dedicated their holidays to the task as well.

For a while, Barclay and Jean slept in separate bedrooms, because each night Barclay literally took the manuscripts to bed with him. Barclay awoke anywhere from 3:30 to 4:00 a.m., and this sleeping arrangement made it possible for him to get up without awakening Jean.

During the entire process of translating and publishing the *Contemporary English Version*, probably the most helpful and dedicated staff member of the American Bible Society was Charles Houser, Manager of the ABS Scripture Resource Development Department. Charles assisted Barclay in every way possible – offering help and encouragement at every stage of the translation process. When the doors of the Bible House in New York opened, Charles was always there to answer any question by telephone that Barclay might have about various aspects of the publication, including such matters as formatting, printing, and appropriate illustrations. If Charles did not have an answer on the spot, he found the answer and got back to Barclay almost immediately. In December 1991, Charles was quoted in the "Religion" section of the *Mail Tribune* as saying:

> The translators paid special attention to how the words would sound when read aloud … What a Sunday School teacher could assume their students knew 30 years ago, they can't assume anymore. Kids have little Bible basics under their belt. In that sense, a lot of churches are concerned that people don't know and read their Bible enough.

On March 22, 1991 Barclay felt his prayers had been answered, when he received a copy of a "Decree" that was announced in writing by the President of the National Conference of Catholic Bishops, Most. Rev.

Daniel E. Pilarczyk. The statement read, "In the name of the National Conference of Catholic Bishops approval is hereby granted for the publication of the *Contemporary English Version*, a translation of the New Testament with explanatory notes submitted by the American Bible Society." To be printed on the reverse of the title page of the book would be *Imprimatur* with the signature: Most Rev. Daniel E. Pilarczyk.

Bryant M. Kirkland, the interim President and Chief Executive Officer of the ABS, responded:

> We are filled with joy these days to see the hearty reception the CEV (*Contemporary English Version*) New Testament has found among Catholics, both at the level of the official text reviewers – Archbishop Whealon, Bishop Wcela, and the members of the review committee, all of whom found it a high quality translation and helped significantly to make it so ....
>
> ...the first CEV New Testament will come off the presses around May 1, just in time for the official "launching" ceremonies at our 175th Annual Meeting on May 9, 1991. And, God willing, also in a few years a full CEV Bible will be available ... in a clear and contemporary English style that can be meaningfully understood by children and adults alike.

Jean remembers clearly the day in early May 1991, when the sound of the doorbell chimes reached her in her upstairs office, and on answering it, she found a special delivery man handing her Barclay's very first two copies of the *Bible for Today's Family* (CEV) New Testament. The two New Testaments had been bound in two bright colors – one brick red and one a royal blue, each with titles and a cross in gold. As a volunteer with the ABS, Jean immediately ordered hundreds of these New Testaments, and for weeks and weeks she received people who wanted to purchase one of each color – one for themselves and one for a spouse. Many ordered large numbers for family members and friends. The first ABS editions of the New Testament sold for $1.75.

One lady from Texas phoned Jean sometime around the early part of June and asked her to mail to her address in Texas several of the Testaments with the promise to send payment by mail. She explained that she and her husband were truck drivers, and as they were passing through the Springfield area, they had heard about the new translation on a radio talk show. Jean mailed the requested New Testaments to the lady and wondered if that would be the last of it. But on July 8th she received a check with a note, "Thanks so much for waiting on payment. My husband and

I drive a truck and have only now come in. I love the New Testament, and everyone I've given one to is really excited about them." Signed: "Brenda Johnson (from Texas)."

Beginning in May and continuing through August, Barclay received copies of newspaper articles discussing the merits of the New Testament from almost every state in North America – from as far west as Washington state and California to as far east as New York and Florida, from Ontario, Canada, Auckland, Christchurch, and Waikato, New Zealand. Various outstanding magazines such as *Time*, *Christianity Today*, *The Christian Century*, and many others published enthusiastic articles about the CEV translation.

In May of 1991 George W. Cornell, a writer for the Associated Press, wrote a compelling article entitled "New easy-listening Bible," which was representative of the numerous articles published in many cities across the States:

> The American Bible Society, which in its 175 years of life had distributed more Bibles than the world's present population, came out this month with a new one. It's made for easy listening.
>
> It sounds different in one way, yet familiar in another. The working is fresh, but it has the familiar tone of ordinary conversation.
>
> "It's the way people talk," said Barclay M. Newman, a Bible scholar who headed the translation team for the new Contemporary English Version of the New Testament....

In February of 1990, the American Bible Society had licensed Thomas Nelson Publishers of Nashville, Tennessee as the trade publisher for the *Contemporary English Version* of the Bible. In early August, seven publishers were selected to make final presentations. During the four to six weeks between presentation and notification, a mutual dialogue was established with each publisher.

Following ... conversations with the various publishers, the contenders were narrowed to three. Based on all ... considerations, the American Bible Society staff recommended that Thomas Nelson become the commercial publisher. Thomas Nelson reaches a much broader constituency than any of the other publishers interested in the translation.

At that time, Thomas Nelson presented the strongest evidence that they could and would focus more attention on nurturing the image and position of the new translation and would fully support it by developing a strong and diverse product line.

Chapter XII

Mission Continues

In May 1991, Barclay received dozens of letters and comments about the *Contemporary English Version* of the Bible. When the CEV New Testament was first introduced during a special service at the First Baptist Church in Springfield, Missouri, one senior member approached Barclay and said, "I'm prejudiced about the King James Bible, but this week I've been reading the new CEV along with my KJV and have found that I've gained many insights into the *meaning* of the Scriptures."

Harold C. Bennett, who served as President and Treasurer of the Executive Committee of the Southern Baptist Convention, and who was a member of the American Bible Society Translations Subcommittee and Board of Trustees, wrote to Barclay on May 13:

> I know you did not do it by yourself, but I commend you on the excellent job you and all the others have done in the translation of the New Testament and the publication of the *Contemporary English Version*. The CEV will be a blessing to millions. Let me thank you for your commitment and for the time you have spent in accomplishing the monumental assignment. God blessed you … May God continue to bless you in what you do to make the Word of God available to everyone.

Hart Wiens, Director of Scripture Translation of the Canadian Bible Society; Hartmut Schroeder in the Translations Department of the Canadian Bible Society, and Harold Fehderau, Translation Officer of the Canadian Bible Society; David G. Burke of the American Bible Society Translations Department; M. Wendell Belew, a member of the ABS Translations Subcommittee and retired Associate Vice President for Missions Strategy Interpretation of the Home Mission Board of the Southern Baptist Convention; Harold C. Bennett's tremendous sense of humor was always refreshing and an inspiration to Barclay; and Carolyn W. Crumpler who served on the Bible Society's Board of Managers and later served as a member of the Promotion Committee was a constant encourager and supporter.

Oswald C. J. Hoffman, who served on the ABS Board of Trustees, was the retired speaker of the Lutheran Hour and the Honorary President of the United Bible Societies. He also served as Chair of the Translations Subcommittee until the CEV was approved. Always a strong supporter and vigilant reviewer of the CEV, he was fond of relating anecdotes about the CEV. Once he told the ABS Board of Trustees that he made a terrible mistake by giving a CEV New Testament to his medical doctor, who was also something of a theologian. Ozzie said the doctor now spends most of his time talking about how much he likes the translation and doesn't give him as much attention as before.

Still other outstanding reviewers were Bruce M. Metzger, who served on the American Bible Society Board and was Professor Emeritus, New Testament Language and Literature at Princeton Theological Seminary; Jan de Waard, a United Bible Societies Translation Consultant living in France; Martin Quigley wrote a letter on April 9, 1992 to Gene Habecker, President and CEO of the American Bible Society:

> Plans should be developed that would result in the placing of CEV New Testaments with Psalms and Proverbs in the library of every public elementary and secondary school in the country … Over the years very little real progress has been made in the use of the Bible as literature or history in our public schools … I suspect that the libraries of a substantial number of public schools do not have even a single Bible. Those that do almost certainly do not have an edition as readable as the CEV.

Graham Ogden, who was a United Bible Societies Translation Consultant in Australia, was a serious reviewer of the CEV manuscripts. He made a meticulous and helpful review, especially of the book of Isaiah; Leonard Greenspoon of Creighton University was a faithful reviewer; Richard Sklba, who appeared late on the scene, proved to be valuable as a special consultant and made careful comments on the Old Testament CEV. And there were others: Aloo Ostotsi Mojola, UBS Translations Coordinator for Africa; David Ekem, UBS Consultant in Accra, Ghana; Sally Shoemaker Robinson, an American Bible Society Board member; Emil Wcela, a special consultant for ABS and who was the Auxiliary Bishop of the Diocese of Rockville Center in Riverhead, New York.

In a letter to David Burke, Bishop Wcela said, "The CEV translation is lively and clear … it conveys the sense of the Scriptures with fidelity. It will be used with profit far beyond the audience of children for whom it was originally intended."

Other helpful reviewers were: Cynthia L. Miller, Professor of Hebrew at the University of Wisconsin (Barclay said she contributed more to the revision of the CEV Old Testament in 2004/2005 than anyone else); Robert Koops, a United Bible Societies Consultant in Gambia, West Africa; Viggo Sogaard, United Bible Societies Media Consultant for the Asia-Pacific Region; Lynell Zogbo, a UBS Consultant in Abijan, Cote D'Ivoire; and John Ellington, formerly a UBS Consultant, serving in Congo/Zaire, Central Africa.

Soon after the publication of the CEV New Testament in 1991, Dr. Eugene Habecker received a phone call from Mr. Irvin J. Borowsky, who identified himself as the Chairman of the Interfaith Institute, an international organization headquartered in Philadelphia. Mr. Borowsky informed Dr. Habecker that he had carefully checked all of the "sensitive" passages related to the translation of the term "Jews" in the CEV, and that he was greatly pleased. So much so, in fact, that he promised to send a check of $100,000 to the American Bible Society and to become an "ambassador" at large for the *Contemporary English Version* of the Bible. He stated that his goal was to see that the CEV, because its New Testament is as close to a hate-free New Testament translation as he has yet seen, might appear in every Jewish home in America.

Irv – as Barclay has come to call him – has kept both of these promises, and over the intervening years, he has sent copies – together with letters of endorsement – to rabbis around the world.

Irv Borowsky has also sponsored other promotional activities with the CEV, including a tour of Jewish communities in Florida, where he and Barclay spoke on its behalf. Perhaps the most unique of all his endeavors has been the establishment of the Liberty Museum in the historical district of Philadelphia, where the CEV has been assigned a place "on a pedestal," as it were.

Over the years, the *Contemporary English Version* of the Bible and Barclay have had no better friend and colleague than Irv Borowsky.

Jean recalls a time when Barclay was away from home, and she took a call that came in the early evening hours. The man introduced himself as Allan Ruben from Florida, a Jewish friend of Irvin Borowsky. Irv had provided him with a copy of the CEV New Testament, and he said to Jean, "If Barclay is not at home, I want to share this with you. I am sitting here reading the New Testament with tears running down my cheeks as I read the stories of Jesus. I want you to know, I pray to Jesus everyday." Just a few years later, Barclay asked Irv about Allan and learned that he had died.

Eugene B. Habecker, President and CEO of the American Bible Society from 1991 until 2005, supported the CEV in every way possible and gave constant encouragement. In correspondence with Barclay in September of 1991, he said:

> Seeing you at the Board meeting reminded me of the fact that I have been derelict in sending you a letter stating how much I have personally been enjoying the Contemporary English Version. I use it all the time in my devotional reading. It states these timeless truths in wonderfully refreshing new ways. Thank you for your willingness to serve Christ in this way.

Maria Martinez, American Bible Society Vice President of the Scriptures Publications Area, was a great influence in the early stages of the CEV and throughout the entire process. Bryant M. Kirkland, past President of the American Bible Society, was a Board member for 26 years and later served as a Senior Trustee.

Other staunch supporters and promoters were Floyd C. Babcock, General Secretary of the Canadian Bible Society, who sponsored Barclay's Canadian CEV tour, and Bruce Pearce with the Australian Bible Society, who wrote to Barclay in November, "Thank you … for allowing God's Spirit to so envelope and control your gifts to produce a translation (CEV) of the Word of such remarkable significance to this waiting world."

There were other supporters: Carl Gross in the Translations Department of the Bible Society of Australia; Glenn Herndon, the American Bible Society Field Representative in Georgia, arranged for several meetings there, so that Barclay could speak and share the goals of the CEV translation. And, of course, Laton Holmgren, former General Secretary of the ABS, phoned from his retirement home in California to encourage Barclay as he continued his work. Gerrit E. van der Merwe from South Africa was a conscientious reviewer and supporter of the CEV.

In December of 1991 Alan Jorgenson (an ardent supporter of the *Contemporary English Version* New Testament) with the Canadian Bible Society wrote:

> For many years the Canadian Bible Society has had a free distribution ministry to new Canadian citizens in courts of Canadian Citizenship across the country. It is our intention to change from the (former translation) to the CEV translation for our next print run. We are planning to produce 80,000 of these special ministry editions in the new year.

T.T. Crabtree, pastor of the First Baptist Church in Springfield, Missouri was very supportive of the *Contemporary English Version.* When he was also serving as Interim Dean at the Redford School of Theology and Church Vocations of Southwest Baptist College in Bolivar, Missouri, he attended the Baptist General Convention of Oklahoma and took with him 500 copies of the CEV New Testament. On another occasion, he and his wife Bennie distributed in a chapel service 1200 copies of the Thomas Nelson edition of the CEV New Testament to the students at the Southwest Baptist Theological Seminary in Fort Worth, Texas.

When First Baptist Church in Springfield, under the leadership of T. T. Crabtree, was making plans for an outreach revival for April of 1994, it was decided that the church would place an order of 10,000 copies of a special imprint CEV New Testament for distribution before and during the campaign.

Roger Omanson, now a UBS Interregional Consultant in the U.S., wrote on July 7, 1991:

> I have worked all the way through the *Contemporary English Version* (New Testament) translation of 2 Corinthians and find that nearly always the meaning is clear. I may not always agree with the interpretation of the translators (or translator), but granted the interpretations which they have followed, the meaning is clear. Because of this, in the Translators Handbook on 2 Corinthians I am citing the CEV regularly as a model translation…

Jean Worley, who was John Erickson's assistant at the American Bible Society, was always supportive and helpful throughout the entire translation process.

Faye Flemister was hired by ABS on October 2, 1989 as Manager of Training and Recruitment in the Volunteer Activities Department. She trained and motivated ABS Volunteers in a variety of settings. At that time Ursula Glanders and Delores Trickel were Volunteer Field Staff members. Later the field staff was increased to include Elaine Nelson and Elmo Familiaran. Faye soon was deeply involved in her work, and she arranged for dozens of 24-Hour Volunteer Conferences, reaching almost every state in the union. She invited Barclay to these conferences to discuss the unique features of the CEV, as well as Bible translation in general. Some years later Faye wrote:

> About the same time (that the Conferences were organized), Barclay was coming out with the individual gospels in the CEV (transla-

> tion). I thought it would be great to have a translator at the conferences. Most volunteers hadn't met one and didn't know the process. It would fulfill my hope to give the volunteers and prospective volunteers some information about translating. Barclay agreed and that began a wonderful ten-year association.
>
> We did the first conference in 1990. We started with three a year, moved to 6 per year and at the end were having 10 to 12(13) a year. ... We held them in hotels and conference centers. Barclay's participation was a tremendous asset to the conferences, and thus to the American Bible Society. Volunteers and participants in the conferences were able to learn what was involved in translating Scripture. ... There was such an ignorance about how one did translation. He made the Bible and the process of giving the Scripture to people in a language they could understand an adventure ... His sense of humor kept people enthralled. They looked forward to his talks. There were fights to sit with him at meals, but it was a privilege if you got to eat with him.

In these 24-Hour Volunteer Conferences, Barclay made his Bible translation presentations by utilizing an overhead projector, where he expanded information from time to time and improved the format of his slides as time went by. On one occasion, a young man who was then living in Texas and had just come to work for the Bible Society, was sitting in the audience and heard Barclay give his overhead slide presentation. Afterward, Matthew Diehl approached Barclay and praised him for his very good slide presentation, but he added, "If you want to make good presentations even better go with power point."

Sara Shailer of the British and Foreign Bible Society got the CEV off to a good start in England; Derek Patton of the Canadian Bible Society accompanied Barclay when he spoke in behalf of the CEV. Derek Hill and Tony Harrop of the United Bible Societies have been and continue to be untiring in their efforts to promote the CEV worldwide. And in this, they had their counterparts: Bill Mitchell, Coordinator for Translation in the Americas; Gilbert Ansre in Ghana; and Father Michael Spillane of the Federation of Diocesan Liturgical Commissions for the Catholic Church. John Jennings, Director of Scripture Division for the Bible Society of Australia, had a sweeping vision of what the CEV could do, and if he had received more encouragement from the ABS, there would have been a CEV Study Bible and other vital resources very soon after its launch in 1995.

From 1991 and into 1992, Barclay received many letters from people who were reading the newly published CEV New Testament. Two letters in particular were especially memorable. One came from his sister-in-law, Ann Sanders of Memphis, Tennessee, who wrote, "We are enjoying our copy (CEV), and everyone we've shown it to really does like the new translation, too." Ann has probably read the New Testament, the Old Testament (after it was published in 1995), and later the *Contemporary English Version* Learning Bible more than any one person besides Barclay. She began reading the 2,363 pages of the *CEV Learning Bible.*

The other letter that stands out in Barclay's mind as very special came from a niece in Oregon. Her grandparents, Carlton and Fran Butler (brother and sister-in-law to Jean) had given her a copy of the CEV New Testament, and on July 25, 1991 Karen Butler Williams wrote:

> My family and I are so pleased to have the *Contemporary English Version* Bible. Reading it is truly a joyful experience. What a privilege it is for me to have an uncle who has diligently worked with the American Bible Society to make God's Word not only more available, but more understandable as well. Thank you.

Carlton Butler and Fran have been instrumental in scheduling Barclay to speak on various occasions about Bible translation in general and about the merits of the CEV in the state of Oregon and in Vancouver in British Columbia.

The New Zealand and Australian Bible Societies asked Barclay to come in August of 1991 to promote the CEV in churches, at the Christian Booksellers Convention, in individual bookstores, in newspapers, on college campuses, and on radio programs.

John Pfitzner, Director of Publications for the Lutheran Publishing House in Adelaide, South Australia, wrote Barclay in September, "My assistant editor here at Lutheran Publishing House, who shares my views on Bible translating and who has a keen appreciation for language, was delighted by the CEV and had found it compulsive reading. I like it more the more I read it."

Soon after Barclay returned from New Zealand and Australia, he held a translation symposium at the Druid Hills Baptist Church in Atlanta, Georgia at the invitation of John D. Baker, their pastor. The gathering included Atlanta area clergy and laity of all denominations, with whom Barclay spoke about the need for a new translation. John wrote, "From the first moment I read portions of my copy (CEV NT), I realized that a wonderful work had been accomplished. I thank you personally for your time and effort."

During January Ralph Allen, Jr., a prison chaplain with Christian Ministries to Offenders, Wichita, Kansas wrote, "I have found the Contemporary English Version (New Testament) to be extremely valuable in my particular setting where there are many levels of reading literacy. The response of the men has been very positive and they are clamoring for more."

A twenty-five-year-old lady was given a CEV New Testament by Haviland Houston of the Volunteer Department of the American Bible Society. The young lady wrote:

> I am a 25-year-old … who at times is like a lost sheep. Over the past years I have been so hungry for the word of the Lord; I have tried all kinds of Bibles and I have been to Bible studies, you name it, I have tried it. I was sharing with a special friend of mine, her name is Haviland Houston; I explained to her how I couldn't keep up on my Bible Study because they kept on jumping all over the Bible, also the King James Version is hard to understand for beginners. Well right about Christmas, Haviland brought me the most precious gift I have ever received. It was your Bible (Bible for Today's Family/CEV New Testament. …

The American Bible Society asked a number of scholars for endorsements for the CEV translation, and several of the Translations Subcommittee members responded wholeheartedly. Bruce M. Metzger wrote:

> The aim of the translators of the *Contemporary English Version* has been to set forth the New Testament, written originally in *koine* or everyday Greek, in down-to-earth contemporary English. Thus the reader is put in touch with God's word expressed in simple and clear English.

M. Wendell Belew wrote:

> The Bible is as relevant to contemporary society as in the days in which it was written. Through the years, translations have sought to make it easily understood by as many readers as possible. Although the biblical message is unchanging, the languages and vernacular of people do change. The American Bible Society has, historically, been much aware of this. Appropriately, upon the occasion of the Society's 175th anniversary, it has released the *Contemporary English Version* New Testament (May 7, 1991 at the Hilton Hotel in New York City)…

Darrell L. Whiteman wrote:

> The new CEV will delightfully surprise readers. It is so clear and lucid that it may first appear as a paraphrase, but it soon becomes

> obvious that the scholarly integrity of this translation has not been jeopardized. Thus, the best of two worlds are combined in a very readable and scholastically faithful translation. Moreover, this translation of the New Testament opens the Scriptures to a wide range of English speakers from young schoolchildren to those who are masters of the English language. This is no mere achievement, but it has been accomplished in the *Contemporary English Version* New Testament.

After the *Contemporary English Version* New Testament had been completed and printed, and the Old Testament translation process had been set up and was underway, Barclay wrote a letter on the 13th of January 1992 to an interested pastor of a church in New York. He explained to him how each Old Testament book had been assigned to a member of the translation team and the procedure used from that point on.

All work was done freshly and directly from the best available Greek, Hebrew, and Aramaic texts of the Bible. For the Old Testament the *Biblia Hebraica Stuttgartensia* text was followed in conjunction with the *Preliminary and Interim Report on the Hebrew Old Testament Text Project*, and the standard lexicons, existing translations, and commentaries were consulted.

Each translator made a draft on the word processor of his designated book, which meant that even before a hard copy was produced, numerous alternatives were considered on the computer screen.

The following step required each translator to read and re-read his material to polish the style. Barclay insisted that style was very important to the success of a good contemporary English translation.

Each drafter then sent his work to the other translation team members for their comments. When all suggestions and comments were received by the original drafter, he considered each one and incorporated them into his manuscript where and if appropriate. The draft was then reworked by the original drafter.

When this stage was completed, the team members met in committee meetings to go over every line of the translated drafts by reading it aloud. How it sounded when read aloud was an important feature of the CEV.

After the committee work, the typist would then re-keyboard each book, and at some point the typist/editor read each manuscript comparing it to a traditional translation such as the *New Revised Standard Version* to determine that nothing had been left out or added in the translation process. Barclay then checked to see if any of the editor's suspected omissions or additions actually existed in the manuscripts. He recalls that he rarely found any omissions or additions.

When the typist had made clean hard copies, the translation team members met in committee again to go over the amended drafts. Finally, when the team was satisfied that the drafts were in good form, the manuscripts were circulated to a broad variety of reviewers. First they were sent to the American Bible Society Board of Managers' Translation Subcommittee, then to a circle of special consultants. A further circle of reviewers included scholars who represented a variety of church traditions and denominations.

In addition to these reviewers, there were approximately fifty United Bible Society translation consultants around the world who have expertise in such fields as linguistics, translation theory and practice, English language usage and style, and biblical studies, who received the drafts and reviewed them and made suggestions.

When reviews came to Barclay's office another committee meeting convened, and all suggestions were seriously considered, after which the typist would again enter these and make clean copies for each member.

It might be added here that at each and every stage, Barclay took it on himself to read all the drafts 6 to 8 times. And before publication of the entire Bible, he and Jean, following the same process that they had followed with the New Testament, very carefully read the proof pages which came to them from Ester Vargas-Manchuca, Anne Schabert, and Liisa Sobottka by way of the American Bible Society office in New York.

Jean assisted Barclay from the very beginning, and she remembers that many days they (in particular Barclay) worked 12 to 15 hours. The New Testament took long hours to complete and prepare for publication, and the Old Testament required even longer hours. Certainly, the translation team had excellent help and support from many staff members in the New York office. So many angles have to be worked out in any publication, such as finances, promotion, marketing, planned presentations, launching, advertising strategies, printing and art work.

On the 12th of February Loyal Funk, Director of Evangelism/Church Planting/Christian Service with the Mennonite Brethren Churches wrote:

> It is a joy for me to recommend and endorse the broad usage of the new CEV. I have personally shared copies with various leaders and both from myself and them, in our fellowship, we give testimony to its captivating readability. For many the past translations have been difficult (lacking background) whereas this is an "up to date" language that the uninitiated can grasp. The Holy Spirit will use this to enter the hearts and minds for many who had been by-passed. I commend American Bible Society for its endeavor

to get the Holy Word to people in a true translation that can be assimilated.

About this same time an interesting article/letter was sent to Barclay with no name attached to it:

> I've never had such excitement over a Christmas gift!
>
> This past holiday season I gave a copy of the American Bible Society's Contemporary English Version of the New Testament to every member of my small congregation at Melissa, Texas.
>
> Not only did every person receive this new translation with gratitude but with delight as they discovered a new pleasure in reading the Holy Scriptures. In fact, several visitors from the Northwest were so thrilled with this new CEV work that they asked for additional copies to take on their return trip....

On the 6th of March 1992 Kevin Schulz, pastor of the Rotorua Baptist Church in Rotorua, New Zealand wrote:

> Thanks for allowing me to look over the new Contemporary English Version of the New Testament. I confess to having a feeling of "Ho hum, another new translation" when I first heard about it. In the weeks that I have had it I have been able to read the whole book and I have to say that I am very impressed. This is a version that is so readable that it's hard to put down, and that's the impact that the New Testament ought to make! It's the Bible that I would like to put into the hands of every New Zealand teenager. I'm sure that they would read and understand the CEV in a way that would not be so with other current versions. It's a book that can be understood by children but is so well written that it also appeals to adults.

By April 1992 the CEV New Testament was experiencing world wide exposure. A letter came to the New York office from Danny Arichea asking permission to use CEV Mark. He corresponded, "I just received word from Mongolia to the effect that they want to print the Gospel of Mark in diglot form, using the CEV and the Mongolian New Testament. They have therefore requested me to get permission for the use of the CEV text."

Robert F. Cullum, Director of Chaplain Services at the Texas Department of Mental Health and Mental Retardation in San Antonio, Texas wrote, "*Bible for Today's Family*/CEV has made a great impact here. Every time I read it from the pulpit, people clap their hands in joy. Know that you have added joy to many lives in a place of darkness."

On the 6th of May Basil Rebera penned a letter to Anthony J. Harrop, Marketing Consultant, located at the United Bible Societies Asia Pacific Regional Centre in Hong Kong, in which he stated, "The New Zealand Bible Society and Bible Society in Australia are promoting CEV widely and using it for a range of products aimed at a number of different audiences. The Ceylon Bible Society (in Sri Lanka) will be using CEV as the text for its English Enhancement multi-Media Project."

The following day Anthony Harrop responded:

> *On Monday in Singapore I saw the CEV... edition of the New Testament with Psalms and Proverbs on Lee Soo Ann's desk, and we spent considerable time discussing the marketing opportunities in Singapore presented by the CEV. ... A number of colleagues who are using the CEV with their families are speaking very highly of it.*

The following November Anthony Harrop penned a letter to Frank Couch of Thomas Nelson Publishers. He reported that the "initial response to CEV among our own staff and early purchasers in Asia-Pacific has been very positive. We believe there is a great future for this version, and are specially pleased at the variety of editions being planned."

By the end of May, the CEV had been printed with the books of Psalms and Proverbs. The *Milwaukee Lutheran* published an article describing these poetic books:

> "The Psalms are poetry with subject matter that is universal. But the form of poetry differs significantly from one language to another and from one generation to another," (Barclay) Newman explained. "With these considerations in mind the translators of the CEV Psalms have tried to accomplish something old and something new." The something old, he said, is the meaning of the text. The interpretation of the CEV Psalms reflects that of traditional, mainstream translations and commentaries. The something new is the style: the appearance of the text on the page, the flow of the language, the sound of syllables and words, and pleasing rhythmic patterns that are important in conveying the full impact of the meaning.... Poetic lines have been carefully measured in order to avoid awkwardly divided phrases and words that run over to the next line in clumsy ways.

On June 6 Meinert Grumm of Stone Mountain, Georgia amply described the work that went into producing the CEV New Testament, "It certainly is a never-ending job (that is, translation of the Scriptures), and from the little I've seen so far of your latest (CEV), it shows signs of beautifully deceptive effortless simplicity."

Basil Rebera of the Asia Pacific region, wrote:

> I read from the CEV Psalms at worship one morning (in a United Bible Societies regional gathering) and had everyone spellbound. Viggo Sogaard, the Media Consultant for the Region whom you will meet in Chiang Mai, Thailand, announced publicly afterwards that CEV is the best English version for reading.

And Rose Baker of the Missouri Baptist Convention Annuity Board said of the translation, "It is so clear and simple, like Christ intended. It just sings to your heart and soul."

In 1991 eight biblical scholars (only four responded) in New Zealand were asked to write a review of the CEV New Testament, and several of these reviews are included below.

Bishop Peter Atkins, Dean of St. John's Theological College (Anglican), wrote:

> This is what the translators for the American Bible Society have achieved for every family member within the reading age. The Contemporary English Version of the New Testament is a chunky paperback with print and spacing large enough for eyes young and old. It is set in paragraph form with clear subheadings. The sentences are clear and crisp, but not clipped, and are straightforward in construction. The text, translated from the original Greek, flows well. Inclusive language in reference to every person is used. Mark's "fishers of men" is rendered, "I will teach you how to bring in people instead of fish." Older teenagers and adults will find the text reliable and no paraphrase. Root notes explain nuances and give alternatives. Introductory material to the whole and to each part is accurate and you can read each synopsis at a glance. A word list explains the essential technicalities. This is indeed Good News for family members of every age in this Decade of Evangelism.

Ron Fountain, National Coordinator of Children and Families Resources for Scripture Union in New Zealand, wrote:

> Those who read English as a second language outnumber native speakers worldwide. They will appreciate the clear use of everyday words and uncomplicated sentences. It is also suitable for reading in churches and a good version for memorization of Scripture. The pronoun "he" is used to refer to God, but inclusive language is used of people.
>
> Despite the large range of English modern translations already available, there is a real place for this one both in the home and in the wider society. I strongly recommend the New Testament (CEV) edition and look forward to the publication of the whole Bible and various parts of it in a range of formats.

John Fuller, Head of Junior and Middle Department, The Correspondence School of New Zealand, commented:

> Reading the familiar passages of Scripture in this new translation (CEV) is an exciting experience. The natural flow of language, enhanced by a vocabulary that is basic yet profound has for those who have read or listened to it created a fresh and lively appreciation of the events, narratives, and truths recorded in the Word. This version is for everyone because of the faithful, accurate translation, making it extremely readable and understandable regardless of age or maturity.

Throughout 1991 and 1992 Barclay participated in a number of phone interviews when he spoke about the merits of the CEV and other translations in general. These conversations were aired by radio stations across the country.

Christianity Today published an article in October of 1992 in which Ken Waters of Pepperdine University interviewed Barclay. Once again Barclay answered the question "Why a new round of translations?" He stated:

> I asked myself that question when the CEV project started in 1984. The short answer is that each contemporary translation meets a different need. With the CEV, we wanted a mission-driven translation. The CEV began as a translation for children. What seemed missing was a Bible for children eight to nine years old that could easily be read aloud without stumbling. We tested the draft translation … in Springfield, Missouri, where the American Bible Society core translation team lives. We used it with evangelical and

> Roman Catholic schoolchildren and their teachers. We found that the adults praised the translation for enhancing their own biblical understanding. In sharing the draft translation with more adults – including street people our church ministers to – we found that the most responsive folks were those with limited English skills, those turned off by traditional Christian jargon, and the un-churched.

It was not until December of 1992 that Barclay wrote a report to John Erickson in the ABS New York office about his time spent in Chiang Mai, Thailand for the Asia Bible Society Executive Secretaries and Distribution Personnel meetings and the Singapore gatherings. Barclay reported:

> I want to affirm that in my opinion this was the single most valuable opportunity that had come my way to speak on behalf of the *Contemporary English Version*, and I am much indebted to Danny Arichea, Soo Ann Lee, Basil Rebera, and Jen-Li Tsai for making it all happen…
>
> Soo Ann Lee (of Bible Society in Singapore) learned that I was to be in the region and invited me to address several important audiences in Singapore, including (1) the Bible Society Staff, (2) Church and Denominational Leaders, (3) the National Council of Churches, and (4) Seminary Professors and Leaders of Christian Organizations … (each) followed by a lecture-discussion period of more than an hour.
>
> As a direct result of the meeting (in Singapore) with leaders of Christian organizations, Mr. Paul D. Hoekstra, Asia Director of the World Cassette Outreach, and son of Dr. Harvey T. Hoekstra, founder of the ministry, has requested that the ABS allow them to use the CEV for outreach.

At the Conference in Chiang Mai, Thailand Barclay had the joy of meeting W. R. Paulraj, Director of Marketing for the Bible Society in India for the first time. In December he wrote to Barclay, "I was touched by your warmth of Christian love and see the wonderful talent God has given you. … We may look forward to introduce it (the CEV translation) in India soon."

On the 1st of February 1993 Delores Trickel corresponded with Barclay telling him about her attendance at a convention of Pastors from the United Church of Christ on Parish Ministry – National Conference in Orlando, Florida. She had arranged to have a display of American Bible

Society Scriptures at the meeting. She shared with Barclay what several had to say about the CEV New Testament, "This is the best, clearest, translation I have ever read. We gave it as gifts to all our Sunday School Teachers. It is great to use with our youth in Confirmation classes." She added, "Several pastors came to the booth, bringing someone with them. Immediately (they) picked up the CEV and began telling that person how great it was and that they needed to use it."

Sometime either late 1992 or early 1993, Barclay had suggested to the American Bible Society staff that it would be good to have the translation of the *whole* CEV Bible completed and on the market by May 1995 rather than on the previously projected date of May 1996. When it was voted on by the Bible Society to go ahead with the earlier date, Barclay and the translation team members knew this would require longer work hours. But Barclay kept remembering what his two oldest granddaughters, Christie and Malea Simkins had said to him, "We are really waiting for the Old Testament."

On the 5th of March 1993 Gene Habecker again wrote a letter to encourage Barclay:

> I never cease to be amazed how God encourages and affirms us in the work we do here at the American Bible Society ... Several weeks ago, as the guest on a secular radio station in Indianapolis, I rediscovered the hunger of American people for God's Word.
>
> The topic of the hour-long call-in show was the relevancy of the Bible to today's society. Before the program began, my host warned me, "Religion's usually off bounds in this business. It's hard to know what kind of response we'll get." As the program began, I read Psalm 23 from ... the Contemporary English Version... As I finished reading the passage, immediately the phone lines began to light up. People were calling with questions about the Bible and its relevance to their lives. Throughout the hour, we offered the *Bible for Today's Family*, a New Testament in the Contemporary English Version, without charge through an 800 number. During this one radio program alone, we received over 400 requests.

Later Gene Habecker reported that the ABS had received thousands of requests for this newly translated version of the New Testament from people who had heard about it on the radio or through other secular media.

In the spring an article appeared in the Northwest Baptist Convention paper in which the writer said:

> ... Carlton and Fran Butler, Northwest champions of this fresh translation, simply say they find it to be "an accurate, very readable, and highly creditable version of the Scriptures."

On the 16th of April 1993 Haviland Houston received an exciting letter from Michael Bangs, Bible Society Representative of the Southwest Region in the States:

> The attached correspondence is the most phenomenal response to the CEV I have ever received. Some time ago, I had the opportunity to share the new CEV (New Testament) with Les Hooper, Director of Westview Baptist Mission Center in Houston, Texas. After a few months had passed, she had become so enthusiastic about this product that she promoted it everywhere! She shared it with the Pastor of Park Temple Baptist Church, an inner city church in Houston. He ordered 200 copies so everyone in the church could have a copy. He then organized (a) "Bible Explosion Sunday"!

The lengthy response from Peter Slagle, pastor of Park Temple Baptist Church to the Bible Society stated:

> ... As a pastor of an old down-town mission church, I felt the need of getting Christians old and new to read God's Word. The reading level of our overall group is third-fourth grade level. I needed a well written, simple English Bible. I was offered for free other versions of the Bible and found none of them to have what I felt would meet the need. While telling this to Les Hooper of First Baptist Church Missions Department, she handed me your new Contemporary English Version of the New Testament. I first told her "no" and then she said look at it. As I read John 3.16 I knew this was what I was looking for. It was easy print, well divided, bound and laid out in a non-threatening way, and the English was contemporary and written in simple English.
>
> As I showed this to some of our people every one of them was impressed. God was in this all the way. I knew I had to give everyone a copy. I ordered 200 copies and God supplied the money. I had none.
>
> ... One man, seventy-two years old said he had never ever read a book of any kind. But he started reading this book (New Testament) and could not put it down. He was the first to complete it, and he just beams when he shares what he read. He has been a

> Christian for over 40 years. "There's just nothing like it. I just had to keep on reading," he stated. One lady said, "I have never been able to understand the Bible but anyone can understand this. Everyone should read this
>
> ... A second grader came to me and showed me what he had read too, and proudly he was in the Gospel of Mark. I asked him if he could understand it, and he said with a big smile: "O yes, I read about Jesus." People keep coming to me telling me what they have read and for the first time they are understanding what they are reading. We are having spiritual growth here in Park Temple. In fact, it is the one single thing that has brought on the most powerful spiritual growth in our recent history....

Late in April of 1993 Gene Habecker received a letter from James D. Ford from the Office of the Chaplain of the U. S. House of Representatives in Washington, D. C., "... you and the Bible Society were kind enough to send me a carton of "Bibles for Today's Family" (CEV), a paperback Bible that was so well received that I do not have any more copies. Another carton would be deeply appreciated and distributed with thanks."

From April the 30th to 8th of May, Barclay attended the Americas Regional Translations Conference (AMRETCON) '93 meeting in Santo Domingo, Dominican Republic. It was here that he and Jean first learned that Althea Nida (Gene Nida's wife of many years) had died. That was a sad day for all the participants at the meetings. Barclay had worked closely with Gene and Althea from the very beginning of his tenure with the United Bible Societies and the American Bible Society

The Canadian Bible Society began giving every new immigrant coming into Canada a copy of the Contemporary English Version of the New Testament.

About this same time Colin Reed of the New Zealand Bible Society asked Barclay if he would consider coming back to New Zealand when the whole CEV Bible was completed. Barclay did make this trip, and it will be discussed later.

In February of 1994 Barclay received a personal letter from Mrs. Ruth Stafford Peale, "It has been one of my greatest experiences to sit on the Board of the American Bible Society and many of its committees. The work has been very much a part of my life. And now we are all having great hopes for the CEV translation (whole Bible)."

February 22, 1994 was a significant milestone for the translators of the Contemporary English Version of the Bible. On that day Barclay reported to the President of ABS, "The Translation Team of the Contemporary English Version is pleased to report that as of today, February 22, 1994 (Barclay's 63rd birthday), we have completed all committee work on the Old Testament ..."

Two days later Maria Martinez, Vice President at ABS wrote the committee members:

> I cannot begin to imagine the joy and pride that you must be feeling as you complete the masterpiece that your hearts and souls have been committed to for these past years.
>
> There will be so many that will come to know Christ because of your gifts and commitment.
>
> We are blessed and privileged to call you colleagues and friends.

Art Linkletter had this to say:

> I'm Art Linkletter with a word for today from the biblical writer St. Paul: "My friends, keep your minds on whatever is true, pure, right, holy, friendly and proper. Don't ever stop thinking about what is truly worthwhile and worthy of praise. You know the teachings I gave you, and you know what you heard me say and saw me do. So follow my example. And God, who gives peace, will be with you." Philippians four-eight in the *Bible for Today's Family*/CEV – from the American Bible Society.

And Eddie Albert wrote:

> The Bible has come down to us through the centuries and generations because it has been read aloud and retold over and over again. This new translation is intended for the ear as well as for the eye. As an actor, I find this important and appealing. It's like a script that comes alive when the human voice recreates printed words into oral and aural messages of faith, hope and love. It tells again the greatest story ever!

Several months later Art Linkletter wrote to Bill Cedfeldt of the American Bible Society:

> My first memories as a child were of the times when my father read to me from his Bible. He was a Baptist evangelical minister and he was determined that I hear and understand every word of the Lord.

Alas, the words I heard were more confusing than inspiring, and the only verse I truly remembered was the shortest one in the good book: "Jesus wept."

Today's children will be blessed, comforted, and taught by this new Bible whose language comes out of everyday usage and whose meanings can truly be understood. I suspect this observation also applies to most adults who have suffered silently through far too many sermons. … What an exciting page turner the Bible can be!

On the 11th of March 1994 the Department of Translations and Scripture Resources invited all ABS staff to a reception in recognition of Barclay's 30 years with the UBS and ABS. The invitation to the staff read:

> Our Department is delighted to announce and to have an opportunity to celebrate this major milestone in the distinguished career of Barclay M. Newman in Bible Translation! Barclay serves our department and ABS as Senior Translations Officer and heads the CEV team currently bringing the *Contemporary English Version* into being. He also served for many years as a translation consultant for UBS in its Asia-Pacific Region…

Again Maria Martinez wrote Barclay after the celebration:

> What can one say to a man of such great accomplishments as you complete 30 years of glorious service to the Lord through the work of Bible Societies.
>
> The day you came to ABS was the beginning of a new golden age in the field of Biblical Translations… The gifts you have been blessed with are given to a very few. Even fewer have the commitment and zeal to develop those gifts – and in the service of the Lord.
>
> I have been richly blessed to have you as a colleague and a friend, and I am so proud to know you and work with you.

In April a very encouraging, but heart-rending letter, was addressed to Gene Habecker in the New York office:

> January and February, 1994, were very trying, traumatic months for me. I'm past 70, live alone and have chronic health problems. The endless nightmare began the middle of January when a crazy man suddenly stepped in front of my car on a busy, icy highway. I had a near death experience but angels saved me in a split second.

Then the pipes froze in my basement and living room plus my oil lines. I was without heat for four days and three nights in below zero weather. The pipes burst in three places and water gushed on my living room floor. My hot water froze and then my living room ceiling started leaking in several places. Plus much more!

But one cold morning in early February a copy of the Bible for Today's Family/CEV arrived. In November I had sent a gift to ABS so people who had trouble reading English could enjoy the Bible and I checked the box to receive one copy myself.

I couldn't believe how easy it was to read. I could have understood it when I was in third grade. With a splitting headache and neurological pains from the cold plus chronic fatigue from sleepless nights I had trouble concentrating on my regular Bible. What a blessing this new one was to me during that awful nightmare period. I read John's Gospel and kept on reading every day. I'm now about to read Revelation – or (more than) 3/4th through the New Testament.

I've developed such an affection for it!! It was a special gift from God! I knew he would give me the grace to be patient and endure and not try me beyond what I could endure. The timing was so perfect – it arrived on the right day – when I was close to despair.

On the 27th of May, Jobsan Midang from Bougainville, Papua New Guinea penned a letter to Ray Jones who had given him a copy of the Contemporary English Version New Testament at a meeting in Brisbane, Australia:

The New Testament in Contemporary English is an excellent piece of scholarship. I find my son Donald who is in grade 3 can just pick it up and read it without much problem. I have also read the whole gospel of John and have come across with lots of new insights. I highly recommend the two Bibles and particularly the Contemporary English Bible to be used in any third world counties with English as their 2nd or 3rd language and more so in Papua New Guinea …

In October two senators wrote to the ABS with endorsements for the Contemporary English Version of the New Testament with Psalms and Proverbs. Senator Dan Coats of Indiana stated, "When my 16-year-old-son read, without any prompting, the CEV New Testament from cover to cover, I knew this translation was a winner. Every family should get, and read together, the new CEV." And Senator Mark Hatfield of Oregon said, "The Contemporary English Version Bible is clear and readable without sacrificing the nobility or authenticity of God's Word. Written in the vernacular, it is an excellent introduction to Scripture. Christians everywhere can welcome the CEV onto their shelves and, prayerfully, into their hearts."

Chuck Colson, Chairman of the Board Prison Fellowship, stated:

> The CEV is a clear and readable version of the New Testament that we have found extremely useful for the Angel Tree ministry to the children of prisoners, and in our work with prisoners. I commend this effort to make God's Word understandable to millions of people.

In the fall David Gowan, American Bible Society Development Representative for the western United States, arranged for a shipment of 6,000 CEV New Testaments to be delivered to various Native American communities in Oregon, Washington state, Montana, Nevada, South Dakota, and Arizona.

In January 1995 Pat Boone corresponded with Thomas Nelson publishers:

> Perhaps a billion people can read and understand this Contemporary English Version of God's Word – including you and your kids! I suppose there hasn't been a better instrument of salvation since the printing press was invented – and I hope to see it in the hands of at least a billion people in our lifetime!

Robert H. Schuller, pastor of the Crystal Cathedral in Garden Grove, California wrote to Sam Moore of Thomas Nelson Publishers:

> Since our culture is no longer church-based, it is both necessary and important to spread God's incredible story to the masses of people in a form that is both readable and understandable.... It will serve as a most valuable tool for churches and ministries whose mission is to reach the unchurched in our communities, and within our network of influence. The possibilities for impacting people through the Contemporary English Version are limitless!

Hundreds of newspapers across the States carried articles throughout 1995 about the CEV, and many letters and stories were received by Barclay. Some of these will be included. One lady closely associated with the work of the ABS wrote about three ladies from her office:

> A woman at work was asking me about the meaning of a certain Bible verse. She used just the King James Version. I explained the meaning to her and brought her a Contemporary English Version of the New Testament. She took it with her to her Bible class that Sunday. Monday when she came to work she wondered if I could get six more for her to buy. The people at her Bible class like it so very much. I gave the CEV to a woman … On her way home from work, when she picked up her five-year old daughter from kindergarten, the little girl saw the book and said, "Mommy, read me a story from this book." The mother always reads a Bible story to her little girl each night, but she said, "Honey, that's the Bible and I think you are not ready for that." The child answered, "I know it's the Bible because it has a cross on it (the cover), but read me some from it anyway instead of the Bible story (book)." The mother did and the next day she told me about the experience. She said, "I had to read five chapters before she conked out!"
>
> I gave a CEV to (another) woman at work. She told me the next day, "I was going to read just one chapter last night from the new book instead of the King James Version, just to tell you that I did it. I started reading and kept on going. When I next looked at the time it was one hour later. I'll really enjoy reading that."

On the 22nd of February Cathy Loden from a small church in Texas wrote a letter to Mike Bangs:

> I would like you to know how very much the New Testament for Today's Family/CEV has been a true blessing in my life. About eight months ago, my husband died and left me widowed with twin baby girls to raise on my own. I was so very hurt and scared; I was truly devastated. At that point in my life, I turned to the Lord above for guidance. Being such a new Christian, I of course thought the King James Version was basically the Bible I needed to read. As I tried reading the KJV, it was very difficult for me to understand. With that being the case, I prayed to the Lord for something that would be easy to understand, comforting and modern. The CEV New Testament was the answer to my prayer….

In the spring, summer, and into the fall of 1995 magazines, such as the *Saturday Evening Post, Christian Century, Christian Print, Christianity*

Today, Catholic Digest, Today's Christian Woman, "Charisma", Pentecostal Herald, Family Circle (Central), *Parade* (South, Central), *USA Weekend* (Southern), *Woman's Day, Good Housekeeping, McCall's, Midwest Today* (Summer), *In Trust* (May 1996), and *Bible Review* (Oct 1996) carried articles on the readability of the CEV and the work of the American Bible Society. Among the dozens of newspapers across the States which carried articles on the new CEV Bible was *The Wall Street Journal.*

From the 21st to the 25th of June the American Bible Society chose to launch the CEV whole Bible by an historic, around-the-clock, non-stop, ninety-hour Bible reading marathon on the Bible House Plaza in front of the Bible House on Broadway in New York. It began at 7:45 a.m. on Wednesday and continued through to 2:00 a.m. on Sunday. 360 participants read for 15 minutes each, and the reading was completed in 90 hours. The readers included political leaders, Broadway and film actors, media personalities, New York schoolchildren, religious leaders and congregants from a broad range of churches and denominations.

From New Zealand Barclay flew to Australia where his itinerary was similar. He worked with the Australian Bible Society staff in Melbourne, Adelaide, and Perth, and on the 25th he was the guest speaker at "An Evening with the Masters," a special event to celebrate the printing of the 10 millionth Chinese Bible printed at the Amity Press in Nanjing, China. On August 22nd Barclay was the guest speaker at a breakfast which had been arranged by the Australian Bible Society and held at the Salvation Army Congress Hall in Adelaide.

From the 27th of September to October 4th, 1995 Barclay traveled once again to Canada at the request of the Canadian Bible Society. With the assistance of Kenneth Peterson, District Secretary of Saskatchewan, Barclay's tour included six major stops (Tisdale, Yorkton, Regina, Swift Current, Davidson, and Saskatoon).

In September Thomas May and Brenda Webber distributed a news release which told of Pope John Paul II's visit to New York in October. The ABS printed a half-million copies of a special, commemorative booklet (book of CEV John), which were given out during the visit of Pope John Paul II. Volunteers made them available in parishes and schools and for the celebration of mass on the Great Lawn of Central Park in New York City as well as the mass at Aqueduct Racetrack in the New York Borough of Queens and Oriole Park at Camden Yards in Baltimore, Maryland.

Pope John Paul II was presented with a full copy of the CEV Bible.

In October Gene Habecker wrote:

> As we began our media outreach campaign to introduce the CEV Bible, we did not know what to expect. On the first day, we received requests for the CEV Gospel of John from 10,000 people. The second day, 12,000 copies were requested! A few days later, I had the opportunity to talk about the CEV on a Philadelphia television program, and in just 15 minutes, over 5,000 individuals called asking for copies of the new CEV.
>
> Right now, we have requests for over 70,000 CEV Bibles and Scripture portions ....

Between the time the CEV was first put on the market by the ABS in June and the 8th of December 1995, more that 185,000 copies of CEV Bibles had been sold in the States alone along with more than 237,000 copies of the New Testament.

In late fall of 1995 a Bible House was opened in Fiji, and at the same opening ceremony the Australian Contemporary English Version was launched by Jen Lai, Colin Reed, Carl and Lyn Gross.

From January 6th to the 21st Barclay traveled to London, England at the request of the British and Foreign Bible Society to help launch the Contemporary English Version of the complete Bible. While there Kim Alexander, Gilly Swan, and Helen Warren had arranged for him to travel almost the full length of the country giving CEV presentations, speaking for television audiences and BBC radio stations as well as other radio stations, and being interviewed by local and national press. It was a whirlwind of activity, and many Bible Society staff hosted Barclay with outstanding meals.

It was later reported to Barclay that the BFBS immediately doubled its order for CEV Bibles from Thomas Nelson after his visit there, and although there were some negative newspaper articles about the CEV, one man called in after a radio presentation and spoke eloquently and favorably for the CEV for more than twenty minutes. Finally, the interviewer asked who he was, and he said, "Dr. Procter, Professor of New Testament Studies, Cambridge."

In the elevators at the New York American Bible Society House a yellow notice was taped which read, "A Star Is Born." Barclay was invited to appear on Public Television, channel 13 for the "The News Hour with Jim Lehrer." "News Hour" producers taped an interview with Barclay in Springfield, Missouri. Barclay was part of a roundtable discussion on Bible translations. He presented the Contemporary English Version.

For 29 years Barclay had assisted his wife Jean in her volunteer work with the American Bible Society. He stated that all he does is tote the boxes for Jean when they are too heavy for her to lift. On April 22, 1996 Jean recorded an incident that took place at a Foreign Mission Board Appointment Service held in Cape Girardeau, Missouri. She had a display of ABS materials, including the CEV Bibles and New Testaments. By this time ABS had come out with a beautiful children's bound edition of the CEV.

A boy of about 9 or 10 years of age literally lunged across the railing of her booth to the side where she had ABS plastic bags stored and a display of Bibles stacked in a circle. The boy grabbed one of the CEV Children's Bibles and began begging his mother to buy him "one of these" because he could read it. The mother was poorly dressed as was the boy. The boy looked a bit bruised, but because he was so active (almost hyper) Jean imagined that he often bumped into things. The mother smiled at him and shook her head "no." He kept begging until finally, Jean strongly felt he should have one, but then she noticed there were six other boys about the same age standing close by watching as the scene unfolded. By this time, Jean was down to about 4 Children's CEV Bibles, and she knew if she gave this boy a Bible, there wouldn't be enough to go around.

A few minutes later, everyone filed back into the auditorium through a door which was in plain view of Jean's booth. She couldn't get it off her mind how the boy had begged so pleadingly for the Bible, and she felt sick that she hadn't figured out a way to give him one without the others noticing.

About 30 minutes later, Jean looked up and coming out of the auditorium was only the bruised boy and his mother. Jean quickly asked the mother if it would be alright to give him a Bible, and she said it was OK. Jean asked him to promise to read it and reached for one. The boy stood motionless and grinned from ear to ear when Jean handed it to him. He dashed away so quickly, Jean didn't see him again, but she thanked God that she had had a second chance to share the Bible with this boy – a boy she would likely never see again.

According to Bible Society Scripture distribution manager, John Jennings, the CEV is fast becoming the most popular Bible version in New Zealand. Sales have exceeded all expectations since its introduction last year.

In June, Barclay received the 1996 Distinguished Alumnus Award from Southern Baptist Theological Seminary in Louisville, Kentucky and was honored as distinguished alumnus at the 1996 Alumni and Friends Luncheon in New Orleans.

From July 31st to August 2nd Barclay was invited to make CEV presentations in Calgary, Canada.

Barclay received a letter written by Carl Gross on the 23rd of August:

> I received the following message from Freddie Boswell, SIL's director in the Solomon Islands about the impact of the CEV in the Solomons. … "The CEV was launched in Honiara at Murray Frew's new (Bible Society) shop back in …. The government minister for Home Affairs, Hon Nathaniel Supa, was the guest speaker … Murray presented him with a CEV after his speech …
>
> "Freddy was in Hon Supa's office the other day, and he said that his wife has been reading the CEV until midnight 'every night,' and 'it has been changing her life.' He can't believe the difference in her! She is a Solomon Islander, from Isabel … He (Hon) is a Gao speaker, which is the next language down from Cheke Holo. He is interested in reading the Cheke Holo New Testament, but he says his wife wants the CEV. Praise the Lord for however He makes His message clear in a language that Mrs. Supa can understand …"

Barclay was off to Scotland for a very profitable Bible Society tour from September 20th to 26th where he worked with Pauline Hurst, Assistant General Secretary of the National Bible Society of Scotland. She reminded Barclay, "For twenty years you have been telling us to use the GNB, and now you are telling us to use a new translation."

Barclay was present for the Glasgow, Scottish Christian Resources Exhibition, and on several occasions gave a presentation "Juggling Eggs on a Trapeze" (featuring the CEV), gave interviews for television audiences, attended several prayer breakfasts, gave radio interviews, spoke at Perth Regional Council and Central Regional Council to Bible Society volunteers, and also spoke at a Rotary luncheon. It was always a joy to work with Fergus McDonald the General Secretary of the Bible Society of Scotland. He also treated Barclay to some sightseeing in beautiful Scotland.

Barclay made CEV presentations at Central Seminary in Kansas City and William Jewell College in Liberty, Missouri on the 16th and 17th of January 1997.

The British and Foreign Bible Society had published in 1996 the "Into the Light" New Testament edition of the CEV and in 1997 the entire Bible. This edition was awarded the 2,000th Crystal Mark by the Plain English Campaign – the first Bible in the world to carry this coveted Crystal Mark for clarity. Their news release stated: … "It captures the vigor and vitality of the original text, making it clear and understandable for today's generation. Every one of the pages is crystal clear, and we believe this is certainly the Bible to take people into the next century."

A press release from Thomas Nelson Publishers reported on the 7th of March 1997 that four million copies of the Contemporary English Version of the Bible had been sold to date. They are anticipating their publication "The Promise Bible for Students" (CEV) to come on the market by March 24th. Throughout 1996 and 1997 Thomas Nelson published many editions of the CEV New Testament and whole Bible.

Barclay traveled to Johannesburg, South Africa the 13th to the 21st of September to attend the African Regional Assembly there. An African delegate described Barclay as "brilliant to listen to, good on the ear, just like the CEV."

In October Barclay made CEV presentations at the Woodbrook Baptist Church in Charleston, West Virginia, and in November at the request of Ray Moreland made CEV presentations at the Bible Society in Baltimore, Maryland.

The ABS announced in October the production of a special imprint of the CEV New Testament translation entitled "Stand in the Gap New Testament" for Promise Keepers. ABS provided 1,000,000 copies for the event which took place in Washington, D. C. on the 11th of October. About half a million participants gathered in the nation's capital for the purpose of encouraging men from all walks of life to commit themselves to church, family, and racial harmony.

In August of 1997, David Neff, the Executive Editor of *Christianity Today,* interviewed Barclay. This interview was subsequently published in the October issue and touched on such questions as, "Why did the CEV translators use gender-generic language where the Bible uses masculine language for people of both sexes?" and "You have pointed out that gender sensitivity in English translations is as old as the King James Version. How so?"

A publication by the American Interfaith Institute called *Explorations*, carried an article authored by Barclay entitled "Challenging the Curse on the Chosen Ones." In this article he deals with the term "the Jews," found frequently throughout the New Testament. To quote a few lines from that article:

> From a cursory reading of the New Testament, it has often been concluded that an eternal curse has somehow been placed upon the Chosen Ones (the Jews), who are now reduced from "favored nation status" to that of God's supreme enemies, because of their rejection of Jesus Christ both during his lifetime and in the earliest days of the Christian Church. Nothing could be further from the truth! … Indeed, whenever the phrase "the Jews" is used of the opponents of Jesus in the N T, it means at the very most "some of the Jews of that time and

> place!" Moreover, the cumulative effect of repeating "the Jews" with negative connotations within the overall canonical context of a New Testament is far more dangerous to truth than the appearance of the phrase would have been within the original setting of the individual books themselves. In effect, this means that a literal translation both generates and perpetuates a hostile environment today that contradicts the overall message of the New Testament itself. … "Christ has made peace between Jews and Gentiles, and he has united us by breaking down the wall of hatred that separated us" (CEV Ephesians 2.14.)

Immediately after November the 18th Barclay flew to the West coast – Portland, Oregon to make CEV presentations at Bible Week Emphasis. David Gowan, Elaine Nelson, Al Fischer, Pat Kreitler, and Richard Koe co-ordinated a program where Barclay would speak at the Rivergate Community Church, Pioneer United Methodist Church, Cherry Park Presbyterian Church, First Baptist Church, Portland, and to the Greek and Hebrew classes at Western Evangelical Seminary, in addition to these speaking engagements.

Barney Field, a local business man in El Paso, Texas declared a city-wide Scripture outreach and called it the Year of the Bible in El Paso. The goal was to encourage every person in El Paso (population 600,000) to read a passage of Scripture every day for the entire year. Seventy-five of the city's church leaders and pastors were encouraged to preach from the daily selections which their parishioners read during the week. The *El Paso Times* agreed to publish each day's Scripture passage for its readers. One pastor commented, "We are reaching people who never took church or Christ seriously before. We are reaching out with the best tool we have." The American Bible Society provided a total of 55,000 Scriptures in the CEV and the Spanish *Version Popular* translations.

Every January in New South Wales, Australia the Salvation Army runs a week-long summer camp for underprivileged children drawn from city and country areas of the State. This January 1998, thanks to the Bible Society in Australia, each child was given a copy of *The Big Rescue*, an Australian edition of the Contemporary English Version of the Bible. Stories were read to the children from the CEV and given Bible verses to memorize. One counselor stated, "I have never seen such a response to the Word of God from children." A full page announcement appeared in the *Guideposts* magazine in February, which stated that a "Positive Thinking Bible" (CEV translation) was available with 365 quotes from Norman Vincent Peale and other motivational ideas.

The summer of 1998 found the Contemporary English Version Bible in the new Bible shop in Tbilisi, Georgia, USSR.

Volunteers Nellie Bicksler (of South Carolina) and Wes and Violet Cox (of Georgia) had a joint CEV launch where participants were invited from both Augusta, Georgia and North Augusta, South Carolina. Along with the launch the program consisted of a "Scripture Fashion Show," featuring young people from the host Church Midvalley Baptist of North Augusta and a delicious barbecue followed.

Sara Shailer of the British and Foreign Bible Society told the story behind the innovative typesetting layout for the CEV Anglicized Bible in England. She stated in the "Publishing World Newsletter,"

> For many people, unfamiliarity with biblical text means that some Bible layouts can appear daunting and create obstacles to an understanding of its message. To help the reader gain a better understanding, the *Into the Light* Bible typesetting focused on making the layout as clear as possible.

In November of 1998, Lynell Zogbo corresponded with Barclay:

> ... We use it (CEV) often as a model in our translation work here in Africa (even with Francophone teams), and I am always interested to see what choices have been made in terms of text, interpretation, etc. I made up models of introductions to Old Testament books in French (because the ones we have are not appropriate) and I relied heavily on the CEV introductions both for content and for their model of simplicity.

The reader of this account may wonder why the Contemporary English Version of the Bible is mentioned so frequently. The desire for Bible translation was perhaps instilled in Barclay from a very early stage in his call to ministry, from the first day he sat in his beginner Greek class at Union University. It would be safe to say that the producing of the CEV was Barclay's very life and breath from the beginning of the task to the end.

From April to September of 1999 the CEV translation was published as a single New Testament book or the New Testament with or without Psalms and Proverbs or the whole Bible as special imprint editions for a number of organizations: CEV John's Gospel Portion for Assemblies of God; Contemporary English Version New Testament/Psalms and Proverbs for Youth For Christ in Ft. Wayne, Indiana; for Nicky Cruz Outreach, Colorado Springs, Colorado; Truckers Ministry, Chandler, North Carolina; Franciscan University of Steubenville, Steubenville, Ohio; the Conference Committee of the Diocese of Alexandria-Cornwall, Ontario,

Canada; CEV paperback Bible for General Baptist State Convention of North Carolina, Raleigh, North Carolina; CEV paperback for Women's Job Corps (a ministry of WMU) 2003.

On the 12th of April, Barclay participated in a workshop for pastors, students, and other interested persons held in Portland, Maine. His topic was "Must Alice – and Others – Remain Lost in Wonderland When Reading the Bible?"

In June, Mike Gahan reported on what the CEV had meant to youth at the Bexar County Juvenile Detention Center in San Antonia. He stated:

> Most of our kids have poor reading skills. Having their own copy of a Bible that is easy to read like the CEV is such a blessing. They will literally read it from cover to cover. It has made a huge impact in these kids lives. We see the change in the behavior of the youth when they begin reading their Bible. Where there once was only anger, hatred, and despair, it is being replaced by peace, love, and hope for their future.

Well before 1999 the American Bible Society declared 1999 as the "Year of the Bible" when it was celebrated across the United States beginning in January of 1999. ABS began many months previous to January to prepare people for this important celebration leading up to the new millennium.

A new daily reading program was designed to help the reader to complete the Contemporary English Version New Testament in one year, reading for just five minutes a day. This program was promoted through churches, ABS volunteers, and individuals so that preparations would be made well in advance. Buttons, bookmarks, bumper stickers, yard signs, and special kits for pastors were provided free; and videos and lapel badges were available for a small fee from the ABS. Also obtainable was a special-edition "Year of the Bible" CEV New Testament, which included the daily readings.

There was a form to fill in, committing the participant to the daily Bible reading. Newspapers in several cities agreed to publish the daily Bible reading passages as a service to the community. For 365 days *The News Leader* in Springfield, Missouri printed the Scripture reading for that day.

Barclay became intensely involved with this nationwide celebration. His wife Jean was a volunteer with the ABS, and she had begun on January 2, 1998 to make plans as how to reach 15 counties in Missouri for the "Year of the Bible." Literally hundreds of calls were made, pastors kits mailed along with "Five Minutes a Day" buttons, bumper stickers, gift envelopes, and more. New Testament were ordered, and her first order of 20,000 New Testaments arrived by Road Way on October 16th of 1998. Jean arranged for 10,000 to be brought to their home and 10,000 more to be housed at the Council of Churches facility, a more northern location. When these some 200 boxes arrived, Barclay was working in his home office. First there had to be a dry space made to store this many boxes of Bibles. The Newman's double garage was the space selected. To make room Barclay's old red car had to be moved out on the street. Then he helped the deliveryman unload and stack these 200 boxes, both in English and Spanish.

Throughout the year Barclay helped Jean distribute the "Year of the Bible" New Testaments in churches, grocery stores, beauty salons, Walmart and other locations for free distribution.

Many stories came back to Jean and Barclay about the effects the reading of the CEV New Testament was having on people all over the States. One story as told by Jose Ruiz will be included here:

> A woman approached me and shared how her 11-year-old son had received Christ two weeks prior. She went on to tell me that the message delivered in his own language through the CEV spoke to his heart. The mother then added that her son had been struggling with an attention disorder that required special medicine. A batch of that medicine didn't agree with his system and he had to be admitted to the hospital. Upon admittance, the staff took his "Year of the Bible" CEV away from him for safe keeping. This was the wrong thing to do. The boy had a fit, and drove everyone in the hospital crazy, so much so that they had to call his mother.
>
> When the mother arrived, she inquired about the problem and asked her son why he was acting like that. He answered, "Mom, they took my CEV away! It is the only one I understand. It is my sword, and I need it – don't let them take my CEV away."
>
> The boy's mother convinced the hospital staff to give him his CEV back. When they did, it was the end of the tantrums.

One lady wrote, "My daughter was filling out a crossword puzzle based on Scriptures. She needed to look up a passage and asked me to hand her a Bible. I gave her my KJV. She looked up the passage and then said, 'Mom, give me the CEV because I cannot understand a word of this.' I was so amazed that my seven-year-old daughter recognized and appreciated the difference in Bible translations."

In October Yeon Sang Lee shared, "There are many translations and all of those have their style. I can find His power, strength and authority through the KJV Bible, and I came to know the world of God much closer through the CEV Bible."

Chapter XIII

Summary of the 1990s

From the beginning of the 1990s, Barclay's time was consumed with his translating books of the *Contemporary English Version* Old Testament, writing articles for Bible Society publications, working on the Catholic Lectionary for Children (published in 1993), holding CEV committee meetings in his home, and traveling (as mentioned earlier) to many states across North America to promote the CEV and the worldwide program of all Bible Societies. Travels were made to many other countries where he gave CEV presentations: Canada, England, Scotland, Wales, France, Spain, Thailand, Philippines, New Zealand, Australia, Singapore, West Malaysia, San Dominican Republic, and Brazil.

Although the entire New Testament had been translated, checked by the American Bible Society manuscript specialists, approved by the American Bible Society Subcommittee on Translation, and published in May of 1991, the Old Testament and Deuterocanonical books remained to be translated.

On October 1, 1990 the first Old Testament Committee meeting was held with four persons participating. Barclay Newman, chairperson, Robert Hodgson, Donald Johns, and Jean Newman, who was serving as secretary and stylist, met to review the translations.

Twelve Committee meetings were held in the year of 1991. Steve Berneking joined the Old Testament translation team in June as the last member, and in December had his first full session as a team member. The Committee meeting scheduled for September 23-27 was designated entirely for the purpose of making one final re-reading of the entire CEV New Testament although it had already been published in May.

Fourteen Committee meetings were planned for 1992, nine for 1993, and seven for 1994. Because the meetings were held in the Newman's home the entire cost of these 44 Committee meetings came to $4,443.13. This amount, of course, didn't include salaries, utilities, travel, computers, paper, ink, postage, etc. but did include coffee, tea, colas, fruit, lunch in a nearby restaurant for each team member, and afternoon drinks and snacks.

From August 10 to September 6, 1991, Barclay visited New Zealand and Australia at the request of the New Zealand and Australian Bible Societies to promote the CEV translation of the New Testament. From New Zealand Barclay traveled to Brisbane, Australia, where he attended an Australian Bible Society Conference of the Marketing Managers, where John Jennings moderated. Barclay also gave CEV translation presentations at several colleges in and around Brisbane. A few weeks after these presentations, John Lane with Scripture Union in Australia:

> Thank you for introducing us to the new *Contemporary English Version* New Testament. A number of us have looked at it, and we are very impressed with it. We wish to explore with you and your colleagues the possibility of several Scripture Union/Bible Society products built on this translation. This version appeals to us because its language and sentence structure is so uncomplicated, so allowing the full force of the message of the Scriptures to come to people of all ages. We endorse the 'dynamic equivalence' principle and enjoy seeing it used so well in the formation of this translation.

In late October, Nancy Schaffer, a highly intelligent Wycliff Bible translator working in Northern Ghana purchased ten CEVs from the Newmans. One of the translators had one copy, and she felt "it was the best help possible for their translation project, but they couldn't get additional copies in Ghana."

In February of 1992, at Union University's annual Homecoming in Jackson, Tennessee, Barclay was honored when he received the Distinguished Alumnus Award along with 3 others, and his well received acceptance speech was filled with humor.

Also in May of 1992, Barbara Bush had been scheduled to give the commencement address for the graduating class at Union University in Jackson, Tennessee (Barclay's alma mater), and at the same time Barclay was invited to give the Baccalaureate Sermon, but when Barbara was unable to keep the appointment, Barclay was invited to fill in for her and did indeed deliver the commencement address for the graduating class, the highest number of graduates in the 167 years of the college.

Barclay continued to receive letters that greatly encouraged him as he and the team members worked on the Old Testament books for the CEV Bible. It was mentioned earlier that Margaret Scroggins of Springfield, Missouri had purchased a large number of New Testaments to give as gifts to friends and relatives. She stated that over the years she and her husband had not had money to spare to buy birthday, graduation, and wedding gifts, but now they could certainly afford the low cost CEV New Testaments, so she bought 35 to give to friends and relatives. And on June 22, 1992 she and her husband James received a letter from Ken James of the Home Mission Board of the Southern Baptist Convention:

> Thank you so much for the CEV New Testament. I have already had time to read rather extensively in it. I am sure that the Lord will use this translation to speak to many who have not been raised in environments where "church-ese" and "bible-ese" have been taught and spoken. The simplicity and clarity of the translation will serve to communicate the life-changing, simple Gospel of Jesus Christ.

On the 26th of August, Barclay received a letter from Judy Landers from Smithville, Missouri:

> I marvel at how rapidly this translation spreads just with people I know. I think nearly every family in our church has at least one and now most of their relatives do too. Our 65-year-old interim pastor uses it in the pulpit. We have given copies to our relatives and they in turn bought copies for their children. My aunt from Virginia is sharing hers at church and ordering for those who want them. A friend from Orlando called and talked for an hour last week and mentioned how much he liked the CEV New Testament we sent him for Christmas. He bought copies for his four kids and for businessmen who he knew would not read the Bible otherwise. He'd gotten the American Bible Society catalog and was ordering other material too. This man has owned a highly successful advertising agency for 35 years doing accounts for the governors, state of Florida. It was fun to hear him so turned on to this Bible.

In the fall of 1992, Barclay gave CEV presentations in Chaing Mai, Thailand, where Asian Bible Society Executive Secretaries and Distribution Personnel were gathered for meetings. He went on from Chaing Mai to Singapore, where he was invited by the General Secretary of the Singapore Bible Society, Lee Soo Ann, to make CEV presentations to audiences there.

In March of 1994 Barclay was honored at a reception for his "30-Year" service with the American Bible Society. All 300 employees of the Bible House in New York were invited and most attended the gala affair. Two months later, Barclay attended the United Bible Societies Triennial Translations Workshop in Chaing Mai, Thailand. In the fall (Nov. 6-9) he was invited to make CEV presentations in Toulan, France. That same month he made a CEV presentation and spoke about the work of the American Bible Society at the Glen Campbell Theater in Branson, Missouri. This event was arranged for by Robert Stevens of St. Louis, Missouri.

On the 9th of August of 1994, Barclay received a significant and thrilling letter from Margaret York, the Product and Special Imprint Coordinator of the American Bible Society. She included in her letter a July article printed by the United Bible Societies *World Report* about a well organized plan by The Pocket Testament League of Lititz, Pennsylvania. The PTL was asking for the American Bible Society in New York to partner with them in the cost of making available in June a Normandy Anniversary Commemorative Edition of the CEV New Testament for D-Day Veterans. The Allied Forces of World War II will gather once again in Europe on the beaches of Normandy, France to commemorate the 50th Anniversary of the joint landing there. This invasion proved not only to be a turning point in the war, but also one of the most costly in the terms of lives lost.

In a January 4th 1995 letter, Michael McCaskey, the Director of Development for Pocket Testament League, stated that the PTL's plan was to have the Commemoration ceremonies held on the three beaches associated with the landing: Normandy, Omaha, and Utah. Each of the major Allied powers – the United States, Canada, and England – was assigned to one of the beach areas, with France occupying the shore lines. The U. S. activities were centered around Omaha Beach. President Bill Clinton closed the ceremony with a meaningful presentation. Teams were set up at strategic locations to provide the commemorative Scriptures to those present. 25,000 CEV New Testaments were provided for the celebration.

The article printed in the United Bible Societies *World Report* read:

> **New York, USA** – To help mark the 50th anniversary of the allied D-Day landings in Normandy on June 6, the American Bible Society in partnership with the Pocket Testament League, printed a commemorative New Testament for armed forces personnel, particularly those who served in World War II.
>
> The 25,000 customized Scriptures which include facsimile pages of the New Testament as it was distributed by the PTL more than fifty years ago, were scheduled for distribution by PTL representatives to veterans and their families during the D-Day observances in Normandy, France, and in the United States in June.

The article went on to explain how the decision was made to use the CEV New Testament:

> The only significant difference between this edition and that provided by the Pocket Testament League in 1941 is that the text in the commemorative edition is the American Bible Society's Contemporary English Version (CEV). The 1941 edition used the King James Version.

Representing the American Bible Society, Charles Houser stated: "We are happy to be able to participate on a partnership basis with the League in providing Scriptures for the Normandy observance, and we hope that the CEV translation will make the Gospel of Christ more real and clear in a whole new way … The CEV is ideal for evangelism of this sort."

In November, Barclay received a letter from a Mrs. Anglin thanking him for translating the CEV and telling him what it meant to her for the PTL and the American Bible Society to make available a copy for her in memory of her husband who had died there at Normandy fifty years ago.

The July issue of the American Bible Society *Abstracts* carried an article listing dignitaries who were present for the Normandy observance. President and Mrs. Clinton, members of the Joint Chiefs of Staff, members of Congress, legendary newscaster Walter Cronkite, veterans and their families were among those present who received one of the 25,000 commemorative CEV New Testaments. This event marked the Allied Invasion of Normandy, France of June 6, 1944.

ABS Board member John Leonard and his wife were there for the chief ceremony on June 6, 1994 with the President and other dignitaries, and in his words: "When I was in the service in 1943, I had gotten a white leather-covered, small New Testament." Now more than 50 years later, he received the red-covered commemorative CEV New Testament while in France. His white one is now 51 years old. "I was moved by the fact that I had held onto the one we got in 1943 and we took it with us, and then to get another one some 50 years later … It was moving and exciting and impressive that the work is continuing." He added, "You don't know where those copies will wind up, whether they will end up with grandchildren, and 50 years from now someone comes up with it. …The ABS involvement in this effort made me personally proud."

The whole CEV Bible was nearing completion by the fall of 1994, and on the 14th of October, the ABS sponsored a seminar around the CEV in New York. Sixty Christian leaders from all over the country were invited to the Bible House in New York for three days to formally announce the launching of the complete CEV Bible. Eugene Habecker, the CEO and President of the American Bible Society, read from John 1.14 which says "… and the word became a human being." He continued:

> The Word became a human being through the incarnation of Jesus Christ. This Word is basically a word of peace and hope. It also becomes human flesh through its ministry in our lives. In a world filled with violence, we must become peace-makers for God. For a world full of misery, it carries a message of divine hope. In Watts, California, the churches use this Word to become agents of reconciliation.

Gene Habecker added that upon reading the free-flowing text of the CEV for the very first time people feel excitement. Bob Schuler of Crystal Cathedral in California requested 60,000 or more copies to send to his TV audiences.

Maria Martinez, Vice President of National Ministries, stated that people are hungry for spiritual truth in an unprecedented way during these days. Maria went on to explain:

> First, the American Bible Society set out to develop a clear, simple, and easy to understand translation for youth, one that was not condescending, regardless of the age of the reader. Second, our goal was to present a translation that was a partner to other existing translations. This translation was developed for people who attend worship services but have difficulty reading the current translations used in worship. And third, there must be an effort to bring the translation to the people through a network of volunteers rather than through the typical mass marketing.

In November, Barclay received a letter from Geraldine Anglin whose husband had fought on the Normandy Beach:

> What a wonderful surprise I received when Ellen McClosky (an ABS volunteer) sent me the 50th Normandy Anniversary New Testament. I heard on TV that all peoples attending in Normandy France were recipients of one of these. I thought of my late husband and wondered what had happened to the one he received the night before the big battle. How I wished for one of those and now our Lord had honored my wish.
>
> My husband was on the Normandy Beach the first hour and lived to fight on for 6 more months until they went to Germany and the war ended.

On the 15th of August, Ester Vargas-Manchuca, Editorial Manager at ABS penned a letter to Robert Sanford of the Thomas Nelson Publishers (commercial publishers for CEV) in Nashville, Tennessee:

> You should receive tomorrow, via overnight courier, one set of master galley proofs for the Contemporary English Version Bible database, Text, Footnotes, Preface, Introduction to the Bible – the Old Testament and the New Testament, Introductions to each Bible book and a Word List. All are included.

In February of 1995, Barclay traveled to Nashville, Tennessee, where he made CEV presentations and spoke about existing Bible translations at the General Board of Discipleship of the United Methodist Church. June 21-25 marked an historic event at the Bible House at 1865 Broadway in New York. The CEV had been completed one year ahead of schedule. And it was launched under the leadership of Haviland Houston, the ABS Volunteer Activities Director, with a 90-hour, cover-to-cover marathon reading. A stage was erected in front of the Bible House from which the participants read. This marathon was publicized in New York newspapers, United Press International, the three network stations – CBS, NBC, and ABC and their affiliates throughout the country.

There were a total of 360 readers over the course of the five-day marathon. The youngest reader was a 7-year-old boy, Lawrence Galvez from the Philippines who spoke English as a second language.

As the marathon progressed, several people walking by responded with encouragement and support. The ABS Bookstore located in the lobby of the Bible House reported brisk business for the CEV and other ABS Scriptures resources.

In the early fall of 1994, Anthony Harrop of the United Bible Societies' Asia Pacific Regional Service Center in Hong Kong had continued with his plans for promoting the CEV New Testament. He had been in correspondence with Vera Buurma in Germany concerning the upcoming Book Exhibition of the Operation Mobilization (OM) Ships Doulos and Logos II in their joint meeting in Toulon, France. Such a joint meeting happened very rarely – only once before. 500 OM staff were expected to be present. Approximately 1,000,000 visitors per year come on board each ship. Many of these are non-Christians, and they might have some knowledge, but none would be fluent in English. Thus the CEV translation would be the most effective Scripture text available for them.

Anthony Harrop added that as part of the CEV promotion in the Asia-Pacific region, he is asking Doulos ship to carry a special section of their Book Exhibition devoted to CEV resources (ABS, BFBS, Thomas Nelson, and UBS Asia-Pacific editions). The ship Doulos is scheduled to return to this region in early 1996. Anthony will discuss with them about utilizing their ship in collaboration with the national Bible Societies as a platform for promoting CEV to conferences of pastors, church leaders, and youth, as well as to the visiting public. Barclay's speaking in Toulon would lay the intellectual, theological, and spiritual foundations for this collaboration.

Anthony stated that he hoped to do several things: (l) to consolidate and extend existing Scripture distribution and use; (2) to promote the CEV New Testament/Bible; (3) to discover attitudes and expectations of multi-national evangelical youth with regard to Bible translations.

Anthony informed Barclay by letter that he was writing to Gene Habecker about supplying 75 copies of the CEV New Testament with Psalms and Proverbs for each Ship's Book exhibition staff member and for main OM Ship's leaders. Anthony also stated: "I am also in touch with Morgan Jackson of Hosanna about getting a similar number of individual cassette tapes of a CEV recording – dramatized if possible ... Barclay, these would be your on-sight tools!"

At the close of 1994, Barclay received a treasured letter from his close friend, mentor, and encourager, Oswald C. J. Hoffman, Honorary Lutheran Hour Speaker and Board Member of ABS. He wrote, "Your contributions to the ABS are simply tremendous. You have stood for something, and I have been glad to stand there with you in support of what I believe to be an excellent translation (CEV Bible)."

In December of 1994, Mary Trammell, Associate Editor with the *Christian Science* magazine interviewed Barclay on the subject of the new CEV New Testament, Psalms and Proverbs.

Her first question was, "Could you tell us what is different about the CEV? How would you distinguish it from every other English translation?"

> ***1. The main thing that differentiates this translation from any existing translation is that it is ear-oriented rather than eye-oriented.***
>
> We live in a society where more people will *hear* the Bible than read it themselves. So, for us, the Contemporary English Version is an *invitation* to read and hear the Word of God as if for the first time. And in that regard, we are trying to produce a text that a person can read aloud without stumbling, that a person can listen to without misunderstanding, and that a person can listen to with enjoyment and appreciation because the language is both lucid and lyrical.
>
> ***2. "Do you use a selective vocabulary in the CEV?"***
>
> No. Not really, though we judge each word. We don't have a list of words that we will not really use, except that we do not use traditional theological terms that aren't understood by the masses of people. One thing we do is to listen to how words are used by people *outside* the church so that we speak to these people. I follow

the prescription of Martin Luther, who said, "We do not ask of the literal Latin what it says, rather we go to the mother in the home, to the children at play, to the men in the market. We listen to the way *they* speak, and we translate accordingly." That's what we try to do.

3. "Do you have a special commitment to children?"

Well, we feel that if you are really writing in a style that children will appreciate, most adults seem to appreciate it, too. Nathaniel Hawthorne said, "Easy reading makes hard writing." And E. B. White, who wrote *Charlotte's Web* said, "The last thing you want to do is to write down to children."

So we spent at least two years in our church here (Springfield, Missouri), checking this back and forth with third and fourth-grade groups, testing responses. There are (also) adult Bible classes – doctors … lawyers … very educated groups – which use the children's edition of Luke with all those pictures in it because they like the text so well. And that was one of the things that got us started into this for a general audience. There was a need, and this new translation seemed to meet the need.

4. "Do you have a sense that it's important to reach the upcoming generation?"

We do. As I said, it's very much a mission-driven translation, and the response has been tremendous – very exciting – in Australia, New Zealand, Canada, and now even in England.

5. "Is any kind of theological slant emerging?"

No, no. Our concern is to stay in the mainstream of biblical understanding, and we have, I think, enough biblical scholars looking over our shoulders to keep us from slanting. Our concern is not to produce a strikingly different, unusual interpretation of the text. Our concern is to follow mainstream interpretations, but with a creative restructuring of the English.

6. "Have you had a good response from non-Christians?"

Oh, yes. And we have been commended for our sensitivity toward the Jewish community. We're not trying to water down or play down the historical confrontation between the Jewish and the Christian communities, but on the other hand, there's no need to stir up problems when they can be avoided, … because people forget that Jesus was a Jew.

7. "What have been the key problems that you've encountered along the way in the translation process?"

… when you're translating you have such a diversity of persons involved – so many readers, so many different denominations. You have all kinds of comments, and so the matter of maintaining the integrity of the text, in terms of its meaning, but primarily in terms of the style through which you want to reach a particular audience, becomes a difficult thing. So you're trying to compromise. But the text is a better text for having gone through that process.

8. "How have you dealt with the gender of divinity?"

The text has been consciously inclusive from the beginning. I would say it is gender-generic but culture-specific. It is also inclusive without being obtrusive. Let me clarify a little. As regards God – in the Jewish culture, God is masculine, and in the English culture, the noun *God* requires a masculine pronoun. …

I realize that God is not masculine. God is not feminine. God is not neuter. God is *God*. God is beyond all human categories … And God incorporates all that is feminine, all that is masculine. God is God, and (he is) unique. But in the linguistic situation, we are stuck with using masculine pronouns with reference to God. We cannot get away from that.

However, we have done several things. In the Psalms, for example, in many passages there is a shift from a third-person reference to God to a second-person reference in the same passage. And so we have shifted the whole passage over to a "You" form.

And we are much more inclusive in our handling of masculine-feminine issues than any other translation. Let me give you an example from Matthew 13:

"The kingdom of heaven is like what happens when a shop-owner is looking for fine pearls. After finding a very valuable one, the owner goes and sells everything in order to buy that pearl" (verses 45, 46).

9. "Now one last question, sort of backing off from all these technical issues that have been so interesting to talk about. You've spent thirty years (actually 45 including college and seminary biblical studies, and teaching New Testament and Greek at William Jewell College) in constant contact one way or another with the Bible, with the Word of God. What does that do to a person? Or to a family? How do you feel about it?"

… when we were living overseas, it was difficult. One's wife has to be as committed to this task as you are. My wife is technically the editorial associate to the translation team. She has very fine English skills and around the table her input is outstanding, I'd say. And then, of course, she and I often read the text over together. We may go through a passage as many as thirty times.

We felt this to be a *calling*. We do this as a commitment, and always with fear and trembling. I often try to sound light-hearted and joke and include humor, but that is because in translation, I think, one of the worst things you can do is take yourself (too) seriously. You must take your *calling* seriously, but not *yourself.* Otherwise, you become defensive of what you do. But you have to listen to what people say, you have to listen to what the text says, you have to listen to what the Spirit of God says.

10. "I guess that no one could work for the length of time that you have with the Word of God, without feeling in a sense transformed by it."

It's a really humbling experience because you realize more and more what's involved. This is the Word of God and it deserves our very best, and that's what we try to do. This new translation is a fluid text, and it doesn't belong to us translators. It belongs to the Bible Society and all the Christian communities who support the Bible Society. And beyond that … it belongs to God.

On June 12, 1995, Timothy Wilt, living and working in Kampala, Uganda wrote:

> I think our Children's Text Committee will simply end up using CEV texts for much of our work. This may enable us to concentrate more on the appropriate presentation of texts for children here than on translating the texts themselves.

As has been mentioned in a previous chapter, Barclay was extremely concerned about the readability of the CEV translation of the Bible. His article on this subject was published October 1995 in *The Bible Translator*. He wrote:

> One of the questions frequently asked about a new translation of the Bible is, "What is its *reading level*?" Too often this question is based upon the false assumption that certain standards exist whereby a text can somehow be automatically "measured" or "weighed" to determine a precise answer. But this is not the case. In fact, the standards for readability testing are not flawless, and any conclusions can never be more than "probability statements." For example, if a text were evaluated to be "grade 4", this would merely be saying that perhaps fifty to seventy percent of persons with a fourth grade education should have little or no difficulty reading it. Most readability formulas focus on sentence length and vocabulary, though others include such factors as grammatical relationships and sentence structure. Un-

fortunately, these measurements tend to be *mechanical* and do not take into consideration the less measurable elements that are equally important. For example, a "short" sentence can be more difficult to understand than a "long" one, if the word order of the shorter one is unnatural and the longer one flows smoothly. Moreover, too many short, choppy sentences in sequence can actually have an adverse effect by reducing the reader's interest. …

He continued in this article by listing seven "other" readability tests:

Somerset Maugham once stated, "There are three rules for writing the novel. Unfortunately, no one knows what they are." Maugham's comment sets the stage for the choice of the seven "other" readability tests suggested below. They are merely an attempt to distinguish some of the less measurable factors that help determine the readability level of Bible translations.

1. Is the text easy on the eye?

The new CEV has attempted to create a text that is easy to look at, with a proper mixture of "white" space on the page. A printed page is similar in some respects to the keyboard of a piano, where the contrast between black and white keys is especially important for the beginner. Not only does the CEV offer "measured lines" in poetry, but the lines are arranged as artistically as possible. And frequent paragraphing in prose sections keeps the text from being threatening, even to an unskilled reader. In a survey where high school and college students were asked to indicate what made books readable, at the top of the list were "short sentences and paragraphs."

Another "user-friendly" feature of the CEV is its use of block indentions for lengthy quotations such as parables and speeches. This avoids the complication of quotations within quotations within quotations; in the CEV there is never more than one set of quotations within another.

2. Is it easy to read aloud?

This factor is especially important in the case of the Bible, since reading aloud often takes place in public worship and in smaller groups. It should be emphasized that the *oral* readability of a text is a result of giving careful attention to a number of stylistic details, some of which will be mentioned later.

3. Does it make easy listening?

Without thinking, many readers at all levels occasionally "sound out" a text, especially if it displays "poetic" qualities. One reader of a new translation – a person with a background in theater – suddenly noticed that as he was reading the Gospel of John, he had unknowingly shifted from silent reading to oral reading, and found himself "listening" with great enjoyment. Another person said: "When I read this translation to a congregation, they don't go 'Huh?' they say 'Hmm.'"

4. Are the words and sentence patterns familiar?

Sentences should follow the informal patterns of everyday *spoken* language. In English this is especially needful for those who have difficulty with the standard form of the language, but this feature is valued by educated readers as well, because it gives a "comfortable feeling," like being with an old friend.

5. Does it capture and hold your interest?

One reading specialist said "*Readability is excitement.* A punchy beginning. Forceful and colorful language. Variety in style, including both long and short sentences."

6. Are the thoughts easy to follow and understand?

Literature that is not "required reading" – and some that *is* required too – will not stay long in a reader's hands, if it is difficult to understand. Even faithful Bible readers complain because traditional translations are often so hard to understand. A young woman said to one of the CEV translators, "I am Polish, and I can understand the CEV better than I can my own Polish Bible that was translated in the sixties. Do you think it is right to make the Bible so easy to understand?" The answer is, "Not only is it right, it is our mission!" For the most part, if someone does not understand the Bible, it is the fault of the translators.

7. Does it "Sing to your heart and soul"?

"Soul appeal"! – above all else – is a necessary ingredient for putting "readability" into a translation of the Bible. This is a feature that is easier *experienced* than explained. It is the "chemistry" that develops between the text and the reader, and it results from detailed attention to all matters of literary style. During a convention someone stopped by the Bible Society booth and was looking at the CEV New Testament with Psalms and Proverbs. The Bible Society representative asked, "Are you familiar with that publication?" She answered, "This is the first time I have seen one with Psalms and Proverbs. But I have read the New Testament, and it is clear and simple, like Christ intended; *it just sings to your heart and soul!*"

The early part of January 1996 began with Barclay giving CEV presentations once again up and down the country of England at the request of the British and Foreign Bible Society; in February he made these same presentations at a workshop in Merida, Mexico, where a translation committee was preparing a Spanish translation based on the CEV. In March Barclay once again traveled to England and Scotland, where he was invited to discuss with various church leaders and professionals the goals and purpose of the CEV. Later in the month he was asked to give CEV presentation in Dublin, Georgia.

April began with many requests for Barclay to present the rationale for the newest American Bible Society translation. On the 5th he appeared on the nationally broadcast Jim Lehrer NewsHour, where he presented the purpose and goals of the CEV Bible. Also in April he made CEV presentations at the Mosaics' Ministries in Chicago and again in Scotland. The last week in April Barclay traveled again to Canada and made CEV presentations. He made CEV presentations in May at Garrett Theological Seminary in Chicago.

June was a very special month for Barclay. He was presented with the 1996 Distinguished Alumnus Award at Southern Baptist Theological Seminary in Louisville, Kentucky where he received his PhD in January of 1960. A few weeks later he was honored as distinguished alumnus at the 1996 Alumni and Friends Luncheon in New Orleans, Louisiana.

Barclay vividly recalls his trip to England and Scotland in September and October, where he was invited to speak on Bible translations. He remembers one very embarrassing incident while attending the Scottish Christian Resources Exhibition. A lull had come in the introductions to and greeting of attendees allowing him to step over to a table of beautifully displayed refreshments. Barclay has always had a weakness for shortbread biscuits/cookies (his ancestry began in Scotland), and nobody can make them like the cooks in the United Kingdom.

Just as Barclay had popped a good size morsel of shortbread into his mouth, a Bible Society friend approached abruptly to introduce him to Princess Ann (British royalty have always been very supportive of the Bible Society cause). Barclay did his best to swallow the ever-growing bite and extended a hand to the gracious Princess. Barclay doesn't remember exactly what he said to her, and neither does he remember what she said to him. He only hoped "the day" was somewhat saved. Shortbread biscuits have a way of expanding once in your mouth. This was Barclay's first time to greet in person one of the British royalty. He and Jean had once seen in Malaysia the Queen and Prince Phillip riding along in their limousine in a patriotic parade.

1997 began another year with an extremely heavy traveling and speaking schedule for Barclay. He made CEV and Bible translation presentations at Central Seminary in Kansas City, Missouri; William Jewel College, Liberty, Missouri; at a Pittsburgh TV and radio station; at a Theological Seminary in Pennsylvania; in Raleigh, North Carolina; in Jackson, Mississippi; at Howard University in Washington, D.C.; in Louisville, Kentucky; for African-American Ministries in Queens, New York; at the Cooperative Baptist Fellowship Convention in Louisville, Kentucky; at a CEF meeting in St. Louis, Missouri with Haviland Houston; at the National Black Catholic Congress in Baltimore, Maryland; at Shorter College in Rome, Georgia (at the invitation of Steve Sheeley); at a Good News Conference in Norcross, Georgia (at the invitation of Violet and Wesley Cox); at the African Regional Assembly in Johannesburg, South Africa and at the Launch of the CEV Bible in several cities across England.

The British and Foreign Bible Society published an article with the statement, "The Bible translation (CEV), which last year hit the headlines with its modern language and phrasing has become the first ever to be awarded the 'Crystal Mark' from the Plain English Campaign." The BFBS publication of the CEV New Testament, entitled *Into the Light* New Testament … now ranks among high-profile winners such as the Arts Council and Comic Relief in the fight against *gobbledygook.* They further stated: "Jesus Christ preached with simplicity, warmth and care. This New Testament reflects all those things for us to share in." *Into the Light* uses the text of the CEV Bible, which they said was specifically prepared to help people who hear the Bible rather than read it for themselves, but now more and more people are finding that this is a translation they can also use in their personal devotions.

Barclay's next travel agenda included Scotland and Wales, where he again made Bible translation presentations. Other speaking engagements took him to Woodbrook Baptist Church in Charleston, West Virginia; the Bible Society in Baltimore, Maryland (at the invitation of Ray Moreland, who has from the very beginning been a staunch supporter of the CEV Bible); Portland, Oregon, a Christian Church in Lebanon, Missouri; and a CEV Seminar at the New York Theological Seminary in New York. On this occasion Barclay and Jean recall staying for their first and only time in the hotel of the Twin Towers in lower Manhattan, New York.

Chapter XIV

Into the New Millennium

Early in 2000, Charles Houser announced the official publication date for the Contemporary English Version *Learning Bible*. This Bible contains 2,391 pages which addresses dozens of topics such as: "How to Use the Learning Bible." Also in the introduction for the Old Testament such topics as "How the Bible Came to Us", "What Books Belong in the Bible?", "Different Kinds of Literature in the Bible", "Translating the Bible", and "Archaeology and the Bible" are addressed. For the New Testament such subjects as "The World of Jesus: People, Powers, and Politics", "How People Made a Living in the Time of Jesus", "Religion and Philosophies in Bible Times", and "Miracles, Magic, and Medicine" are just a few that are discussed. This Bible contains 16 color maps, 35 charts and 227 color reproductions of fine art images from around the world, hundreds of explanatory notes, and, most important, the full text of the CEV translation of the Bible.

Steve Berneking and Charles Houser were the driving force behind this tremendous undertaking in which they invested many long hours. Literally hundreds of credits are given for numerous articles throughout the book and for the charts and religious art work. The work was begun in 1992, and the official publication came in September of 2000. As Barclay has said *The Learning Bible* (CEV) is user-friendly. Its carefully laid out pages are easy to read, and its references are clear and direct.

Barclay traveled to the Philippines on the 27th of January, where he lectured on Bible translation along with Annie del Cora, Gene Nida, and Danny Arichea until the middle of February. The intensive Translations Workshop was held in Baguio City in the northern part of the Philippines where prospective Bible translators and pastors attended.

Throughout the year of 2000, Barclay attended a number of meetings and spoke on Bible translation a total of 17 times. From June to October he welcomed into his home office three of his colleagues from the New York office, David Burke, Maria Martinez, and Patrick English. He authored seven articles during the year.

Charles Houser wrote an encouraging letter to Barclay in June:

> I am on the Church Council at Holy Trinity Lutheran Church (Dick Jeske's old church on Park Central West in New York City). Last night the president opened the meeting by reading 1 Corinthians 12 as our opening devotions. We are an NRSV congregation but she chose the CEV for her reading (with no prompting from me). The council members seemed to really feel the impact of Paul's message about gifts. One woman actually said "wow" after the reading. There certainly was no misunderstanding about what Paul was saying.

From the 17th of June to the 2nd of July 2000, Barclay attended and participated in the United Bible Society Triennial Translations Workshop in Torremolinos, Malaga, Spain.

Barclay learned from his colleague in New Zealand, Colin Reed, that the *CEV Children's Daily Devotional Bible*, a Thomas Nelson publication won the "Children's Book of the Year" award. Colin added, "The easy to read and understand style and format were significant features which made this a winning book with the New Zealand Christian Booksellers' Association."

Thomas J. Brown, the Bishop of the Anglican Church in Wellington, New Zealand wrote a letter to Colin Reed in which he stated:

> I warmly commend the Contemporary English Version Bible to you. (It is) written in today's language, it is both easy and enjoyable to read, bringing greater clarity to what we affirm as the Good News. When it comes to personal reading and reflection as well as publicly reading scripture, it is my preferred version.

Between January and December of 2001, Barclay spoke either on Bible translation, the CEV, or the individual books of the Gospel of John, 1, 2, 3 John, and Revelation a total of 46 times and attended 8 meetings either in California or New York.

From the 9th of February to the 4th of March, Barclay traveled in Africa, working with Peter Renju in Moshi and Arusha, Tanzania and Aloo Majola in Uganda and Nigeria. On the 13th he wrote:

> This morning we left the pleasant surroundings of my clean, though not ritzy hotel and drove some six hours to Moshi, Tanzania ... En route we had to stop numerous times: passport control, several police checkpoints with metal pieces full of six-inch metal spikes across the road, holes where the road has simply disappeared...

We found the Lutheran Hostel with no difficulty and ate lunch there, while waiting word from the man who was to meet us from the Bible Society of Tanzania. I took my stuff up to my room, and my UBS colleague (Peter Renju – who lives in Moshi) discovered that they do not accept credit cards of any kind. This is all right for Peter, since he will spend the night at home, but other arrangements had to be made for me.

The place is from the ancient past, and they had to look around to find a room with an outlet for me to use for my computer. This single outlet now looks like some kind of mutation with two lights and one computer hooked up to it, …

The setting is beautiful at the foot of Mount Kilimanjaro – or so I am told; clouds cover it now.

On the following day Barclay again wrote:

I've had a terrific time today (Tuesday) – first speaking at a Lutheran "Theological" School on a mountain dirt road at the foot of Mt. Kilimanjaro, then spending time with several translation committees. These people are true servants of God, working under almost impossible circumstances. Makes you wish you could do something for them, other than offer translation help and words of encouragement…

We drove through a "market" on the way back to the Lutheran Hostel, and even I got a culture shock. It was much worse than I had ever seen in Asia. This was "wholesale" day and the ground was strewn with piles and piles of secondhand shoes and clothing. As we were leaving, I saw where it came from – bales of clothing bound like cotton bales, though not as large. The road was like a war zone with more holes than road. And dust was everywhere, as were the masses of humanity. I was told that the average person here doesn't have enough money to buy the Gospel of Luke in Swahili. Those few who have enough money for food "today" are the lucky ones, because having food is something you have to be concerned about on a day-by-day basis.

Barclay wrote home on the 22nd of February, his birthday:

I had a wonderful time last night, having dinner with the board of the Bible Society. They presented me with a walking stick (carved ebony and heavy), which they said was a sign of "honor," not age!

> Today I am to meet with the pastor of a Pentecostal Church with 8,000 members. He is reading through the CEV and preaching from it this year.

The latter part of March was spent in New York, where Barclay lectured on New Testament Survey to the staff and made CEV power point presentations and spoke about translation in general at Fordham University.

In April, he returned to New York where he made CEV power point presentations to a group of Bible Society donors from Savannah, Georgia, Atlanta, Charlotte, North Carolina, and Greenville, South Carolina. The third week in April brought Barclay's colleague Trevon Gross, ABS Vice President for Programs, to his home/office.

During the second week of November Barclay made CEV presentations at the University of Pennsylvania "Spirit of Liberty Symposium" for the 300th Anniversary celebration of William Penn's Charter of Privileges. At the same gathering Barclay and Howard Clark Kee spoke on the "Biblical Foundations of Religious Liberty," followed that evening with an award dinner held in the John Wanamaker Building where there were close to 600 guests.

Again in December, Barclay made CEV presentations at St. Francis Episcopal Church, Modesto, California and to a number of other area churches. After a meeting in the New York office, he then flew to St. Louis, Missouri where he made CEV presentations at the Zion United Methodist Church, which had been arranged for by Bob Stevens.

In 2001 Barclay spoke about Bible translation or lectured on certain books of the Bible a total of 38 times.

The year 2002 began another year with a heavy travel schedule for Barclay. He made CEV presentations in Baltimore, Maryland with Ray Moreland as his host. He traveled once again to England and Scotland where he spoke afternoon and evening at the British and Foreign Bible Society Roadshow in Northampton; had a meeting and gave a presentation at Warwick University, and met with personnel at the Bible House concerning the CEV Concordance.

And in Scotland, he made CEV presentations to the staff of the Scottish Bible Society; held interviews with a number of Scottish Bible Society staff including Douglas Campbell, Executive Director; Colin Hay; Programs Manager; Marketing and Computer; John Binnington, Information Officer; John Lloyd, Public Relations Officer; Robert Pollock, Sales Manager; and Maisie Rendall, Field Manager. He preached and made Bible translation presentations at Holyrood Abbey Scottish Presbyterian Church in Edinburgh. Barclay was privileged to spend Sunday in the home of Neil McTaggert, Chairman of the Scottish Bible Society Board.

At the request of Irvin Borowsky, Barclay made a total of 6 CEV power point presentations in Palm Beach, West Palm Beach, Boca Raton, and Sarasota, Florida to a total of 211 of Irvin's Jewish friends. The purpose of these sessions was to examine how the CEV Bible might be placed in hotels and motels across the States. On the final evening in Sarasota Barclay was presented with the Exemplary Citizens Award by Irvin Borowsky of the National Liberty Museum and the American Interfaith Institute.

Trevon Gross of the ABS office was Barclay and Jean's guest for a Saturday night the 4th of May where he proceeded to preach a special sermon at their church on Sunday morning. Before his sermon began Barclay and Jean had to rush to the airport to catch a plane on their way to the AMRETCON meetings in Cuzco, Peru, in South America.

In the year of 2002 Barclay spoke or gave interviews approximately 51 times.

Barclay attended meetings during the month of January 2003 in New York and Washington, D.C., and in March he and Steve Berneking completed Committee work on the CEV Global edition of the CEV.

In March of 2003, he completed developing "The Challenge." From the 15th to the 29th of June he attended and participated in the United Bible Society Triennial Translations Workshop in Iquacu, Brazil. Barclay made CEV presentations in San Antonio, Texas, and once again he traveled in December to the Philippines where he gave CEV presentations.

The CEV Bible had been completed and published in 1995, and now Barclay and Gene Habecker agreed that a revision should be underway for a 2005 publication.

On February 6, 2004, Barclay wrote a report on the beginning of the CEV revision:

> It pleases me to announce that the CEV Revision Project is now on schedule … All of this is the direct result of the harmonious "environment" in which we are privileged to work at the NIDA Institute (at ABS). Please be patient as we review some of the events that make such a statement possible. On July 12, 1999, as my wife and I were driving Eugene Habecker to the Springfield, Missouri airport, he raised the question of how often translations should be revised. I indicated that as a rule, we thought of every ten years. To this he replied that we should then plan to have a revision of the CEV ready in 2005.

However, the revision process did not actually begin until April 29, 2003, when Trevon Gross sent a memo to me in which he said: "You are in charge! DO what needs to be done." This I *knew* to be a mandate – DO something, and Do it *now*.

Francis Bacon, the noted English essayist, once wrote, "A man may be young in years, but old in hours, if he has wasted no time." Trevon is such a person – he possesses wisdom and insight beyond his years, and he moves patiently and methodically until his goals are accomplished. Trevon is a genuinely caring person of absolute integrity, who inspires us to perform at our highest level, and to do so with happy hearts. …

When Trevon told me to "DO what needs to be done" to get the CEV Revision on track, I immediately asked Steve Berneking if he would be my partner in this important enterprise. Steve responded by saying that he had been hoping for such an invitation. Then I knew we would soon be both on track and on schedule.

Bob Hodgson, Interim Dean of the NIDA Institute, has played a significant role in making our assignment both fruitful and joyful. He has been absolutely supportive, as well as gracious and generous with his time. … For years Charles Houser's exemplarily work ethic and highly professional skills have contributed immeasurably to the production of the CEV. And now Steve and I are extremely fortunate to have the support and encouragement of other colleagues in the NIDA Institute. For example, Joseph Crockett, a consummate scholar whose vast knowledge makes my head spin; Liana Lupas, "Mother" of all Bible curators and archivists; Barbara Bernstengel, imaginative, creative, and industrious; Sonia Tellez, who sometimes substitutes as ad hoc dean; Choi Yee, champion of the computer and collector of data; Dorette Saunders, whose research is impeccable; Scott Elliott, a budding Biblical scholar; Susa Simms, thorough and methodical; Jacquelyn Sapiie, who expresses profound truth in ordinary language; Andrew Seltz, master magician of multimedia; Gail Warren, amicable mediator between us and Trevon. …

… Steve (Berneking) and I met when he was a university student and, we were members of the same church. He showed an interest in and a proclivity for Bible translation, and we kept in touch while he was in seminary, where he did some outstanding contract work for the ABS. When the CEV was underway, he accepted my invitation to become one of the translators, which he did with remarkable diligence and dedication. There is no one better qualified to co-chair the CEV Revision than Steve …

On the 6th of March, Barclay and Jean flew to London to represent the American Bible Society at the 200 Year Anniversary Celebration of the British and Foreign Bible Society which was held in London at St. Paul's Cathedral. Jean recalls that they were seated very near The Lord Mayor of London Ken Livingston. The Queen was invited but she was unable to attend since she was out of the country for the celebration of one of her son's birthday.

The last week in April, he was a Facilitator representing the ABS at the idiomatic Translations Workshop in Reichenau Peninsula, Germany.

The first week in June Barclay traveled to New York where he was honored at the American Bible Society for his "40-Year" service celebration, and from there he went to Washington, DC to visit the ABS office in Washington. He spoke twice on Sunday at a church in Alexandria, Virginia at the request of Mike Perez.

A number of Bible Society Workshops have been alluded to throughout this account and according to Barclay's Curriculum Vitae he was involved in Translation Seminars and/or Translation Workshops for a few weeks to a month in at least the following locations: Limuru, Kenya (1965, 2001); Ponape, US Trust Territory (1967); Baguio, Philippines (1968, 2000, 2003); Cipayung, Indonesia (1967, 1970); El Escorial, Spain (1969); Octacumund, India (1969); San Jose, Costa Rica (1970); Banglamund, Thailand (1971); Pyramid, Irian Jaya (1973, 1974, 1978, 1986); Ruschlikon, Switzerland (1972, 1975); Bangkok, Thailand (1978); Chania, Crete (1981); Legon, Ghana (1983, 1985); Stuttgart, Germany (1984); Harper's Ferry, West Virginia, USA (1987); Charlemont, Massachusetts, USA (1987); Taipei, Taiwan (1984); Fiji Islands (1984); Chaing Mai, Thailand (1992, 1994); Santo Domingo, Dominican Republic (1993); Malaga, Spain (2000); Uganda, Africa (2001); Tanzania, Africa (2001); Iguacu, Brazil (1998, 2003).

In July, after a routine physical and angiogram, Barclay's primary physician, William Moore, indicated to him that now was a good time for him to undergo open heart surgery to replace his bicuspid heart value with a tricuspid valve. Barclay was born with a bicuspid valve, and it was now leaking. After two visits with David Zolfaghari, a heart specialist, it was decided that Barclay would have the procedure done on the 31st of August.

As it turned out, Barclay and Jean were all set for an early arrival at the hospital on the last day of August, when David Zolfaghari called the night before and said because of an industrial accident in a southern city, the ICU department at Cox South was filled to capacity. Barclay's operation was then postponed until the 3rd of September. Barclay took the delay calmly, but Jean confessed that she was disappointed and anxious to get the procedure over with. So on the 3rd of September, Barclay received a bovine pericardial heart valve and came out of surgery beautifully. Jean marveled at how brave he was through the whole ordeal. She fretted enough for both of them.

On the 19th of October, Barclay was inducted as a fellow of the Ryan Center for Biblical Studies in recognition for his contributions to Biblical studies as a Union University alumnus. A reception was given in his honor following a number of lectures in various Religion and Greek classes. Jean recalls having to drive Barclay to Union University Jackson, Tennessee because he was still recovering from open heart surgery.

From February 5th to the 11th of 2005, Barclay traveled to Ghana and Nigeria to promote the Global edition of the CEV. Barclay's visit to Ghana was in conjunction with National Bible Week, and he had the good fortune both of being introduced to the overall program of the Bible Society of Ghana and of participating in certain programs, especially those related to the promotion of the CEV. On Sunday the 6th, he participated in the service of the North Kaneshie Assemblies of God Church, and the following Sunday he took part in the Ridge Church, first with an Anglican Congregation, then with a combined Presbyterian-Methodist Congregation, where Rev. Kofi Owusu, the General Secretary of the BSG, delivered an inspired and inspiring sermon in each service.

During the week, Barclay had the joy of introducing the CEV Global Youth Edition to the Labone Secondary School, the Presec Boys Secondary School, the Ridge Church School, and then at two theological institutions, including Trinity Theological Seminary, and at a Scripture Union gathering, as well as at two other meetings. Except for the theological schools, where there were about a hundred in attendance, the schools each had approximately a thousand present, and Barclay was informed that between fifteen hundred and two thousand were at the Scripture Union service.

Mr. Kofi-Kabraba Afful, the Youth and Children's Program Officer for the Bible Society of Ghana, was Barclay's constant companion. Kofi was absolutely indispensable, as was their driver Samuel, who said to Barclay: "If you'd stay and give your pep talk for another week, we'd sell all our CEV Bibles."

Barclay wrote about his visit:

> Never have I met anyone more gracious and caring than Rev. Kofi Owusu, General Secretary of the Bible Society in Ghana, who did everything possible to make my stay in Ghana both pleasant

> and worthwhile. In fact, the entire staff was both thoughtful and helpful, especially Rev. Jacob Aguda (Associate General Secretary), Mr. Kofi Agamah, and Ms. Esther Lomo. I am forever in debt to my dear friend, Dr. David Ekem (Translations Consultant for Bible Society of Ghana) and his wife Ivy, with whose family I spent a relaxing evening. As a bonus, I was able to visit in the home of Gilbert Ansre, my long time colleague and retired United Bible Society Translations Consultant.

At the Bible Society in Nigeria Barclay found Dr. Fred B. Odutola, General Secretary and CEO, to be an energetic and inspirational leader, whose work ethic sets a constant example, not only for the staff of the Bible Society, but for all others who came into contact with him. For Barclay it was a genuine joy to have the privilege of spending time with Fred and of learning about some of the many exciting avenues of service being pursued by the Bible Society in Nigeria.

One of the items on the agenda that Fred had planned was "Meeting with Church Leaders on CEV." The final of these valuable meetings was scheduled for five o'clock on Wednesday afternoon with representatives of The Apostolic Church. It was then that Barclay discovered that miracles still happen! As they approached the massive compound of this mega church in Lagos, Barclay asked how many would attend a Sunday service here, and Fred replied, "About 100,000 – that is on the inside; there would be more than that on the outside!" At the gate they were informed that they would have to leave the CEV Bibles with a man who would come out to greet them. But instead, he invited them inside, where twenty-five or more national leaders of this denomination (of more than five million) were seated. Fred has a way with people, and in a few minutes they were on friendly terms with them all, and he was promoting the CEV as a Bible for the Youth of this denomination that otherwise is bound to the KJV. Barclay and Fred left with high hopes!

The climax to the visit to Nigeria came on Thursday with the launch of the CEV in the auditorium at The Bible Guest House. It was preceded by a press conference with representatives from all of the major TV stations, radio stations, and newspapers. Then after the meeting, these reporters flocked around Barclay and the Bible Society people there for personal interviews. That night some of these interviews appeared on two or three of the major TV news programs.

Anthony Harrop, United Bible Societies Publishing Services Consultant at the World Service Center in Reading of the United Kingdom, wrote in February of 2005 concerning the Global CEV:

> Growth of English use and English Bible purchase in the continents of Africa and Asia is set to rise dramatically in the coming decade. Bible Societies are well placed to meet this audience demand. We see expanding sales of GBT, particularly to Catholic audiences. But most of the new English readers in these continents are youth. The CEV text is ideally placed to meet their needs. All Anglosec Bible Societies recognized this. Hence the enthusiastic response to the (very welcome) ABS offer at Anglosec 2002 to promote CEV globally under special terms for a period of time. There were only two cautions with regard to this globalization of the CEV (= GCEV: Global Contemporary English Version).
>
> (1) The African and Asian Bible Societies at Anglosec said that the success of launching a new English version in an already crowded English-speaking marketplace currently dominated by the KJV and NIV depended on (a) funds directed to publicity and promotion sustained over a period of years, and (b) a range of value-added GCEV products being produced year-by-year, such as Study Bibles, Youth Bibles etc.
>
> (2) Bible Society in the West Indies (Jamaica) was already engaged in a major promotional exercise to wean their churches away from the KJV to the GNT. Although in full agreement with globalizing the GCEV, for tactical reasons BSWI did not wish to complicate their marketing by promoting GCEV at the same time as GNT.

Anthony Harrop added a post script to this e-mail addressed to Charles Houser of the ABS office:

> You'll be pleased to know that orders for GCEV reprint are already coming in, just two months after the first printing reached Bible Societies. Both Philippines and New Zealand have placed orders for the same quantity again, with immediate effect.

On the 8th of April 2005, Barclay penned a letter of resignation addressed to the American Bible Society's President Eugene Habecker, but planned to wait until July the 1st to mail it when the Bible Society's fiscal year began. But on the 13th of June, Bob Hodgson visited Barclay in his home office in Springfield stating that because of reorganization of the ABS the position as Senior Translations Officer had been eliminated. This new development now freed Barclay to go ahead with the Greek project for the United Bible Societies/German Bible Society. On Barclay's last day (June 30th) as Translations Officer with the ABS, he and Jean celebrated a long and enjoyable tenure by going to their favorite eating place in Ozark, Missouri.

August 21st marked the "100 – year" Anniversary of the Fruitland Baptist Church in Fruitland, Tennessee – Barclay's first pastorate while he was attending Union University and later the Seminary in the early 1950s. For Barclay it was a joy to go back to the little church where his early official Christian service began. Only a handful of people remained in the congregation from his time as pastor there.

In the early part of 2004, Daud Sosielo, United Bible Societies Translations Coordinator for the Asia Pacific Region and Chair of the UBS Human Concerns Texts Committee (HUCOTEC), invited Barclay to teach a Bible course at Trinity Theological College in Singapore. With permission and support from the American Bible Society, Barclay accepted this invitation. It was decided he would teach a three-week intensive course on the Gospel of John, beginning the last half of April and extending through the first week of May, 2005.

When Barclay arrived on the campus on April 14, he learned that his class consisted of two graduate students, who needed this course in order to meet their requirements for graduation. They were Edgar Ebojo from the Philippines and Huang Ao-You, a young active priest from the Chinese congregation of St. James Anglican Church in Singapore. Another student, Ernest Christopher from the Bible Society in Pakistan, often joined Barclay and Edgar in biblical and translation discussions, although he was not one of Barclay's students.

Barclay had already had the privilege of working with Edgar on at least three previous occasions. Edgar made the statement to Barclay, "I grew up on your Greek dictionary when I was learning Greek." Edgar was now being groomed to take over the office of Translations Officer for the Philippine Bible Society. So Barclay felt privileged to work once again with this promising young man who was certain to be a real asset to the Bible Society. Barclay has always had a special place in his heart for the people in the Philippines. This is where he and Jean and their two daughters had first gone when Barclay agreed in 1965 to work as a Translations Consultant for the United Bible Societies.

Barclay began his classes on Monday morning April 18, and all sessions were held for two and one half hours each day. Although the Gospel of John was the primary focus of the lectures, Bible translation was also included, since both students were eager to learn about the translation principles involved in creating the CEV.

Barclay had insisted that Jean join him on this trip and before Jean arrived, Barclay was quick to admit he had felt a bit lonely, especially on his first weekend, when the sky grew black and heavy rain had poured down all day on that first Sunday. His only activity outside the classroom had been to walk down to a nearby small grocery store where he bought bananas, grapes, soy milk, and cereal for his breakfasts. The open-air café on the campus served wonderful meats and vegetables for lunch and dinner, but in all the years Barclay had lived and traveled in Asia, he had never learned to enjoy fish ball soup over noodles for breakfast.

After Jean arrived in Singapore (April 27th), Huang Ao-You and his wife prepared a wonderful Chinese meal in their home, where Barclay and Jean were honored to meet and spend time with their two young children. It was a delight to be in their high-rise apartment overlooking the great city of Singapore. Their apartment was on the ninth floor, and Ao-You explained that the higher up the apartment in the complex, the more expensive the purchase price was.

While at Trinity College, Barclay found the office staff members to be extremely helpful. Mercy Koh, Catherine, and Poh Geok, in particular, answered many of his questions, supplied classroom equipment, duplicated materials for him, made detailed arrangements for meeting and spending time with the General Secretary Lim K. Tham of the Singapore Bible Society and other staff members at the Bible Society. In addition, they supplied bus passes, made telephone calls, and gave helpful directions for going into the city and elsewhere.

Barclay was excited about visiting the Bible Society of Singapore once again, where he had worked so closely with Peter Hsieh (then General Secretary) for so many years. Lim K. Tham, the current General Secretary, invited Barclay to speak to the staff, and afterward in the conference room at the Bible House, several staff members spoke about his or her responsibilities with the Bible Society. It was thrilling to hear such a dedicated and enthusiastic group and to view some of their recent publications. They had published first in 1996, again in 2004, and yet again in 2005, the CEV/Chinese diglot with the English and Chinese texts in parallel columns. The Bible Society of Singapore reported that this edition was extremely popular. Many young Chinese are buying it, in order to improve their English, and in the interim they are being exposed to God's Word.

Another reason for publishing such a New Testament was to meet another need. There are many readers who want to be able to switch between reading Scripture in English and Chinese. This edition makes it possible for these readers to do so.

Barclay was informed that the UBS Concise Greek-English Dictionary which he had prepared years ago had now been translated into Chinese and was currently available on the shelf of the Bible Society bookstore.

Already the Dictionary had been translated into a number of languages, including Spanish, Japanese, Indonesian, German, French, and now Chinese. It is currently being translated into Urdu as mentioned earlier.

Mercy Koh, Assistant to the Dean at Trinity, made arrangements for Barclay and Jean to have dinner and visit in the home of Lee Soo Ann, a former General Secretary of the Bible Society of Singapore in the 1980's. Although Barclay knew and had worked with Soo Ann in the early 90's, he had not seen him since.

When Jean arrived on the 27th of April with their friends, Lois and John McCullars from University Heights Baptist Church of Springfield, Barclay had already been teaching for about 12 days. Roland Chia had arranged for the Newmans together with their friends, the McCullars, to be housed in the visiting professors' quarters on the campus, which proved to be very convenient to all of them.

Barclay had also been invited to speak at the "20-year Anniversary" celebration for the Bible Society of Malaysia. And since that organization did not exist (except as the Bible Society of Singapore, Malaysia, and Brunei) when the Newmans lived and worked in West Malaysia, this occasion was extremely rewarding to both Barclay and Jean. They each expressed profound joy at having the opportunity to return to this beautiful tropical country and to the people they had served. So three days before they were scheduled to fly back to the States, they flew to Kuala Lumpur in West Malaysia. Looking out of the plane and seeing literally miles of cocoanut palm trees and tin mines, gave both Barclay and Jean occasion to remember the years they had lived and worked in Petaling Jaya, just outside Kuala Lumpur, the capital city of Malaysia. As their plane came near the airport a few miles from Kuala Lumpur, the Newmans recalled the old Subang Airport where Barclay had departed from so many times while they were living in Malaysia.

On landing at the new airport, Joel Ng, the General Secretary of the Malaysia Bible Society and Lee Min Choon, a lawyer and Consultant for the MBS met them and treated them to a fantastic Chinese meal in Petaling Jaya. Joel was a young Chinese Christian, but very efficient in his role and dedicated to the mission of sharing God's Word with the churches in Malaysia. Later he gave Barclay and Jean a tour of the Bible House and its bookstore and encouraged them to attend the Board meeting in the afternoon before the big celebration later that evening.

In October Lee Min Choon e-mailed Barclay:

> Again, on behalf of Malaysians I wish to express our gratitude to you for the work you have done in the translation (in the late 1960s

> and 1970s) of our national language Bible (the Malay Bible). There is now a struggle to make the Malay Bible available to all Malaysians. The Government has banned the Alkitab (Indonesian Bible Barclay worked on) for Malaysians except Christians. Shipments of imported Alkitabs are being seized.
>
> The work of the church today is to do all we can to make the scriptures accessible to everyone. Please remember us in your prayers as we remember you.

At the Bible House in Malaysia Barclay and Jean also had the privilege of meeting and spending time with the President of the Board, Kong Yeng Phooi, who was one of the most gracious Christians they had ever met.

On May 7, 2005, the night of the 20-Year celebration where Barclay was honored to speak, the Newmans were thrilled to see their old Petaling Jaya neighbors seated at the head table with them, Eng Kiat Koh and his wife Kim. Oh! What good memories surfaced…

On one occasion, the Newman family had gone away for a week's vacation when Eng Kiat and Kim had volunteered their daughter to care for the Newman's small Chihuahua. The dog would remain at home, and their young daughter would come over each day to the house to feed, water, and let the small dog run around outside for a few minutes. When the Newmans returned home, the white tiled floor in the living room was messy in between layers of newspapers, and Brownie was starved. The little dog thought it was her duty to guard the house and everything in it and would not let the neighbor's daughter in. The little dog was so ferocious that all the girl could manage to do was to shove through the barely cracked door a little food and water. Brownie had rushed over to their house every chance she got to be petted by their children, and for this reason the Newmans didn't think there would be a problem.

Once when Barclay was away from home, Jean noticed strange droppings on the white tile floor each morning when she came downstairs. She asked the Kohs about it, and they suggested that perhaps a shrew was coming into the house each night. When Barclay returned home he bought a mousetrap and put a square of cheese on it. The next morning the cheese was gone, but the trap had not been set off. But the droppings were still there on the floor. The Newmans tried this same procedure another night and the same thing happened. No cheese and no mouse or shrew. The Kohs then offered one more solution. They would loan the Newmans their big cat, and surely she would pounce on the mouse or shrew, and that would be the end of the intruder.

The next morning there were still more droppings around the edge of the room, and the cat was sitting in a corner looking frightened and bewildered. Barclay decided he would try another trap. He bought a large rattrap, placed a small piece of cheese securely on it, and waited for the outcome. Next morning, there was a big, flattened shrew with cheese still in place.

Back to the "20-Year Anniversary Celebration." Also at the head table was the President of the Malaysia Bible Society Board, Kong Yeng Phooi, a dignified and dedicated Chinese Christian. He was a gracious host at the table and made certain Barclay and Jean had all they could possibly eat of the beautifully prepared Chinese dishes. Barclay and he seemed to bond from the minute they met one another, and there was a noticeable sadness in his eyes, as well as in Barclay and Jean's, when the evening came to a close. It was as though they had met a fellow on his Christian journey in a faraway place, became very close in just a few short hours, and then they had to say goodbye – perhaps never to see each other again until that time when all believers will have the joy of meeting again in our heavenly home.

On the 8th of September 2005, Barclay and Jean made a trip back to New Zealand and remained there until the 19th. This was their third journey to this beautiful land of enchantment…

Their flight was met early on Saturday the 10th in Auckland, North Island, by Colin Reed, Chief Executive of the Bible Society in New Zealand, who immediately escorted them to the domestic terminal, where the three of them flew to Wellington, the headquarters of the BSNZ.

Early Monday morning, Colin, Barclay, and Jean flew to Christchurch, South Island, where they visited several Christian bookstores and talked with their staff members in the morning and afternoon. Barclay also had the joy of making a CEV presentation to a number of book dealers at the Copthorne Hotel during the noon hour, before they returned to Wellington late that afternoon.

Tuesday included visits to more Christian bookstores during the morning (in Wellington) and afternoon (in Palmerston North), but the climactic event was the opportunity of visiting with the Bible House staff in Wellington at noon and discussing the CEV with them before and during the lunch hour.

Friday began with a breakfast to which all Auckland bookstore managers and staff were invited. Then Barclay had a thirty-minute interview at Radio Rhema, the most important Christian broadcasting station in New Zealand. After visiting bookstores during the late morning and early afternoon, they traveled to the home of Julie Beldin, editor of *DAYSTAR*,

"New Zealand's Christian Monthly," where she interviewed Barclay for a forthcoming article in this informative and colorful publication.

Earlier in the year (June) Allan Davidson reported to ANGLOSEC that the "CEV accounted for 77% of New Testament distribution and half of portions in the last 12 months, due largely to Bible Society's preference for the version for self-published outreach Scriptures."

The BSNZ's paper *Word at Work* included a story in the summer 2005 edition:

> Stop at the Waihola Service Station, south of Dunedin, and it's quite possible that petrol may not be the only thing that you drive away with. You might notice the display of paperbacks on the desk – "Good News For You" – and on enquiry, be invited to take one away, free, and be encouraged to read it. Every week the service station owners, Noel Symons and his wife Maryanne, give away as many as twenty New Testaments. It was an idea that came through conversations generated at the time of *The Passion of the Christ* movie. As Noel says, "people are searching. There is so much going on in the world that people question and the Bible has the answers."
>
> Noel says it's very important that the version they give away is one that is easily understood. The "Good News For You" in the Contemporary English Version hits the target because it looks like a regular book, is printed in single columns "just like the books kids read at school" and is easy to understand. Noel is quite definite about that: "the Bible has to be real to people," he says. "It's not as effective if you can't understand the words."

From the pages of the United Bible Societies' World Report a story is told of how a Mexican American came to use the CEV:

Although Jorge Roque's parents worked hard to provide a good home for Jorge, … by the age of 14, he had already joined a local Chicago gang.

Like many teenagers, he sought approval on the streets instead of at home. His role models were the petty crooks who had made a name in his neighborhood for fighting, making money, driving fancy cars, and having women around them. Members of the Two-Six gang provided the longed for attention and support that his hard-working parents did not have time to give him.

Jorge admitted, "The gang became like my second family." Soon after entering his freshman year in high school at the age of 15, he was expelled for throwing a rival gang member out of a second-story window.

On a Friday night while he was walking alone, he threw bricks at a car full of a rival gang. He was clearly outnumbered and the chase began. He was pinned against a fence by the gang's car with a gun held to his head. The gunman looked into Jorge's face and declared him to be a mere child and let him go.

Fearing for his safety, Jorge's mother sent him to Kansas to live with his uncle for a while. His uncle expected him to follow house rules, such as cleaning, cooking, and helping with the laundry. And twice every week he took him to church. Jorge felt loved and accepted. On New Year's Eve, Jorge, now 16 walked to the altar and prayed: "Come into my life, Jesus, I need you." Peace and joy came into his heart and he felt God changing him from the inside out.

Five months later he returned to Chicago, eager to share with his family about his new-found faith. Now he would have to leave the gang, and he feared they might not let him leave so easily, but finally he was "blessed out" with no worry about retribution.

While he was with the gang, he had recruited some 50 of his childhood friends for gang membership; now he would have to try to get them out, and he started by inviting them to church. After some time, Jorge was asked to work with the Youth For Christ prison ministry. Because of the strength he drew from Scriptures, Jorge always traveled with cases of Bibles to give away – Bibles that Youth for Christ had obtained from the American Bible Society. The ABS's CEV, in particular made the word of God easily understood for the young people he met.

At the beginning of this account the writer stated that funny things happen to fun loving people. Over the years it still holds true. The 10th of October, 2005 Barclay made an e-mail inquiry of Hart Wiens of the Canadian Bible Society. In two days Barclay received an e-mail response from Hart answering his question. On that same day Barclay replied with thanks to the e-mail from Hart. The Subject matter (Re:) addressed to Hart was in perfect Chinese. So much for the technology of the computer. Barclay does not speak or read Chinese.

On the 10th of November 2005, Barclay received a letter from Gail and Carol Dunning of Louisburg, Missouri:

> About 25 years ago the owners of Joseph's Colleges of Beauty in Nebraska … asked us to train the interns who were "going on the floor" and servicing clients who came in for hair cuts, etc. … The owners wanted these students to learn how to treat their clients well. As is always the case, each class had a star pupil or two. In the first class a young girl named Debbie was unusually alert and eager to put the concepts of appropriate human behavior into practice

> ... She is also now a committed believer in our Lord Jesus and a good witness.
>
> The witness includes having a display in her shop of the Contemporary English Version Scripture portions which she encourages her clients to read. I always carry with me a stock of the materials ... to refurbish the "Debbie stock" ... Barclay, the years you labored in producing the CEV still are having their rewards.

On the 20th of November 2005, Barclay traveled to Philadelphia to meet with his German Bible Society colleagues, Florian Voss and Bertram Salzmann. Almost immediately Barclay began the "On-Page" Greek Dictionary (later entitled "Running" Greek Dictionary), but the software which had been set up was not functioning properly. The three of them investigated the problem and came to the conclusion that it was indeed the software which was malfunctioning and not Barclay's equipment. After contacting the company which produced the software, the problem was solved in a little over two months, and Barclay began once again on February 10, 2006 to produce the material for the On-Page Greek Dictionary for the text of the Greek New Testament.

From that February date, when the software and his computer began to cooperate, Barclay put in many hours from early morning until late afternoon on the project and often put in working hours on Saturday. By midsummer he was into 2 Corinthians, and by the first of September he had completed the drafting of all the material through the book of Hebrews.

In the meantime, Barclay signed an agreement with the German Bible Society to produce the Dictionary, which was to include contextualized translations of all words in the Greek New Testament that occur thirty times or less, together with the identification of difficult forms of these and other words. The anticipated date of publication was the spring of 2008, but Barclay completed the project before the deadline, and it was published in the fall of 2007 as part of the UBS Greek New Testament: A Reader's Edition. Barclay received his first published copy on November 19 – a beautifully bound edition.

Barclay had made plans to visit the German Bible Society in Stuttgart in September of 2006 in conjunction with a vacation he and Jean had arranged for in southern Germany. At this time the progress of the dictionary was discussed with Florian and Bertram.

Now that Barclay was semi-retired he began to plan a visit with his only living first cousin Jimmy Westbrook, so on a beautiful June day Barclay and Jean drove to Springdale, Arkansas. They found Jimmy's home and spent a long, delightful afternoon reminiscing about the many good times they had together as little boys growing up in Mississippi. Jimmy was the cousin mentioned in the account of Barclay's early childhood whose mother had died when he was still a very young child. Jimmy (now Jim) reminded Barclay that he used to call him "Befford," Jr., all in one breath. It was concluded that Barclay had heard his mother refer to him as "Junior" to distinguish him from his father Bedford, and Barclay found it easier to pronounce the "ff" sound rather than the "d" sound.

On the 26th of June 2006, Barclay received an e-mail from the Bible Society in Singapore announcing information about a Chinese-English New Testament with Psalms: "This bilingual scripture, featuring the texts of the Chinese Union (Simplified Script) and the Contemporary English Version (CEV) in parallel has been published by the Society. Each copy is beautifully bound with quality leatherette covers."

The third week of July found Barclay and Jean traveling once again. They drove to Gatlinburg, Tennessee to join Jean's brother and two sisters, their spouses, nieces and nephews for a "Butler" family reunion. At the end of three wonderful days in the Smoky Mountains, Barclay and Jean were anxious to visit R. C. Briggs who was living in Raleigh, North Carolina in a rest home. Barclay had not seen his beloved college Greek and New Testament professor since he and Jean were married. With the help of Libby Barnes (Briggs' daughter), arrangements were made for the Newmans to get together with him for dinner the first evening they were in Raleigh. What a joy! Seeing R. C. Briggs once again meant the world to Barclay, and they both beamed with delight as they endeavored to catch up on all those many years. The next day Barclay and Jean spent the entire morning visiting again with Briggs (as he is affectionately called) and listening to him recall old times. The conversation was almost magical and filled with excitement as the two bantered back and forth. Barclay feels a very deep sense of gratitude for this man who inspired him to acquire a profound knowledge of the Bible and its original languages.

On October 2007 Barclay and Jean made a "down memory lane" trip to Greenwood and Vicksburg, Mississippi. Quite by chance Barclay sat next to a table at breakfast with two older gentlemen who knew intimately some of his old buddies that he grew up with in Greenwood. To Barclay's sorrow his long time friend Marvin Tillman had died a couple of years earlier. But they also knew well his older sister, Tennie. When Barclay inquired about her, he learned that she was out of town. So Barclay and Jean spent some time at the cemetery where Barclay's mother and stepfather were buried, at old downtown buildings, and at school grounds before heading to Vicksburg.

Now that the On-Page Dictionary was completed, the German Bible Society gave Barclay the go-ahead to begin the revision of the Concise Greek-English Dictionary. This dictionary was first published in 1971 by the United Bible Societies. It has proved such a valuable tool that the German Bible Society, which now owns the copyright, signed an agreement with Barclay on September 10, 2007 to revise and enlarge it with the addition of several new features. These important new features are: (1) each word that is used only once in the Greek New Testament will be so indicated by book, chapter, and verse at the end of the entry where it occurs; (2) each word that is used more than thirty times in the Greek New Testament will be so indicated by a plus sign enclosed in brackets at the end of the entry where it occurs in the dictionary; (3) as a didactic, mnemonic, and phonetic device, compound words will be divided by hyphens according to their basic components; and (4) words closely related to another New Testament word are enclosed within arrows immediately following the entry. In addition, an article ("A Sampling of Some Greek NT Words That Share Similar Meanings") will be included as a separate entry apart from the dictionary itself. The expected date of publication is the spring of 2010. This dictionary is sold as a separate edition and also as an appendix to the UBS Greek New Testament.

On December 22, 2006, Barclay received the following email from Anthony Harrop:

> Good news on CEV: gone to print last week was order # 9 for a further 150,000 copies. It continues to be a best seller in African countries – Ghana, Nigeria, and Kenya. (They) are the largest purchases. We're now close to 750,000 in print since August 2004.
>
> In March of 2007 Barclay received an email from Aries Aguilar of the Philippines in which he stated:
>
> Let me begin first by updating you on the CEV acceptance here in the Philippines. Currently, more and more Young People are switching to the CEV as their personal Bible. Even one of the major publishers of Christian Curriculum is making CEV their primary resource Bible for their Youth Curriculum. We even have SMS contents containing the CEV text that people download everyday, (and) a newspaper Bible verse published daily (using) CEV! We see in the future a more influential CEV that helps people to better understand and apply the Scripture in their lives.

While Anthony Harrop was visiting Springfield in July of 2008, he shared with Barclay that the Global CEV had sold a total of 800,000 copies -- 170,000 in China and 630,000 in Africa.

Barclay worked long and tedious hours throughout 2008 to complete his second and last project for the German Bible Society. He finished reviewing his work in late December 2008, and on January 7, 2009 he e-mailed the final draft of the revision of the Concise Greek-English Dictionary to the German Bible Society.

Forty-six years later, he had now come full circle with his work for the Bible Societies. His very first project for the American Bible Society was creating and writing the Concise Greek-English Dictionary begun in 1963 during his fourth year as professor at William Jewell College in Liberty, Missouri.

Now at 78 years of age Barclay continues teaching on occasion and writing articles with the same enthusiasm and deep understanding of the Scriptures that he had in the beginning of his ministry. His wisdom has increased with experience and age and is surpassed by none other.

After completing two major projects for the German Bible Society, Barclay still felt the burning desire to translate from the original Greek New Testament another easy to understand New Testament, which he completed two years later. This translation is known as "Scriptures Plain and Simple," published by PaperWood Publishers, Josie Ruiz of Birmingham, New York.

Conclusion

In closing, the writer of this account includes the following benediction offered by Barclay at the University Heights Baptist Church, Springfield, Missouri in 2001, because it so accurately summarizes his Christian faith:

Our Lord and Ruler,
your name is wonderful
  everywhere on earth.

We confess that we often
  look in the mirror
and believe the image
  we see there is God.

In this sacred hour of worship,
  may we see you as you truly are –
the God who offers
  love in place of hate,
  mercy in place of justice,
  and forgiveness in place of revenge.

Lord, the next time
  we look in a mirror,
may we see someone there
who reflects something
  of what you really are like.

Our Lord and Ruler,
your name is indeed wonderful
  everywhere on this earth.

Now, as we continue to worship,
  bring honor to your most wonderful name.

Acknowledgments

The word "acknowledgment" is too weak to describe my debt to the many persons who are mentioned in this account of Barclay Moon Newman, Jr.

The author has been the beneficiary of all kinds of help with fact checking, copyediting, and encouragement all along the way.

First, I want to thank Doyle O. Kinder (known affectionately as "Doc" for reading the manuscript I wrote twelve years ago. By the way, this is the first book I have ever written. Doyle read the entire manuscript in three days, called on the phone to say the work is "readable and inspiring." Now call our good friend, Paul Bass, who is a widely published author himself. And I have never dreamed a man with his busy schedule could be so helpful. Paul put in many hours at his computer since I have become computer illiterate. He offered suggestions on how to organize the entire volume, how to handle deletions, what photographs to include, and what to expect from the publisher, Doug Sikes, from Acclaim Press in Sikeston, Missouri.

Then Jan Bass, a qualified editor, spent many hours reading, correcting errors, and making helpful suggestions.

I would be amiss if I didn't thank Barclay's much loved Greek professor Robert Briggs, who he studied under while a student at Union University in Jackson, Tennessee.

It was Eugene A. Nida who hired Barclay as a United Bible Society Translations Consultant to Asia.

Thanks and appreciation are due to many others: David Burke, Barclay's colleague and friend of the American Bible Society in New York; Steve Berneking, who assisted in translating the Contemporary English Version of the Bible; Donald Johns and Robert Hodgson, who contributed a great deal to translating the CEV; Eugene Habecker, then president of the American Bible Society, who always encouraged Barclay in his work; and Trevon Gross, who helped in many ways also.

The final projects Barclay was involved with before he retired was initiated by Florian Voss and his colleague of the German Bible Society in Stuttgart. Barclay's work with the United Bible Societies around the world gave him insights he never dreamed possible.

Thanks are due to many other individuals throughout the world who wrote letters of encouragement and gave helpful insights during the many years Barclay worked with both the American Bible Society/United Bible Societies.

The omission of any names throughout this volume is regrettable.

Resources for Other Information on Barclay Moon Newman, Jr.

"Disease in Warfare Basis of Japan's Secret Weapon, Chemistry Professor Says," by Howard W. Blakeslee, *The Commercial Appeal*: Memphis, Tennessee, July 16, 1944 (newspaper article about Barclay Newman, Sr.)

"Historectomy: The Nonsense of a Non-Sexist Bible," by Barclay M. Newman, *Mission Journal*, March 1981, pages 3-5

"A Bible for the Entire Family," January 24, 1992, *Pittsburgh Catholic*

"Stop! Look! Listen! (The CEV is on its way!)" *(personal notes-* Simple and Straightforward, Sound, Sequence, Succinctness, Sensitivity, Sense, Shape, Style! Style! Style!)

"New Bible Translation," Summer 1995, *Midwest Today*, pages 24-25

"The Man Behind the CEV," Summer 1995, *American Bible Society*, page 5 Ad for the CEV in *McCall's Magazine*, October 1995

"Making Peace Between Jews and Gentiles," 1996, American Interfaith Institute

"CEV: Hearing God's Word for All Its Worth" by Barclay Newman American Bible Society *Record*, October/November, 1999 Pages 10-11

"A Response to the Episcopal Commission on the Doctrine of the Faith's 'Objections to the Contemporary English Version on Doctrinal Grounds'," by Barclay M. Newman, *A.M.E. Church Review*, July-September, 2001, pages 73-78, (presented to the Catholic Bishops Fall 2000)

"Turning to the Good Book," October 7, 2001, *Springfield News-Leader*, page 1G

Amazon.com has over *sixty* of Barclay Newman's books available on line.

About the Author

Jean Butler Newman was born in Jackson, Tennessee, in 1931 to two loving parents, Clyde R. and Leora T. Butler. She had one brother, Carlton, two sisters, Ann and Lucy. All four of them went to Union University in Jackson, Tennessee.

While still in junior high, she began to develop a life-long love and aptitude for art. Painting came naturally to her as did wood carving in her later years. Today her home features a wonderful collection of exquisite carvings and paintings.

As her skill in art developed, she has also illustrated three children's books:

Gingko Tree
Long and Short of It
How Much is 12?

She has written numerous articles for various periodicals through the years, leading up to this full-length book, her first. As if preparatory for this work, she had always found great joy helping edit Barclay's correspondence throughout his career and her own part in reviewing the *Contemporary English Version* translation of the Bible. She graciously proclaims of her work, "GOD has been good, indeed!"

Index